VICTORIAN CAMBRIDGE

Josiah Chater's Diaries

1844–1884

VICTORIAN CAMBRIDGE

JOSIAH CHATER'S DIARIES

1844-1884

by
Enid Porter

PHILLIMORE

1975

Published by
PHILLIMORE & CO. LTD
London and Chichester

Head Office: Shopwyke Hall
Chichester, Sussex, England

ISBN 0 85033 213 3

Printed in Great Britain by
UNWIN BROTHERS LIMITED
at The Gresham Press, Old Woking, Surrey

CONTENTS

ILLUSTRATIONS

(between pages 14 and 15)

INTRODUCTION

Josiah Chater

Josiah Chater was born, on 12 November 1828, in the Essex town of Saffron Walden where his father, William Chater, was a well-known nurseryman and landscape gardener. There is still a Chater's Hill in the town perpetuating the family name, while the Bridge End Gardens, laid out by William Chater to the design of Francis Gibson, remain a pleasant memorial to his skill.

Josiah was the third child in a family of nine. His mother, who was born Elizabeth Jay, died in 1839; two years later his father married Mary Ann Cock. Educated in Saffron Walden, first at a dame school then at a private boys' school, Josiah left the latter at the age of 12 and spent the next two years helping his father in the nursery gardens.

At the end of 1843 however, he began, as he later recorded in his diary, 'to find home a burden'. Prehaps the 15-year-old boy did not, at first, welcome the arrival of a stepmother in the home or the birth of the first of his five half-brothers and sisters.

William Chater junior, Josiah's elder brother born in 1827, had already left home and was working in Cambridge, in the woollen drapery and tailoring firm of Simpson and Basham in Petty Cury. William Adams, a wealthy relative of the Chaters who had married into the Simpson family and become head of the firm, from which he retired at a comparatively early age, had brought William to Cambridge. In 1843, learning of Josiah's desire to escape from what the boy was discovering to be an unsatisfying life at home, William Adams arranged that he, too, should come to Cambridge to be trained in book-keeping and in general business methods at Mr. William Eaden Lilley's drapery shop in Market Street.

On 26 December, therefore, the young Josiah arrived in the town—Cambridge did not receive City status until 1955—in which he was to spend the rest of his days. We know nothing of his first impressions of life in Market Street, where he lived above the shop with other apprentices, because he did not begin to write his diary until 1 October 1844. He was then to give, however, a detailed account to his working conditions, of his social life and of his enthusiastic efforts to improve his mind by serious reading and by attendance at lectures in the Mechanics' Institute and similar institutions.

In 1850, his apprenticeship at an end, he left Mr. Lilley's employment and embarked on the great enterprise of setting up business, with his brother William, as a woollen draper in Sidney Street. Three years later he married Agnes Barrett, daughter of John Barrett whose linen drapery shop adjoined Mr. Lilley's premises in Market Street, and niece of Robert Barrett, senior member in the china and earthenware firm of Barrett & Son, which had been established in 1792 on Market Hill. The growing affection between Josiah and Agnes is recorded at length in the diary, for the young couple had to wait for some time, on account of Agnes's youth—she was five years younger than Josiah—for Mr. Barrett to give his consent to an engagement.

From 1850 onwards the diary records the young man gradually establishing himself in the commercial life of Cambridge, extending his business and moving it to larger premises on Market Hill where he and William were joined, next door, by their younger brother Alfred, who was in partnership with Charles Osbourn in the tailoring firm of Chater and Osbourn.

At home, first in Chesterton Road, then above the shop in Sidney Street and later in Fitzwilliam Street, Josiah and Agnes brought up their family of 15 children of whom two died in infancy. With his painstaking account of life in the Chater household from 1853—the parties, the amateur theatricals, the outings into the country and holidays at home and abroad, troubles with domestic servants, deaths and burials—Josiah has left us with an intimate picture of Victorian family and social life.

From 1850, too, the diary shows Josiah playing an ever-increasing role in Cambridge affairs. A deeply religious man and, from his earliest years in Cambridge, a member of and a Sunday School teacher at St. Andrew's Street Baptist Church, Josiah was a founder member of the Young Men's Christian Association, whose Cambridge branch was established in 1852. He served for many years on its committee, represented Cambridge at the International Conference held in Geneva in 1858 and, as Buildings Secretary, was tireless in his efforts to raise money for the large new Y.M.C.A. building, which was opened in Alexandra Street in January 1871. This building was demolished in 1972 in a re-development scheme, so the same problems which Josiah and his fellow committee members faced a century ago have had to be faced by their successors.

In the middle years of his diary-keeping he attended classes at, and served on the committee of, the Working Men's College, founded in Cambridge in 1857, and was, for a while, a lieutenant in the 8th Cambridgeshire Volunteers. He was a committee member, too, of the Cambridge Building Society and a Trustee of the Penny Savings Bank and of the Borough Charities. Though never very robust, he had a fund of nervous energy which enabled him to take on these commitments in addition to running a business and shouldering the many responsibilities which faced him as the father of an ever-increasing family. His enthusiasm for everything he did was boundless, whether it was the photography which he took up as a hobby in the 1850s or learning to use the electric pen he purchased in the 1870s.

In 1876 the partnership with his brother came to an end. Josiah, whose role in the firm had chiefly been the keeping of the accounts, became alarmed at what he thought was unnecessary extravagance on William's part in employing a traveller to do the work which, until then, William himself had done. Always anxious—usually unduly so—over money matters, Josiah began to have doubts concerning the future of W. G. & J. Chater. At the age of nearly 50, therefore, he took the bold step of leaving William to continue on his own and of setting out himself on a new career. Because of his early training under William Eaden Lilley and his years of experience in his own firm, accountancy was the obvious choice and in 1880 he became one of the first chartered accountants in Cambridge.

The final years of his diary are a record of his new professional life as well as of his home affairs. In these last years he took on many important duties, becoming secretary of the Cambridge Improved Industrial Dwellings Company, of the Cambridge Reform Club Building Society, of the Cambridge Steam Laundry Company and, most important of all, of the Cambridge Street

Tramways Company. His work in the last-named resulted in his writing in the diary a unique record of the day-to-day development of the company and of the early trials and tribulations which attended the establishment of horse-drawn trams in Cambridge.

The diary is not, however, merely a record of Josiah's personal and professional life although, insofar as it is such a record, the journal provides an intimate study of its writer. We see Josiah emerging from his early light-hearted days as an apprentice to become a responsible young business man, a loving father and, a professional man with an important position in the town. What is even more interesting, however, is that this portrait of the diarist is painted against a background of Victorian Cambridge.

The Cambridge in which Josiah arrived in 1843 was a small market town of some 25,000 inhabitants, including under-graduates. Following the Enclosure Acts of 1801 and 1807 some building had taken place on what had once been open fields, but the countryside still lay all round the town, a fact which enabled Josiah to record seeing, from Market Street, outbreaks of fire in villages some six or seven miles away. There were no buildings beyond the top of Castle Street where it merges, today, into Huntingdon Road. Chesterton Road, in the 1850s, was only just beginning to be developed with the erection of a few houses, one of which was Josiah's first home after his marriage. Beyond these lay open country up to the fringe of Chesterton village.

New Town, to the west of Hills Road from Hyde Park Corner, had been growing since about 1810, but the railway station which Josiah saw opened in 1845, when the Eastern Counties Railway came to Cambridge, was built well away from the town on part of the former Barnwell Fields. The choice of the site was mainly influenced by the University, which viewed with some misgivings the advent of the new method of travel and the possible arrival of hordes of strangers to disturb the academic peace of Cambridge.

After 1845 the Mill Road area began to grow—Josiah found, 'almost a little town', there in 1847—although the development of the Romsey Town end of the road did not come until after 1879. The Barnwell district grew too, with the coming of the railway, its numerous poor cottages, crowded into insanitary courts of which there were many in central Cambridge also, helping to spread the typhoid and cholera outbreaks which Josiah recorded.

By 1883, in which year Josiah ceased to keep his diary, the population of Cambridge had increased to just over 35,000 and the number of inhabited houses to 4,000. No houses lay beyond Cavendish College—now Homerton College—in Hills Road; on the north side of Mill Road there were still none between Petersfield Lodge, on the corner of East Road, and the parochial cemetery. A level crossing and a footbridge, now over the railway on Stourbridge Common, carried Mill Road traffic and pedestrians over the railway line. In Milton Road *Hurst*, the new home to which Josiah's friend Mark Ives Whibley moved in 1879, stood in rural surroundings on the north side of the road near the modern Hurst Park Avenue, which was not made until 1928. The house, which Josiah visited so often and whose gardens he watched being laid out with lawns and paths, flower beds and croquet ground, is now replaced by a block of flats.

By 1891 the land known as Cavendish Park, on the east side of Hills Road, was being developed by the Rock Freehold Land Society of London. It was to one of the houses in this area, in the newly-made Hartington Grove, that Josiah moved in 1894. The house, named by him *Agnes Holm* in honour of his wife, remained his home until his death on 8 January 1908. Agnes stayed on in it until her own death on 16 January 1919, and it continued to be occupied by their son Augustine until he died in 1941. Even in his own days in Hartington Grove Josiah would have seen this district of Cambridge rapidly expanding.

Throughout the period in which Josiah wrote his diary he worked, and for part of the time lived, near the market place, the hub of the then small town of Cambridge, as today it is the hub of the 'historic centre' which attracts the tourists. In 1846 he saw the very existence of this area threatened by a fire at Headly's iron foundry, a fire which, had the wind been in another direction, might well have destroyed the whole of Petty Cury. Three years later he saw the blaze which swept through the block of old shops which then occupied part of what is now the site of the market stalls. Following the Corporation's subsequent purchase of the whole of the property lying to the east of Great St. Mary's Church, he watched the new market place emerge and saw the removal of Hobson's Conduit from its old site in front of the Guildhall to its present position in Trumpington Road.

From his vantage point in Mr. Lilley's shop, in the early years, and later from his own premises in Sidney Street and on Market Hill and, finally, from his office in Alexandre Street, or when walking briskly about the town, Josiah was able to record numerous interesting scenes and events which he either witnessed himself or heard about from his wide circle of friends. He described the excitement of parliamentary and municipal elections, the noisy scenes at the hustings on Parker's Piece, the trials for election bribery and corruption, royal visits, Plough Monday dancing, the peace celebrations of 1856, the consecration of St. John's College Chapel and the opening of the new Corn Exchange. He wrote of the brief re-appearance of a stage coach in Cambridge after the opening of the railway, of a public hanging on Castle Hill and of the almost comic incidents that occurred when a new gas company tried to light the streets of the town.

He saw, too, many of the Town and Gown fights and other disturbances; the burning, by angry undergraduates, of an effigy of the Mayor in 1875 and, by jubilant Conservatives, of a dummy figure of one of his own Liberal friends in 1880. Yet, at the same time as the diary recorded the outbreaks of hostility between the townsmen and the University it also recorded the co-operation which could exist between the two. At the Mechanics' Institute in his early days and, later, at the Working Men's College and the Y.M.C.A. Josiah, and many of his fellow townspeople, attended lectures given by University dons; on many occasions these tutors invited their pupils to the college rooms for social evenings. An anonymous Cambridge resident, whose memories of life in the town in the 1850s were published in 1900 in *The Cambridge Graphic*, could also recall, 'the chief people of Cambridge mingled more with the dons than they do now . . .'

As secretary or committee member of so many organisations, Josiah was able to see the role that many senior members of the University played in the life of the town, and the interest and concern they showed in the betterment of the less prosperous inhabitants. Evangelical students, too, did much to help the poor, especially in Barnwell, through social and religious work and in the Jesus Lane Sunday School, by teaching reading and writing as well as Scripture to the under privileged, and largely illiterate, children of the area. Involvement in the life of ordinary

Cambridge citizens, which many undergraduates are seeking today, is no new thing.

On nearly every page of Josiah's diary appear the names of Cambridge people which, in many cases, can still be read above shops in the modern city centre even though, sometimes, the businesses are no longer family concerns. William Eaden Lilley's store, now occupying much of Market Street, would be unrecognisable to Josiah, but it is still continued by his first employer's great-grandsons. Barrett & Son's china and glassware shop in St. Andrew's Street is still owned by a direct descendant of Agnes Chater's great-grandfather, founder of the firm in 1792. It stands not far from the large shop of Robert Sayle who began in business a year before Josiah arrived in Cambridge. The store still bears its founder's name, although the business is now a branch of John Lewis Partnership.

Only in the 1960s did the grocery, wine merchant's and restaurant business of Matthew & Son in Trinity Street close its doors; Josiah knew both George and Henry Matthew, his son, who began in partnership in the early 1870s. Only in 1962 was the ironmongery shop of A. Macintosh & Son Ltd., at 14 Market Hill, closed and later demolished. Throughout his life in Cambridge Josiah was friendly with Alexander Macintosh whose father, in 1816, had established a coppersmith's business in Market Street. Josiah saw Alexander expanding his business until, in 1884, he purchased the ironmongery and ironfounding firm of Edward Beales at 14 Market Hill, moved his stock to the new premises and continued there, to be followed by his descendants.

Josiah put his own roots deep into Cambridge. Two of his sons, Vernon and Augustine, joined him in 1895 in the accountancy firm which was known from then as J. Chater & Sons. Although Vernon subsequently left Cambridge, Augustine remained, to be joined by his brothers Bertram and Leonard. Today the firm is continued by Josiah's grandson, Mr. R. Chater Blows, while the accountancy firm of Chater & Myhill, founded by Leonard Chater at the end of the First World War, continues under Mr. Norman Chater and his son, grandson and great-grandson of Josiah.

The people so often mentioned in the diary formed a closely-knit community whose members, in some cases related by marriage, were united by common political views and religious beliefs. Many, in those days, were Liberals, as was Josiah, and many of them were Baptists or Congregationalists. All of them played an important part in Cambridge life; all of them were connected with the Y.M.C.A. and were benefactors of that and of many other institutions in the town.

There have been many diaries kept by distinguished members of the University, but Cambridge town journals, and certainly any as detailed as Josiah's, are comparatively rare. The overall impression given by his records is of the liveliness and friendliness of Cambridge in the middle years of Queen Victoria's reign. True, he wrote almost wholly about the central area, because this was the one he knew best. It was the most prosperous area, too, even though, as he recorded, the trade in corn, coal, butter and other commodities was temporarily dislocated by the coming of the railway. The diary shows, however, that its writer was not unaware of the poverty and overcrowding that existed elsewhere in Cambridge.

The Diary

Josiah Chater's diary was presented to the Cambridge Folk Museum, in 1964, by the late Mr. Leonard Chater. The journal was kept regularly, apart for the three years 1863-6, from 1 October 1844 to 3 May 1883. It is not known why it was then abandoned, unless ever-increasing professional work allowed Josiah no time to continue it.

By the last entry he had filled 17 quarto notebooks; an additional book contains the records of his holidays in Scotland and in Germany in 1856 and 1857, and of his adventures in Switzerland in 1858 when, with a party of friends, he went on a tour of the Alps before going on to Geneva to represent Cambridge at the International Conference of the Y.M.C.A. The hotel bills for both trips abroad are pasted into the notebook along with two passports, each of the latter a single sheet of paper. The first sheet, dated 1857, was issued in the names of Josiah, his two brothers and two friends; the second bears Josiah's name only. In the event, one of the men named on the first passport was unable to travel and another friend took his place. No alteration to the document, however, seems to have been necessary.

I must express my sincere gratitude to the members of the Chater family for allowing the diary to be published. I know that Mr. Leonard Chater, when he gave the volumes to the Museum, wished that his father's valuable historical and social record of Victorian Cambridge could be more widely known. I can only regret that his wish was not fulfilled in his lifetime. I am especially grateful to the late Mr. R. Chater Blows, who answered so patiently so many questions about his grandfather.

I am indebted, too, to Mr. Kenneth Eaden Lilley and to Mr. Howard Lilley, to Mr. Henry Barrett and to Mr. Stuart Whibley for supplying me with details of their families. My thanks must also go to Miss Kathleen Johnson and to Mr. Andrew A. Smith for information about the history of Nonconformity in Cambridge.

ENID PORTER

I

1844 to 1849

APPRENTICESHIP

Living Conditions

It was on 1 October 1844 that Josiah Chater began to keep the diary that he was to continue to write for so many years. He was then 15 years old and was living, with three other apprentices, above the shop at No. 12 Market Street of William Eaden Lilley, draper, carpet warehouseman, paper merchant and seller of oils, colours and brushes.

It is difficult, when looking at the large modern store of William Eaden Lilley & Co. Ltd., which now occupies Nos. 10 to 15 Market Street, to imagine what the premises were like when Josiah lived in them. An engraving of *c.*1840 indicates, however, that they rose to a height of three storeys. They were undoubtedly old, for No. 12 had, since the mid-18th century, when the street was known as Cordwainer Row, been occupied by a succession of drapers and oil and colourmen.[1] Beside and behind the shop lay a yard containing the various warehouses which, in 1845 and again in 1856, were largely restored or re-built.

The room in which the apprentices took their meals seems to have been on the ground floor, at the back of the building. Their bedrooms were, undoubtedly, on the top floor, for on one occasion Josiah, after looking out of the windows one bright moonlit night, described the view of roofs and chimney-pots which met his eyes.

Acting as housekeeper, until November 1846, was a Mrs. Fanny Goody who lived on the premises with her husband and children, Mr. Goody being employed in the shop. Little love, however, was lost between the Goodys and the apprentices in their charge, and the diary has many references to, 'the unpleasant state of our domestic affairs', and to the numerous occasions on which Josiah and his companions complained to Mr. Lilley.

For the most part their complaints were trivial ones. There was the occasion, for example, in December 1844 when Mr. Goody, for some reason not stated, took away the carpet from 'our bedroom'. Josiah shared a room with Stephen Cook, his senior by two years, and seems to have shared the bed too, for on 5 May 1845 he recorded, 'they have been cleaning our room today and have placed the bed differently'. This led to a slight disagreement with Stephen because, 'he wanted to lie opposite the window and I had got there first, not knowing he wanted to sleep on that side . . . so we moved the bed as it was before', an action for which they were both severely reprimanded by Mr. Goody.

More than once the Goodys disciplined the boys by beating them, as on 19 November 1844 when Mrs. Goody 'laid the stick on to poor John so hard she has broken it'. The punishment was given because, on the preceding day, Mr. Goody had been reprimanded by Mr. Lilley following a complaint from John to his employer about 'how ill the Goodys used him'.

Josiah himself was twice threatened with a beating. The first time was on 30 October 1844 when, on going into the counting house before breakfast, he found the Goody children playing there:

> I gave them a good talking to and made George cry, so when we went into breakfast there was such a row . . . Goody promised he would lay the stick on my back.

On the second occasion, in May 1846, Josiah went to sweep the counting house as usual before breakfast, and found that his broom had been taken by one of the servant girls, who was using it in the yard. He took it away from her, probably none too gently for,

> on going into breakfast Goody began by asking what business I had to take the broom from the girl; I told him, and he said if he had been there he would have broken my head with it, and brought up a variety of things against me, and so did Mrs. Goody.

For the most part, though, the apprentices' grievances were concerned with the food. Often it was badly cooked and sometimes there was not enough to go round, so that when two vegetables appeared on the table the boys were given one or the other, Mrs. Goody making the choice. At breakfast the bread seems often to have been sour or mouldy, so that more than once, even though he first grumbled at the boys for complaining about it, Mr. Goody himself had to admit that it was uneatable and to send out for a fresh loaf.

The apprentices, being still growing lads and having to work long hours, were always hungry. Josiah, however, received from home each week a box, which he collected from the *Eagle* Hotel where it had been delivered by the Saffron Walden carrier, and which he returned to the hotel to be sent back and re-filled. In the box, along with clean linen and an occasional small gift of money, was always some food - sausage rolls, apple turnovers, a bag of sugar, some fruit or cakes and always, on his birthday, a plum pudding. These delicacies he shared with the other boys. His older brother William, who was apprenticed to the drapery firm of Simpson and Basham in Petty Cury, also received a weekly box and often gave Josiah something from it.

Sometimes, it seems, Mr. Lilley's apprentices cooked supper for themselves in the counting house, buying the food out of their own pockets, though whether this meal was in addition to one provided by Mrs. Goody, or in place of it, is not clear. The fare, on these occasions, was usually some potatoes roasted on a shovel before the fire, or a penny loaf which was either made into bread and milk or was eaten with roasted onions.

Mr. Blumson, one of the senior employees who, though married and living in his own home, took his meals in Market Street, often bought the boys something to eat - chestnuts, a herring or some sprats which they toasted before the counting house fire. Once, on 7 February 1845, he took Josiah to

> The baker's over the way and got a penny twist and divided it, and then went to our fishmonger in the Cury and had 5 or 6 oysters - such great ones too. They went down beautifully with the twist.

On most Sundays Josiah and his brother had tea and supper at their uncle William Adams's house in Trumpington Street;[2] often, too, they and Mr. Lilley's other apprentices went to meals at the houses of their friends so, all in all, there was little danger of the boys starving.

Relations between the Goodys and the apprentices deteriorated from the spring of 1846. There was fault on both sides. Mrs. Goody certainly was not the best of housekeepers and she does not, moreover, seem to have looked after the boys when any one of them was ill. They were left to find their own remedies for the colds, coughs, toothache and chilblains from which they often suffered. Josiah, who was never very strong and who was always much preoccupied with his health, meticulously recorded the pills, the salts and the castor oil he took, the 'poor man's plasters'[3] which he applied to relieve a cough, and the oil of tar with which he treated toothache until he was forced to go to Mr. Hargreaves, the Petty Cury dentist, and pay two shillings for an extraction.

But the boys for their part, must often have been very annoying, and in their dislike of the Goodys they seem to have gone out of their way to find excuses to complain about them. Towards the end of 1846 Mr. Lilley decided that a radical change was due. He dismissed Mr. and Mrs. Goody and appointed in their place, a Miss Aikin, who kept a lodging house in Green Street, which she continued to run, with the help of servants, even after she went to live as housekeeper in Market Street.

Improvements in the boy's sleeping arrangements were made at once. On Saturday 7 November Josiah was able to write, 'Four new bedsteads came in this evening, with the palliasses' and on the following Tuesday,

> This being the day for the final departure of Mr. Goody and his family, Smith's men came to put up our beds. John and I are to sleep where Goody's children used to sleep, and Hayes and Stephen where the girls slept. About ten o'clock Mr. Lilley came in and read a few regulations to us and also read a chapter in the Bible and prayed, a practice we are to continue at eight in the morning and nine in the evening. After that he left us and we went to supper, our new housekeeper, Miss Aikin, presiding. I do not dislike the looks of her at all. We had some very good bread and cheese and we are to have a washing stand and its accompaniments.

What washing facilities the boys had had before is not known, but there is an early reference in the diary to Josiah brushing his teeth, 'at the pump in the yard'.

On the next day:

> We got up at 7 o'clock this morning. Stephen and I dressed ourselves and at eight o'clock a large bell was rung and in to breakfast we went in good earnest. There was a round of bread and butter cut for each and laid on a plate, and the rest of the loaf was on the table so that the rest we cut ourselves. We had boiled leg of mutton and dumplings for dinner - the bell was rung again at one o'clock, Goody dined with us and he looked very queer sitting at the table as one of the rest of us. We also tea'd exactly at half past four. After I left the shop I went into the house to supper - had cold mutton and cheese - and after supper Cook

and I had a game of chess . . . We have a new looking glass in our room, also night candlesticks and all the necessary requisites.

From then on things went much more smoothly. The boys liked Miss Aikin and she got on well with them. She played games of draughts, bagatelle and chess with them in the evenings, lent them books, looked after them when they were ill and even gave Josiah lessons in French. To show his appreciation of this he helped to look after her garden in Green Street; indeed, the two remained firm friends for several years. Mr. Lilley, on his part, was determined that the improvements should be maintained and when he found, early in 1847, that the boys were slipping back into their old practice of going late to bed, he insisted that they must be in bed by half past 10, and drew up a list of rules which he read out on 8 April. 'He wishes to have them strictly observed', wrote Josiah, but unfortunately did not leave on record what the rules were.

Working Hours

Although Josiah spent the greater part of his time in the counting house, he was also expected to serve in the shop, to assist in the carpet and linen warehouse with such tasks as fixing price tickets to goods, and in the 'pitch warehouse', the 'sperm place'[4] and the paint warehouse in the yard behind the shop.

The shop closed, in the summer months, at nine o'clock, but in winter the shutters were put up at seven o'clock.

'This is the first night of our shutting at seven', Josiah wrote on 2 December 1846, while two years later, on 2 November,

Mr. Sayle[5] has shut up his shop at seven o'clock tonight to set others an example, and almost all the others have agreed to it.

Josiah's first task each morning was, with the other apprentices to sweep out the shop and the counting house before breakfast. Both of these had gas lamps - Josiah refers to taking off the burners and cleaning them - but they were, apparently, not lit early in the morning, for on 10 October 1844,

It was so dark when we came down this morning that we were obliged, for the first time this year, to have a candle to sweep the shop.

Having cleaned and tidied the counting house Josiah usually, in his early apprenticeship days, went round to see his brother William in Petty Cury, returning for breakfast at eight o'clock. Then on 31 October 1844 Mr. Lilley gave him fresh instructions:

He said to me, I think Sheldrick brings the letters up to my house[6] in the morning . . . I thought you would like to bring them in the future, for the benefit of the air. I told him that I should, and he replied that he would think about the matter . . . meanwhile, I might do my counting house work and after that go where I liked till breakfast, but he would advise me to go for a walk somewhere because I was kept late at night and could not go out when the others did, and he thought the confinement would be too much for me after being in the open air at home.

Early in 1845, it was arranged that Josiah should take the letters to Mr. Lilley, an errand that he carried out daily for the next two years.

He certainly often worked late. Mr. Lilley and the senior assistant, Mr. Blumson, were frequently away from Cambridge all day on their separate 'journeys' to neighbouring towns and villages, taking samples to other drapers and tailors, and collecting orders and debts. Mr. Lilley, too, made regular visits to wholesale suppliers in London, travelling by the 'Star' coach until the railway opened. Both men would return in the early evening, and Josiah was then needed in the counting house to do the paper work which resulted from their journeys. Sometimes Mr. Lilley did not leave until half past nine or ten o'clock, and until he went his apprentice could not go either.

In January 1849 to Josiah's delight, his employer purchased 'a letter copying machine - an apparatus for copying letters instead of writing them; it will lessen the trouble considerably'. He does not give details of this labour-saving device, and it may have been a copying press in which the letter, written in ink thickened with gum or sugar, and a thin, absorbent sheet of paper placed beneath it were squeezed between two flat metal plates. The original letter was thus copied, in reverse, on to the thin paper, but could be read by holding it up against the light. As he calls it a 'machine', however, it was, more probably, a roller copying press, which had been patented by James Watt in 1780. This apparatus consisted of two rollers, the upper one having a handle. The letter to be copied was placed, with the semi-transparent paper, between two pasteboards and then passed between the rollers.

There were three occasions in the year when all the employees of Mr. Lilley were especially busy; these were the annual stock-taking in January, the days in September when Stourbridge Fair[7] was held, and the visits of the village and parochial clothing clubs. These clubs, into which villagers and parishioners paid small weekly sums throughout the year, usually spent their funds in November and December, although there are a few references in the diary to those which did so in September, doubtless because harvest wages had then been paid. So, on 29 September 1845, Josiah wrote,

> We have been very busy all day; had the Landbeach Club and Mrs. Whewell's. The shop and warehouse were literally crammed all day.

On 2 December 1844,

> We have been very busy getting the things ready for the Barnwell Club. We started one waggon off about a quarter to three and another about five, full of goods.

On 7 January 1846

> Drayton Club here; 34 members came.

At Stourbridge Fair time it seems that a stall was set up in the yard of the shop, and work in the counting house increased because traders coming to the fair paid off their outstanding debts:

> *25 September [1846]*
> We have had an extraordinary day of business, both in saddlers and other wholesale customers. Have not been so busy for a long time, and being one porter short we have had as much as we could fairly manage ... It has been a very good fair, but goods were dear.

> *24 September [1847]*
> We were all afloat early this morning, being Stirbitch[8] Fair. Got our stall set out very tastily in the yard but were not very busy.

> *25 September:*
> This is Horse Fair Day[9] and we began early to be busy, and busy we were all day long. I did not leave the counting house till ten o'clock, which is late now as I generally leave on Saturdays by nine. It has been the finest fair day we have had since I have been here.

> *25 September [1848]*
> Stourbridge Horse Fair Day. Business has been exceedingly good, and the leather and horse fair being condensed has made us doubly busy; we have taken in debts £500.

It was, apparently, the custom for the porters and the warehousemen to have a special dinner on Horse Fair Day, for on 25 September Josiah wrote,

> The men dined in the yard off a piece of beef and pudding according to the general rule.

The same custom was observed in other shops, too, and on

27 September 1847 Josiah was invited to dinner by Mr. Ingle,
a currier whose business premises were at No. 24 Market Street:

> We had a good lunch of a wonderful piece of beef which, when whole
> weighed 80lb. 9oz. the like of which they make it a rule to have every
> Stirbitch fair.

At stock-taking time the apprentices worked very long hours
and it was a task they were thankful to see completed. All the
goods had to be 'taken down' from their various resting places,
and then 'called over' or checked by Mr. Lilley or by Mr. Blumson.

27 January [1845]
> Stephen and Cook got up this morning at a quarter past three to take
> down the haberdashery. When I came down they were making some
> toast and chocolate for breakfast, so I got a slice of my plum pudding
> and a sausage roll and so made a very good breakfast. After breakfast
> Mr. Best and I did the carpet warehouse and we finished that completely
> this evening, and Mr. Blumson and Stephen have nearly finished the
> warehouse upstairs.

28 January:
> When I came down this morning I took down the stockings in the
> middle warehouse, and when Mr. Lilley came in he called the prints over
> and we finished upstairs completely. Mr. Lilley wanted to take the shop
> down tonight but they were not near ready, so it was deferred till
> tomorrow evening.

29 January
> Mr. Lilley came down before breakfast and called over the landing and
> Barrett's place[10] . . . this evening they began on the shop. John and I
> took down the haberdashery on his side excepting the ribbons; Mr. Lilley
> called over the greater part of the drapery side. We did not go into
> supper till half past ten.

31 January
> A little before one o'clock this afternoon Mr. Lilley and I went to call
> over the warehouse, and we finished that before four o'clock. I had to
> read, and very cold it was. Mr. Lilley said he had not been so cold for a
> very long time.

Apparently Josiah's work satisfied his employer for, on the
following day, he records,

> Mr. Lilley said to Mr. Blumson that I was quite an altered boy; he
> thought that when I first came that I should not be fit for anything,
> but now he thinks he shall do something with me, and that I had
> improved very much lately.

In January 1849 Josiah again gives a long account of stock-
taking, describing the taking down of the Brussels carpet and
chintz warehouses, and the blanket, string and flannel ware-

houses. One day, he recorded they did not finish work, 'till half past nine o'clock.

On 18 January he and Stephen got up at four o'clock in the morning and took down a great deal of the stock in the shop, pausing at half-past five for a breakfast of bacon, sausages, chocolate and bread and butter. Mr. Lilley arrived at six o'clock and work continued throughout the day, though, 'a little hindered by the customers', and on the two following days, so that on the 21st Josiah could write, 'Having finished that most odious of all work, stock taking, we have been engaged in clearing up the oddments'.

To celebrate the end of the 'odious work', the assistants, a month later, held a supper which they seem to have paid for themselves:

20 February [1845]
At half past seven exactly we met at the *Coach and Horses*[11] in the Cury and had a good supper of sausages, hot potatoes, and bread and beer . . . we could not eat them all so I pocketed 2 sausages and 2 large pieces of bread for lunch tomorrow, Mr. Blumson took 4, Hayes 3 and the rest some each, so that we cleared the dishes. After supper they had pipes and ale, and some had brandy and water and cigars, and we broke up just at ten o'clock . . . Mr. Blumson treated me. Some of the sausages we brought home for Stephen as he could not come; Mr. Hayes is now warming them at the fire in the counting house, on the cinder sifter with a piece of board laid on it, so it is quite clean.

In the following year the stock-taking supper was held in the *Black Bear*[12] in Market Street, the main dish being, as before, hot sausages.

Any employee of Mr. Lilley who was found guilty of dishonesty was punished instantly and severely. On 17 March 1846, Josiah wrote,

The first thing this morning Sheldrick took six shillings for a stone of soap, but he only put 3/6d. in the till, keeping 2/6d. for himself. He was detected by Reece, but he stoutly denied it and said he must have dropped the money. But Reece saw him put his hand in his pocket as he stooped down to look for it, and he saw the 2/6d. in his hand and told him so. Sheldrick denied it, but would not show his hand, and afterwards the 2/6d. was found against the rag basket, four yards from the place where he took the money. So when Mr. Lilley came down he was acquainted with the circumstances. He had a policeman in and Sheldrick was taken to the Town Hall[13], examined and remanded till tomorrow. Reece had some suspicion of him last Saturday and had told Mr. Lilley.

On the following day Sheldrick appeared in court and was committed to the next sessions; these were held on 7 April when he was found not guilty. There is no more mention of him in the diary, so it is probable that he did not return to the shop. Ironically, the assistant named Reece, who reported him to Mr. Lilley, was himself dismissed a fortnight later for taking the day off to attend Newmarket races after he had been refused permission to do so.

Leisure and Recreation

Josiah usually attended at least once on Sundays St. Andrew's Street Baptist Chapel where, in September 1845, he became a Sunday School teacher, and where he was in charge of the library. From November 1848 he went also, fairly regularly, to the Independent Chapel[14] in Downing Place, off St. Andrew's Hill, because a minister, the Rev. George Burden Bubier, whose sermons he much admired, had just been appointed there. He records the 'day of recognition', on 23 January 1848, when George Bubier was formally installed, the occasion being celebrated by a service, which lasted two and a half hours, and a public dinner in the Town Hall. Josiah did not attend the latter, however, probably because the tickets were expensive - 5s. 0d. for men and 3s. 0d. for women. Half a pint of wine, however, was included in the price, a fact which Josiah noted with some disapproval.

The St. Andrew's Street Chapel and the one in Downing Place had both played an important part in the early history of Nonconformity in Cambridge. On Hog Hill, as St. Andrew's Hill was once called, a Presbyterian Church had been established in 1689. To it came, in 1691, a minister named Joseph Hussey who, five years later, persuaded his large following - the Great Meeting as they were called - to adopt Congregationalism. But some members objected to the change and deserted him, joining the congregation of a chapel in Green Street which had been erected in 1689 and had adopted the Congregational way of managing its affairs. The new arrivals however, succeeded in imposing their views on the minister and the church became a Presbyterian one.[15]

When Joseph Hussey left Cambridge, the Great Meeting passed through a period of divisions and quarrels among its members. The wealthier section of the congregation wanted, as pastor, a Mr. Throgmorton, while the poorer preferred a Mr. Davis. A temporary arrangement was made whereby one man preached in the morning and the other in the afternoon, but in 1720 the wealthy members refused Mr. Davis access to the pulpit. So, with about 100 supporters, most of them Baptists, he hired and fitted-up a stable and granary in St. Andrew's parish, in a place called the Stone Yard, and began to preach there on 16 April 1721. This barn was purchased, in 1764, by the congregation and a new, and larger, meeting house was built on its site, to be replaced, in 1836-7, by the present St. Andrew's Street Chapel.

Josiah Chater held very liberal religious views. He had, until coming to Cambridge, attended the parish church in Saffron Walden, where he had been baptised. It was doubtless through his uncle, William Adams, who had become a full member of the Baptist Church in 1806 and who was a deacon at St. Andrew's Street Chapel from 1823 until his death in 1849, that he joined the congregation of that Chapel. But this did not prevent him from going also to Church of England services, to which he was drawn by the many eminent preachers of his day. So he often went to Holy Trinity Church, to Great St. Mary's and, especially between 1844 and 1849, to St. Michael's where the Vicar, the Rev. James Scholefield, Regius Professor of Greek in the University, delivered sermons which greatly appealed to him. He was, though, always more in sympathy with the Nonconformist than with the Established Church, and the whole of his diary reveals his deep religious sincerity.

The mid-19th century was a time when young men of the middle class sought conscientiously to improve themselves by serious reading, by attending lectures and classes, and by joining - or even forming - debating, literary and philosophical societies. Almost as soon as he was settled in Cambridge, Josiah became a member, as his brother William already was, of the Cambridge and Cambridgeshire Mechanics' Institute, which had been established at a public meeting held, in response to many requests for such an institution, on 12 March 1835. The Institute rooms and library were in Sidney Street, and throughout the years 1844 to 1849 there are many references in Josiah's diary to his going to them, in the late evening after work, to read the newspapers and the copies of *Punch*, the *Spectator* and the other periodicals, to borrow books, to attend lectures and, from 17 October 1848 to take a course of French lessons. These last cost him £1 for the quarter, a considerable sum for him to pay

out of his small salary of £20 a year, but the tutor very kindly
gave his pupils a few extra lessons at the end of the course, for
which he charged them nothing. Considering that Josiah had
left school at the age of 12, the amount of serious reading to
which he applied himself is remarkable, especially in view of the
fact that most of it was done round about midnight, 'sitting up
in bed with my greatcoat about my shoulders'. Not only did he
borrow fiction from the Institute, including all the latest numbers
of Dickens's novels as they appeared in serial form, but he read
books of sermons, poetry, political works and speeches and
volumes of biblical criticism. That he *did* read what he borrowed
is evidenced by the comments he often makes in his diary on
the books.

On 1 December 1847 he was taken by Mr. Blumson,

> to hear a debate at the Philo-Union, and a very interesting hour I spent
> there . . . it is a very nice room and the meeting was very well attended.
> I should very much like to join but I cannot afford it.

The Philo-Union or Cambridge Literary Society had been
founded in 1826 for, 'the diffusion of general knowledge and
the discussion of all subjects not of a theological nature'.[16] The
first meetings were held in the *Crown and Woolpack*[17] Inn in
Sidney Street, but in 1846 the Society found new premises in
the *Wrestlers*[18] Inn, Petty Cury; in 1851 it moved again, this
time to No. 63 Sidney Street where it stayed until 1887, when
the Philo-Union was dissolved. A reading room and a well-
stocked library were open to members, and debates were held
once a fortnight. The annual subscription, at the time when
Josiah could not afford it, was 15s. His brother, however, was
able to join, for on 1 February 1848, Josiah recorded, 'William
went to the Philo this evening and held forth for the first time'.

In the Autumn of 1848 Mr. (later Sir) Isaac Pitman came to
Cambridge, with an assistant, Mr. Reid, to lecture on phonography, his newly-devised system of shorthand constructed on a
purely phonetic basis. His three introductory lectures in the
Town Hall were followed by a course of instruction. Josiah
attended the lectures, paid 5s. for the course and 3d. for a class
book, and, on 21 October, went to the first lesson at half past
eight in the evening and came away, 'highly delighted'. He
followed the course on the two following days and, on the
third, recorded,

> I borrowed a shilling of John Moden and after tea I went to King's in

the Cury and bought a Phonographic Manual with it. Mr. Lilley came down a few minutes after eight and so stopped us from going to the Town Hall till a few minutes to nine . . . but we heard Mr. Blumson's letter read that he wrote to Mr. Pitman.

Several letters appeared in the three Cambridge newspapers[19] at this time, but as most of the writers hid their identities behind pen names it is not possible to say whether Mr. Blumson's was published or was sent privately to Mr. Pitman. The majority of the letters condemned phonography as being inaccurate and, to anyone with a knowledge of other systems[20] of shorthand, unnecessary. This seems, eventually, to have become Josiah's opinion too, for on 2 November he wrote,

This evening we went for the last time to the Phonographic lesson, and I think I would much rather have had the money in my pocket. I have no doubt it is all very well for those that do not know a shorthand, but I confuse the one I know[21] with Phonography, so that it bothers me.

Others, however, did not tire so easily, for five days later Josiah heard that it had been decided to form a, 'Society for Instruction in Phonography'.

Many University dons gave lectures at the Mechanics' Institute so that Josiah was able, on 5 March 1847 to hear 'a very pithy and dry lecture from Professor Pryme[22] on *The Progress of Civilized Nations from Barbarism,* the first of a course he is about to pursue'. Late working hours, however, prevented him from attending more than three out of the five; indeed, it was not often that he was able to hear any complete series, and on many occasions he was able to get to only the second half of a single lecture.

In October and November 1847 he heard a Mr. Marriott speak at the Institute on Phrenology, a subject that fascinated him so much that,

I went along to the lecturer and had my cranium examined, and certainly it was greatly to my satisfaction and, I may say, surprise. I have looked into the science a little and do believe there is a great deal of truth in it, and I should advise every one to try it. I have succeeded in getting a class of eight or nine persons.

In the early summer of that same year, the temperance lectures which a Dr. Grindrod had delivered in the Town Hall had also won praise from Josiah, who declared the speaker to be,

a very clever man. He has a splended collection of drawings of parts of the human frame to illustrate the evils arising from the uses of alcoholic beverages, and very well satisfied I was with what he said.

Four days later he declares his intention, 'to stick to total abstinence', and on the following day, 2 June,

> I signed a declaration of my principles up at the Town Hall after hearing some very convincing arguments in its favour by the learned Doctor.

He did not, however, remain for very long a total abstainer. Early in 1848 Josiah's enthusiasm was aroused by a lecture on hydropathy[23] which he heard delivered at the Town Hall by a Dr. Ross,

> I never heard a better lecturer in my life; he kept us till half past ten, but felt no fatigue from sitting so long. He had an extraordinary mode of keeping your interest in the facts he relates. The plates were held at the door and I gave sixpence.

The lecturer seems to have inspired Josiah to put his teachings into practice, for on the following day,

> This morning I tried a new plan of washing. Instead of a sponge I take a towel and saturate it with water and lay it over my head and shoulders, then all over my body, and I find that is the best way of doing it. It is a plan recommended by Dr. Ross.

Two nights later he tried sleeping in a wet sheet, again following Dr. Ross's instructions:

> I have made preparations to have a wet sheet tonight, but the worst of it is that I cannot get anyone to roll me up.

He got very little sleep, for his efforts to envelop himself in the damp sheet were not very successful, so, 'I laid until four o'clock, then I got up and had a good wash in cold water'. And that seems to have been the end of his interest in hydropathy.

But he *was* interested in what he saw at the Observatory[24] on Madingley Road when he went there on 5 October 1848 with his brother, who had obtained permission for them to be shown round:

> At eight o'clock William and I walked up to the Observatory; it was a glorious night for observing. He introduced me to Mr. Todd, a very nice young man, and very clever. He took us over the place; showed us the instruments, three of which we had a peep through. One was placed to see the stars as they passed the meridian; through another we saw the moon, and I could discern the shadows of the mountains thereon, a very interesting sight. Then through the Northumbrian Telescope we saw a star of the 8th magnitude. I must add that through the first instrument we also observed the planet latest discovered, called Neptune[25], about as big as a star of 6th magnitude. The young man has afforded us a very great deal of useful information, inasmuch as we

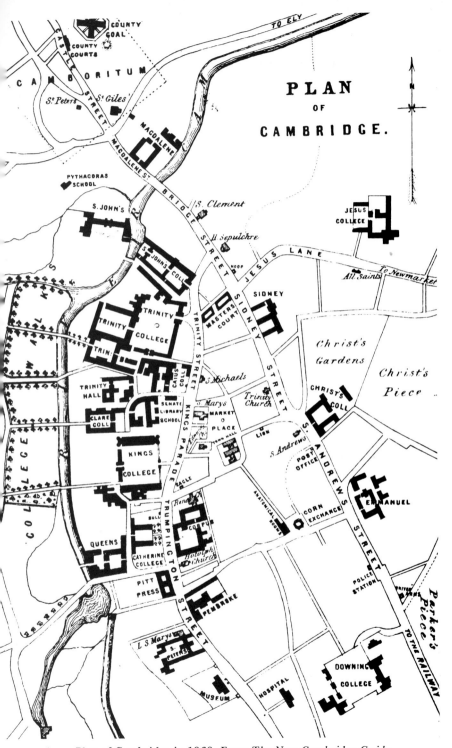

1   Plan of Cambridge in 1868. From *The New Cambridge Guide.*

2   Josiah and Agnes Chater in 1903.

Started this morning in a nine...
peculiar way Mr Lilley went out & did
not come down again after three
Oclock nothing particular tonotify this
day

Mr Lilleys intended togo to London
this morning but on account of his
being out last Evening threw that
project aside wrote agood long letter
to Tom to day to cheer up his time
a bit

Mr Lilley went to London this morning
& Mr Blunson went the Cottenham
journey after dinner. I had to
go to Mr Lilleys with a letter to Smell...
as far as Mr Blunsons house Mrs B
was very gracious I went for Meeting
in the Evening Mrs B came down &
asked me to go for her to Mr Scotts in
the Ram Yard but afterwards she came
& countermanded her solicitation which
I was not at all sorry for on account
of Phrenological lecture at the Mechanics
Institute by a Mr Marris it it before us
till past ten could not go to the nigg...
class

3   A page of the Diary for 1847.

4   Saffron Walden, Essex. From an engraving by C. Mottram in the possession of Mr. G. W. Seaman-Turner.

5   Cambridge Railway Station in 1847. From the *Illustrated London News*

7 Market Street in 1880.

6 Holy Trinity Church and Market Street. From
J. Le Keux's *Memorials of Cambridge*.

8 Petty Cury in 1867. *Copyright* Ramsey & Muspratt, Cambridge.

9   The Market Place in 1842. From J. Le Keux's *Memorials of Cambridge.*

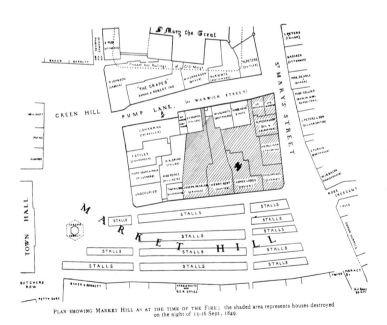

PLAN SHOWING MARKET HILL AS AT THE TIME OF THE FIRE; the shaded area represents houses destroyed
on the night of 15-16 Sept., 1849.

10   Plan of the Market Place before the Fire of 1849. From A. B. Gray's
Cambridge Revisited.

11   The Market Place in 1853

12   The Old Guildhall.

14 Bill of Chater & Osbourn 1867.

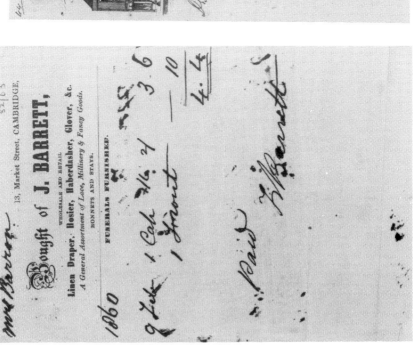

13 Bill of John Barrett 1860.

17   Laying the Foundation Stone of the Cambridge Y.M.C.A.

18   The Cambridge Y.M.C.A. in 1970.

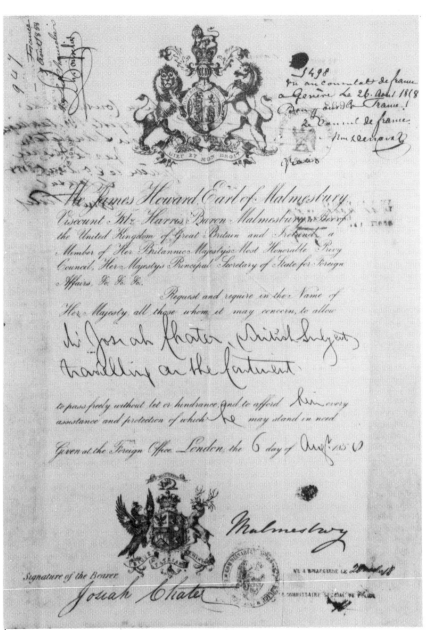

19   Josiah Chater's Passport 1858.

20   Foster's Bank in Trinity Street.
From W. B. Redfarn's *Old Cambridge* 1876.

Knight & Mortlock's Alms Houses. Rebuilt 1818. (by W. Mortlock Esq.)

21   Knight's and Mortlock's Almshouses. From *The Cambridge Guide* 1840.

22   St. John's Street in 1862. Reproduced by permission of the Master and Fellows of St. John's College.

23   A. Macintosh's Ironmongery Shop, 14 Market Hill, in 1880.

24   A Cambridge Tram.

25   The Tramway Terminus by Christ's College.

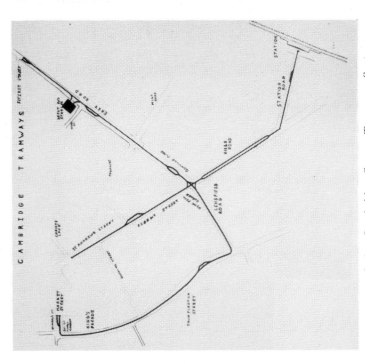

27   Plan of the Cambridge Street Tramway System.

26   The Tramway Track from Senate House Hill to St. Mary's

were both highly gratified by our evening's entertainment. The object glass alone of the Northumbrian Telescope cost £800. The telescope was given by the Duke of Northumberland - a very handsome present.[26]

On 4 July 1848 Josiah paid his first visit to the Fitzwilliam Museum; he wrote, however, no detailed account of what he saw, merely recording in his diary that he went to see over the building, 'as it is now open to the public twice a week, Wednesdays and Saturdays, from twelve o'clock till four'.

The books, pictures, etc. which had been bequeathed to the University in 1815 by Richard, 7th Viscount Fitzwilliam of Merrion, together with £100,000 for a building to house them, had been exhibited, since 1816, first in the Perse School in Free School Lane and, from 1842, in the University Library. The first stone of the permanent museum had been laid in 1837, but building was, from 1845, delayed, first because of the accidental fall from Ely Cathedral tower of the architect, George Basevi, and then by lack of funds. In 1848, however, as the library and galleries were completed, the collections were transferred to them. The public were admitted, first on two days a week and, later, on three, provided they were respectably dressed and were willing, if required, to give their names and addresses.

Ever since October 1846 Josiah had been an active member of a society which as the diary records, his brother had helped to form,

William and G. Battell[27] are trying to form a society for discussing useful knowledge; they have been to look at a room in Sidney Street,

Eight days later, on 9 October, the society was in full swing:

There was a meeting of the Society for discussing useful knowledge. They have hired a room in Sidney Street and there are 19 members who pay a penny a week. My brother and G. Battell are the two chief promoters.

16 October
In the evening I went to our new society. They have elected the officers and agreed for a room at ten shillings a quarter, with fire and candles; nicely carpeted and everything comfortable. I paid 4d. for the first month. Mr. Ginn put the first question, which was upon Education. Several spoke, and well, too. We parted at ten. I think there were 17 or 18 there altogether.

27 October
In the evening I went to our new Society. They call it the Mental and Moral Improvement Society. There was some very good speaking.

The society, which came to be referred to as the Mutual Improvement, flourished for some years, its rooms being later in Wheeler Street, above Thring's coffee house. The members read papers on and discussed such controversial issues as War, Capital Punishment, and the Reform of Parliament, and produced a manuscript magazine to which Josiah contributed articles on *The Influence of Ignorance* and *The Model Mayor*.

It may have been this society that inspired him to encourage his fellow apprentices to improve *their* minds on the evenings which they spent at home, for on 23 November 1848 he wrote,

> After supper we formed a Debating Society in our room; the first meeting is on Thursday. The first question is Is Vocal or Instrumental Music better adapted for public worship.

There is no report of this proposed meeting under the date of the following Thursday, nor is there any further reference to the Debating Society. Either enthusiasm waned or Josiah was well enough occupied by his other activities.

But not all his leisure time was spent in attending lectures, debates, classes and discussions. Soon after he came to work for Mr. Lilley he joined the Cambridge Choral Society[28], sang sometimes in the chorus, and went to many of its concerts, as well as to those given by local and visiting singers and by the University Choral Society. He was not, however, able to get a ticket for the visit of Jenny Lind[29] on 12 March 1849, but managed to hear her because,

> As soon as I could get out I went to Mrs Pink's[30], the cork-cutter's, and asked her if she would let me go in her back premises to listen, and I did. I had a capital place on the roof of a shed just under the window of the Town Hall where I heard her to perfection. I never heard such singing in my life - it was scarcely like a human voice, and so divinely managed. Mrs. Pink gave us a good supper - sandwiches, custards and lots of good things - and would take no more than a thank you.

The apprentices, after the coming of Miss Aikin, often held their own musical evenings. In March 1847 Josiah borrowed from a friend's father, Mr. Ingle, an old violin which, after he had renewed the strings and the bridge, was quite playable. Mr. Ingle also lent John Cook a flageolet so, 'there is a nice row with us'. Josiah practiced regularly, usually early in the morning, and kept up his violin playing for some years.

On 12 February 1848:

> Miss Aikin asked us whether we knew anyone that wanted to hire a
> piano for 2 sovereigns a year. I said I would have it, and it came this
> evening. It is Miss Thodey's[31], but she cannot take it with her, and
> does not want to part with it. Miss Aikin has lent me a book of
> instructions and I intend to learn it.

By 18 February he could write,

> After breakfast, for half an hour, I continue to practice the piano and
> can run up two octaves with both hands pretty tolerably (slow of
> course).

On the following day he could, 'manage one tune decently',
but he was not able to make much more progress because,
exactly one week later, Miss Aikin was asked to send the piano
to London where, presumably, Miss Thodey had managed, after
all, to find space for it. Josiah, to his regret, was thus, 'deprived
of a large source of amusement'.

Because his brother was already in Cambridge when Josiah
arrived in 1843, the latter was at once drawn into the circle of
William's friends. These were, almost wholly, the sons and
daughters of prosperous tradesmen in the neighbourhood of
Market Hill: of John Ingle, the Market Street currier, for
example, of George Shippey, the Sidney Street ironmonger, of
William Macintosh, the coppersmith and tinman, of Joel Smart,
the hatter and clothier, and the families of the tailors John
Johnson, Edward Battell and Simpson and Basham.

Many of these families were Baptists, and so the young people
met regularly at chapel and at the Sunday School. Most of the
girls had been, or still were, at school together, at Miss Sutton's
school in Regent Street, and most of them belonged to the
Choral Society or were keen concert-goers. Many of the boys
belonged to the Mechanics' Institute or to the Mutual Improvement Society.

All of them met, however, at more frivolous events than
chapel services and lectures. They went to the wild beast shows
and the circuses which regularly visited Cambridge and which
Josiah recorded in his diary, although they appealed little to
him. So on 8 November 1844 he noted, 'Van Ambury is building a large brick place on Midsummer Common for the keeping
of his wild beasts and to show off his horsemanship', in
November 1845, 'Wombwell's wild beasts are on the Common',
and on 14 May 1847 that Hylton's menagerie was in the town

and had, 'sent the elephant round this morning with a girl riding on its back'. In the August of that year he *did* go to see Cooke's Riding Circus and reported,

> the performances are very well indeed for that sort of thing, but nothing satisfying to my taste. I could see how it was all done, and there was much imperfection in it. We got out about ten o'clock and the charge was one shilling. It was crammed to excess and very hot indeed.

He had been better pleased by the exhibition of Waxwork Anatomical Models which he had visited for sixpence at the Town Hall on 30 December 1846. He always enjoyed, too, the shows arranged by the Cambridge Florists' Society for which he was usually given a ticket by his cousin, John Chater of Haverhill, who always exhibited at them.

Josiah attached great importance to exercise, which he considered essential for his health. That is why he so often took a long walk before breakfast before he delivered the letters to Mr. Lilley, or after breakfast if that were at all possible. On Sunday afternoons he and his friends would walk to Grantchester or Coton, or along the Trumpington Road and Madingley Road which, in the 1840's, were not yet built upon. Summer evenings, when lectures at the Mechanics' Institute were temporarily suspended, would see the young people strolling along the Backs of the Colleges or about the streets of the town. King's Parade, Trinity Street and Petty Cury were usually crowded with promenaders, some less respectable than others, for the local newspapers commented, from time to time, on the 'disgraceful state' of central Cambridge due to the presence of so many prostitutes. On one occasion Josiah, walking with a friend, was accosted by one of these 'bad women'; the friend lingered to speak to her but Josiah thought it 'prudent to cut away'.

With his fellow apprentices he went regularly to swim in the river at Newnham, although this meant that they had to get up at half past five in the morning in order to be back in Market Street at seven. In winter there was skating whenever conditions were favourable. The nearest skating ground for the boys was the pond in the gardens of Emmanuel College, and Josiah often managed to get on to it on his return from taking the letters to Mr. Lilley.

An annual summer spectacle to be witnessed was the Procession of Boats[32] after the University May Races. Josiah wrote of, 'the vast crowds of spectators on both sides of the river' who had gathered to watch the eights, decorated with flowers and floats, row past in order and line up, side by side, across the river. Each crew, in turn, was cheered by the others who stood to in their boats, oars raised, while a band played *For he's a jolly good fellow.* When the last boats had been acclaimed, the procession re-formed and, led by the crew which had gone Head of the River at the races, rowed back to the boat houses.

For an apprentice, Josiah had generous holidays. He was able to go home, with his brother, for Christmas, the two boys setting out late on Christmas Eve and returning on 26 or 27 December. After 1845 they were able to travel by train to Audley End[33], where their father waited with his pony and trap to take them on to Saffron Walden. In 1844, although they might have travelled by carrier's cart, they walked nine miles to Hinxton and were met there by their father. They returned on 27 December, being driven to Stapleford Turnpike and left there to walk the remaining five miles to Cambridge. This journey took two hours and Josiah was back at work in the afternoon. The brothers, too, had a week's holiday in summer.

Having such a number of friends of their own age in Cambridge, both William and Josiah received many invitations to meals, parties and musical evenings. On 2 January 1845 they were asked by Mr. Smart, the hatter and clothier in Petty Cury, to a New Year's party:

> Mr. Lilley went over to Waterbeach this afternoon which gave me an opportunity of getting away a little earlier in the evening, so that I got to Mr. Smart's very little after eight. They were then playing at Charades, so I joined them and capital fun we had. Then we went to supper and after that had a game at Twilight; I had 3 forfeits and we had rare kissing. After that we had Cross Questions and Crooked Answers . . . we broke up a little after eleven. There were about 24 there altogether, 12 young ladies and 12 young gentlemen. I certainly have not spent such a merry evening for many a day. Just as I was coming away I could not find my hat, so I went home in a barge-man's worsted cap[34] with a long red and green tassel to it.

He returned the cap next day - it was probably borrowed from Mr. Smart's shop - and retrieved his own hat and gloves. That evening, perhaps feeling the effects of the party, he,

> fetched a pint of milk from the Crane and a penny twist from Scrafield[35] and boiled it in Mr. Hayes' copper mug and made a famous supper for twopence halfpenny; and after that I took two pills.

On 23 January 1847 Josiah went to a party given by William's employer, Mr. Basham. It began at 6 o'clock with, 'a very comfortable tea', after which,

> We had Charades and also played Mr. Pickwick and Oliver Twist; we also had a Magic Lantern. Supper at ten - a glorious repast.

In summer there were picnics or, as Josiah called them, *gypsy parties*. He was invited to one in 1848:

16 June

> Of course I worked well this morning and when Mr. Lilley came down I asked for the afternoon which was readily granted. At three o'clock I went over for my charges. Agnes Barrett and Susannah Macintosh,[36] but they were gone on, so I cut after them and caught them at the Mill Road railway gate. We had a hot and long walk, but afterwards came the treat, for at tea we all sat on the grass. After tea came cricketing with sundry other games, and a delightful walk to the chalk pits where there are the best scenes across Cambridge that I know of. We came back and set the ladies all racing, and at nine we cleared up and departed. It was a most splendid day. The walk home I enjoyed most, as we were occupied in conversation on very rational and intellectual topics which we (my two ladies and I) discussed with spirit. There were about 16 or 18 of us in all, a nice round party, and very agreeable indeed.

A little later in the same year, Josiah and his fellow apprentice, Stephen Cook, were invited to a 'Gipsy party' given by the young sons and daughters of John Barrett, the draper whose house and shop at No. 13 Market Street adjoined Mr. Lilley's premises. On this occasion Mr. Lilley was not so willing to give either Josiah or Stephen the afternoon off:

> Soon after Mr. Lilley came down this morning he called me in and asked me why I and Cook wished to go out together, and I told him where we were going. Then he began a short harangue, saying: I might perhaps think him inquisitive in wishing to know, but he only intended it for my good. He said it was not well for me to associate too familiarly with the young ladies so as to give them an opportunity to think I meant more than I intended . . . But what he said, and the sentiments he expressed were administered with such a kind spirit that I could not take it otherwise than as an act of kindness on his part . . . He said he liked me to have pleasure and would always do so when opportunity afforded, and therefore Cook and I might go . . .

At three o'clock therefore, Stephen and Josiah made their way to the meadow belonging, 'to a Mr. Martin[37] and used by him as an archery ground; it is a famous place a little on the road to Grantchester'. They found the rest of the party there and so, the first thing was to have a game at bat and trap[38] and then we had tea. There is a nice little house there and everything comfortable. After tea we played at Hunting the Wild Rabbit and lots of other things till half past seven when once again we adjourned to have some fruit and syllabub, and at nine we started for Market Street. We went to Mrs. Barrett's house, had a good wash and took our seats at the supper table which was sumptuously laden with delicate viands. After supper came singing and music. Miss Fox sang a very nice song - *Jeannette and Jeannot.*

In 1849 Josiah was invited by the Barrett family to join them, on 15 June at Impington where there was to be,

a very large dancing party at Mr. Saunders' to commemorate the putting down of a stone to the memory of a Mrs. Woodcock[39] who was buried in the snow on her way from Cambridge Market in the year 1799 . . . it is a shilling subscription to pay for the stone and they give tea and supper.

He decided, however, not to accept the invitation because of the difficulty of returning home; the Barretts intended to stay the night with relations in the village. He heard, later, a report of the affair:

There were 140 invited; 90 sat down to supper. Some did not get away till four o'clock in the morning, and quite tipsy.

Amidst all his social and cultural activities, and his work, Josiah Chater managed to keep a watchful eye on everything that went on around him in the town. From his meticulous record of major events and minor incidents can be painted a lively picture of the Cambridge of his day.

EVENTS IN CAMBRIDGE 1850-5

The Opening of the Railway

One of the most exciting events in Josiah's early years in Cambridge was the opening of the railway between Cambridge and London. After many proposals - the first was made in 1821 - for the establishment of rail communications between Cambridge and the capital, it was only on 4 July 1844 that the Act which enabled the Eastern Counties Railway to construct a line from the Northern and Eastern Railway at Newport, Essex, to Brandon and Peterborough by way of Cambridge and Ely, received the Royal assent. Shortly before this, a working arrangement had been authorised between the two companies so that,

as from 1 January 1844 the two worked as one. The line from
Newport to Cambridge was built by the Eastern Counties, and
the station at Cambridge was erected on its present site on what
had, until then, been part of the common field of the town.

The University authorities viewed with some alarm the
possible disruptive effects of the new mode of travel on the
quiet peace of academic life. They managed, therefore, to have
inserted in the Act the same clauses which had been included
in the Great Western Railway's Oxford Railway Act of 1843.
Thus the Vice-Chancellor, the Proctors, the Heads of Houses,
the Tutors, the University Marshal, the Yeoman Bedell[40], with
any others who might be deputised by the Vice-Chancellor,
could claim free access to any part of the station when trains
were about to arrive and depart. They could obtain, from the
railway officers, information concerning any member of the
University who was actually on the station, or was coming to it
at these times, and could impose a fine of £5 for failure to
provide such information.

If the Vice-Chancellor, or any of his deputies, heard that a
member of the University who was not a Master of Arts, or a
Bachelor of Civil Law or Medicine, had informed the railway
officials that he intended to travel by train, then the officials
had to refuse to take such a traveller, even if he had already paid
his fare. The University further insisted that, on Sundays, no
passengers were to be set down or picked up at Cambridge
station, or within three miles of it, between the hours of 10
o'clock in the morning and 5 o'clock in the afternoon, unless
the morning train was unavoidably delayed. A donation of £5
was to be made to Addenbrooke's Hospital, or any other county
charity, by the Railway Company if this rule were not observed.

Josiah Chater, living in the centre of the town, did not have
many opportunities to view the actual construction of the
railway, nevertheless, whenever he could he went to see how
the work was progressing. Thus, on 9 October 1844 he went in
the evening for a walk with Mr. Blumson,

> as far as the turnpike gate up the Newmarket Road, and I saw where
> they have begun the railway. They have just finished the little piece of
> new road to use while they are making the bridge over the main road.

On 19 November:

> This morning I went as far as the rail in Newmarket Road, and certainly it is wonderful what a lot of earth they have thrown up since I was there last.

In April 1845 he, 'went a good way up the Cherryhinton Road to see the railway' and reported the men to 'be getting on with it very fast'.

On 1 July he saw his first train when he and his brother walked up Mill Road and across the fields to Cherryhinton Road:

> Just as we were on the bridge a steamer was ready to start, so we waited to see that off. That is the first we have seen running on this line.

The grand opening of the railway was originally planned for 1 July but the event did not, in the end, take place until the 29th, resulting in some confusion - 'a complete bungle', the *Cambridge Chronicle* called it - amongst local tradesmen as to whether the day, when it came, was to be a whole holiday or not. A Parliamentary bye-election in the borough, early in the month, may have had something to do with the postponement. On 29 July Josiah wrote,

> About ten o'clock I had to take a note and happened to meet of Mr. Blumson, who was going to the railway, so I went with him and stayed there till half past eleven. [He does not say whether his long absence from the shop was noticed]. I saw the Grand Train come in - it was a beautiful sight and I have no doubt it is very comfortable riding. Then I came home and found they were going to shut up shop. So I would not wait for my dinner but ran round for Henry Smart who wanted me to go in the water with him . . . About four o'clock several of us went to the Railway; it rained very fast as we were going there so we got rather wet. When we got there Henry Lilley joined us and we played about, jumping and one thing and another, till half past six when we saw the train start for London, and then came home to tea. There were grand doings at the Rail, they had a splendid dinner and there were omnibuses cutting about all day which gives life to the town. There were thousands of people there.

The food for the 'splendid dinner' for the Directors and their friends, was provided by the famous London catering firm of Gunter. It was served at three o'clock in what the *Cambridge Chronicle*[41] described as, 'a very elegant marquee . . . 150 feet in length and 36 feet in width', which had 'a boarded floor and was lined throughout with scarlet and white drapery . . . Tables were laid in the principal pavilion for 300 persons, and adjoining and communicating with it was a smaller marquee, lined and boarded in like manner, in which there was a table for 30 persons. On the opposite side was a third tent in which was stationed the band of the Coldstream Guards . . . A substantial dinner was provided for the labourers in the luggage house which was tastefully fitted up'.

The station itself was decorated with flowers and flags, many of the last being lent by the University Boat Clubs, and with flowers and plants[42], while on the top of the building, so the *Chronicle* reported, 'were numerous cannons which kept up an almost continuous popping, until the most timid lady got brave enough to bear those warlike noises without so much as a start'.

Josiah cannot have heard those cannon, or he would surely have mentioned them. They must have been fired when the Grand Train, which had left Shoreditch station at 8 o'clock that morning, filled with Directors and their friends, returned from Ely, together with the Norwich train, to arrive together in Cambridge for the dinner. At that time he would have been bathing in the river with Henry Smart.

On the following day, when the first passengers were carried on the line, Josiah wrote of the omnibuses from the *Hoop*, the *Lion* and the *Bull* hotels being extremely busy taking people to and from the station, while on 31 July, when he had to go on an errand to the Mill Road Workhouse, he could not resist the temptation of running farther along the road,

> to see if perhaps there might be a train in. I had not been there more than ten minutes when the 3rd class came up from Ely and one was going down to Ely from London, so I had a good view of them.

On 1 August the first parcel - a box of gold leaf - arrived at Lilley's shop by rail from London, but it was not until 20 November that Josiah noted the first delivery by rail from Norwich of three chests of soap. He does, however, mention the accidents which occurred in those early days - a train being derailed, for example, at Chesterfield on 4 August, causing the death of one man, and another mishap on 'the line near London' on 4 November, when, 'a great many sheep were killed and an engine spoiled. Two gentlemen very much hurt and injuries to a great many'.

The first excursion train from London to Cambridge travelled on Monday, 1 September 1845. Josiah wrote, 'it brought down a great many strangers but not so many as was anticipated, about 350 is the calculation'. The *Cambridge Chronicle*[43] gave 'the total influx of Cockneys', whose tickets cost 5s. each, as 286 and reported, 'an immense concourse of persons assembled at the station to watch the arrival of the curiosities who, by the way, conducted themselves very well during their stay here'.

The initial effect of the railways was, on many towns, an adverse one. Cambridge took some time to become used to the new form of transport for the goods which hitherto had been conveyed by river barges, and Josiah was to refer later, in the 1850s, to the numerous local firms which went bankrupt. But already, by the end of 1845, he recorded, 'the markets are so very low and suffering from a most wonderful depression, that they hardly know what to do in consequence of the great speculation in railroads.

The new method of travel deprived many of the old coach drivers of their livelihood, though some found work on the railways and the first Station Master at Cambridge, Mr. Clarke, was a former stage coachman. The town was, however, to see a brief return of the old vehicles.

In September 1847 the Eastern Counties Railway Company unexpectedly increased both its passenger fares and its freight charges. On the 14th of that month Josiah recorded,

> At the Town Hall this evening a public meeting was called respecting the stage coach conveyance which is about to be put into opposition to the Railway Company, and it is to start on October 1st. 200 shares at £5 each. 150 are already taken by separate individuals, one individual not being allowed more than one share.

This was not, in fact, the first meeting. At least two had already been held at the *Crown and Woolpack* Inn in Sidney Street, at one of which, 'a great deal of merriment was occasioned by a letter which had been received from Mr. Bates who proposed to place a steam coach at their service, affirming that he had nearly perfected that mode of locomotion, and that by availing themselves of his invention the company would be able to run the Eastern Counties Railway Company off their own line[44].

At the meeting on 14 September it was formally resolved that a coach to and from London should be immediately established, and there was some discussion as to what name should be given to the vehicle. It was finally agreed that it should be called *The Defence*. An advertisement was duly inserted in the *Chronicle* on 9 October stating that the 'new light four-horse

post-chaise' would leave the *Woolpack* Inn every week day at
10 o'clock and, after calling at the *Blue Boar* in Trinity Street,
would set out for the *Catherine Wheel* and *Green Dragon* Inns
in Bishopsgate Street, London and the *Old Bell* in Holborn, and
return daily from the *Old Bell*. Inside passengers would be
charged 10s. 6d., outside passengers 3s. 6d. Parcels under 7 lb.
in weight would cost sixpence, under 21lb. 10d. and under
28lb. one shilling.

On the following Monday, 11 October, Josiah watched,

> The new coach start this morning . . . with the bugle playing and a loud
> hurrah. It was very animating, I should think there were about 500
> people to witness the starting.

The reporter to the *Cambridge Chronicle*[45] believed, 'not less
than 100 were collected about the *Woolpack*, and all along the
street, as far as the Conduit Head, were groups waiting for the
unwonted, but not forgotten, sight of a real four-horse coach
rolling over our pavements at 10 miles an hour. A lusty cheer
burst forth when the vehicle dashed off, and what with the
bugle playing *Should auld acquaintance be forgot*, and *See the
Conquering Hero comes*, the affair was as exciting as need be'.

The experiment proved successful at first. A meeting of the
Cambridge Coach Association held on 1 January 1848 agreed
to continue for a further three months, but by late spring the
Association was forced to retire from the contest with the
railway. In June, however, it tried again, sending a coach up to
London on one day and back to Cambridge on the next; but by
then even the most timid were willing to entrust themselves to
the railway, and tradesmen were finding it more convenient to
send goods by rail, so in a few weeks the Association ceased.

Elections

Parliamentary elections were lively affairs in the first 10 years
or so that Josiah lived in Cambridge. His diary records the noisy
scenes at the hustings[46] on Parker's Piece where rival candidates
addressed the crowds and where the voters climbed up the
wooden steps to the platform and publicly recorded their votes
in the presence of a booing, cheering crowd. It records, too, the
processions of the candidates and their supporters to and from
their headquarters, the fighting that often broke out after the
poll was declared, the heckling at the meetings, the bribery and
corruption. The Tories alone were, in Josiah's eyes, guilty of the
last, for he was a staunch, even bigoted, supporter of the

Liberals. Municipal elections were less exciting but in these, as assessor to one of the wards, Josiah was eventually to take a part, and he went regularly to political meetings of both parties.

The first Parliamentary election described in the diary was that of 1845 when the two candidates[47] were Fitzroy Kelly and Robert Adair:

8 July

This afternoon the Conservative Band came out of the *Blue Boar* and marched towards Market Hill. Mr. Adair came to solicit Mr. Lilley's voting interest this morning, so I had a good look at him. He is a nice looking man, middle size with dark whiskers . . . After we shut up Mr. Blumson and I went to hear Mr. Adair speak at the *Black Birds*, Barnwell.

9 July

I went to the *Red Lion* to hear Kelly - there was much hissing and groaning, and after they had cheered him someone in the crowd shouted three cheers for Adair.

11 July

Mr. Kelly came to solicit Mr. Lilley's voting interest but he soon got his answer . . . This morning I took two yards of ribbon to Elizabeth Smart to make me a favour.

12 July

John and I have been counting up the buff and blue satin ribbons that have been sold for the election, and we made it out, at a rough calculation, to be 428 yards. That was this morning and we have sold a great deal more since then.

14 July

I went down to the end of the street to see the Whigs go up to the Hustings. About eleven I went on to Parker's Piece and there was such a row. The Tories actually engaged about 200 of the navvies[48] to come and kick up a row, but the Whigs ordered them off the Piece . . . Instead of going in to dinner I went again to the Piece and saw the show of hands, which certainly was 3 to 1 in favour of the Whigs. After that the Tories sneaked home, but the Whigs went up the Hills Road, down Coronation Street and Trumpington Street, across the Hill and down the Cury and up Market Street into St. John's Street and on to the *Hoop*[49]. A splended turnout it was.

15 July

At a quarter past ten I went to the Hustings to see what was to be seen. Kelly was ahead by 69. After dinner I went down again and stopped till a quarter to three, came back and saw Mr. Lilley going home for dinner, so away I cut and did not get home till five o'clock. Kelly was elected by a majority of 17. It was a very sharp contest and he paid dear for it, for they say the last 40 that voted for him cost him one thousand pounds. However, they had no procession, only marched to the *Eagle* and the Whigs to the *Hoop*. There was a severe fight between the rail-road men, who overturned a Whig fly and some of the Whigs. Three of the men are dangerously ill. Just as the Whigs were coming down Regent Street the Tories were coming down Downing Street. The Whig flys and the gentry had just passed that street when the Whigs flew at the Tories, tore down their colours and, it is stated, killed one man.

16 July
A little after eleven o'clock this morning the Tories went marching up Sidney Street to the Hustings, so I went with them to hear what Kelly had to say for himself. The Mayor opened the meeting by giving the state of the poll, which was as I have stated it yesterday. Then Kelly spoke . . . it lasted about 20 minutes and then I came away, and he started off for London, without any chairing or any procession whatever.

Young Josiah certainly seems to have taken a great deal of time off - doubtless unofficially - at election times.

The rumour that a man had been killed in the *fracas* on 15 July was, happily, without foundation, although the fight between the Whigs and the Tories was a desperate one, according to the *Cambridge Chronicle*[50], started by 'the hired ruffians of the Whigs, the leader of whom was a fellow known as Tambourine Sam'. Followers of both parties were injured, and some had to be taken to hospital; flags were torn to pieces and flagstaffs were used as weapons.

The diary devotes less space to the General Election of 1847, when the Cambridge candidates were Robert Adair, the Hon. William Campbell and the Hon. John Sutton, Adair and Campbell being duly elected. Josiah does note, however, on 31 July, 'instead of the two representatives being chaired, they are going to present the money to the Hospital'.

The Chartist Fiasco

In 1848, the Chartist movement, which had remained quiescent after the serious riots it had caused 10 years before, became more energetic under the leadership of Feargus O'Connor. His intention was to present to the House of Commons a petition, signed by five and a half million people throughout the country, setting out the movement's demands[51].

On 5 April Josiah recorded that the whole of Cambridge was talking about the Chartist meeting arranged for the following day, but on 6 April he could only report,

Twelve o'clock came (the time appointed to commence) but no Mr M'Grath. Two o'clock - no information from London. Three o'clock - all getting impatient; so they went to their homes in peace without the satisfaction of hearing anyone speak on the subject of the People's Charter, and many were dissatisfied. But the reason why the learned gentlemen did not attend remains a mystery.

The *Cambridge Chronicle*, however, was able to explain the mystery. On 1 April it had reported that, for several days, a man had been stationed on Market Hill with a petition for the Charter lying on a table for signature. 'We do not believe a dozen sane men put their names to the absurdity, but boys without number displayed their proficiency in writing over and over again. The guardian of the document was generally surrounded by school-boys'.

Describing the meeting that never took place, the newspaper, on 8 April, expressed the opinion that it might have been the Market Hill man who had placed placards about the town inviting working men to attend and hear P. M'Grath speak. The placards aroused interest, 'the people wanted amusement, and as few of them had seen a real live and speaking Chartist, although they had heard a great deal about such curiosities, they began to talk about the matter and to anticipate fun'.

The local magistrates met in council to decide what measures to take should any rioting occur, and they put up notices warning Cambridge people not to attend the meeting, and announcing that special constables had been sworn in to keep the peace. However, as Josiah saw, a good many people did decide to see what was going to happen, but with no speaker appearing the only 'fun' they had was the sight of 'a splendid race between an offender of the law and a rather stout policeman' the latter pursuing his quarry across the Piece to the accompaniment of shouts and jeers from the crowd. There was, later, a scene outside the Gaol on Gonville Place when the man who had, in the past week, been gathering signatures to the petition, announced that Mr. P. M'Grath would not be coming. A mob set on him, but he appealed to a policeman who escorted him as far as Melbourne Place where, being threatened by another noisy group with a ducking in the river, he took to his heels.

Town v. Gown

Because he lived and worked in the centre of Cambridge, Josiah was able to watch and record the many outbreaks of violence which, from time to time, occurred between the under-graduates and the townspeople. 5 November was a traditional day for such outbreaks to occur, but after 1845, when there was 'much fighting between the Town and the University', the threat of severe penalties often restrained the undergraduates from celebrating Guy Fawkes Day too enthusiastically.

But fighting could break out at any time, and once it had begun it often continued for several nights on end, as it did in early March 1846, when:

> About half past nine Mr. Blumson came and rapped at the counting house window and told us there was a row between Town and Gown. So we cut out directly, and a rare row there was, just in the Crescent. Four gownsmen were taken to the Station House. It lasted till eleven. Lord Stamford was one of the leading men, but Tooker of Jesus was taken first. I went to the Station House with him. The last they took had a poker in his hand.

9 March

> The four University men were tried this morning at the Town Hall. One was fined £1.0.0., one ten shillings and one 2/6d. and pay their costs. The other was let off. There were a great many people on the Market Hill and the University men vow vengeance to the police tonight. About half past eight the gownsmen assembled in the Rose Crescent to the amount of, as near as I could guess, 300, and from there they paraded the streets till a little after nine; they began to kick up a row; they had tremendous cudgels. I got out about half past nine and was going up to Miss Reed's[52] but could not get there till nearly ten. There I found my brother and we walked about together for some time till the University men were all taken up. The Proctors and Masters were all out, but to no purpose - there has not been such a tremendous row for many years. After they were taken up, the gownsmen threw glass bottles on to the townsmen's heads, and water and stones, which so enraged the townsmen that they went to all the Colleges and smashed the windows to pieces. Christ's have got it worst. There are above 80 panes broken.

10 March

> I went round this morning on purpose to see the smashed windows at Christ's and Emmanuel Colleges - there are a great many squares broken. The Vice-Chancellor has issued a notice stating that whenever 4 or 5 University men are found assembled together they will be either rusticated or expelled as he shall think fit. I think this, in a great measure, will put a stop to more violence.

On 2 March 1846 Josiah was given permission to leave off work early so that he might go to the Town Hall with his brother, and some of the Smart family, to see the famous dwarf, 'General' Tom Thumb[53]. He paid a shilling for a ticket and was 'highly gratified with the little General who performed his feats very well'. The entertainment was marred, however, by the noisy intrusion of a number of undergraduates, who stormed into the hall, causing Josiah to think 'we must have been crushed to death'. He and William managed to protect Jane and Elizabeth

Smart from the mob, and to carry their little brother to safety. There was more trouble at the performance on the following evening, and more fighting in the streets.

In February, 1848, there were Town *v.* Gown riots on nearly every evening between the 9th and the 21st. On the 19th Josiah wrote,

> The gownsmen have become as bad as they were when Tom Thumb was here, for last night they marched about the town in regiments of about two or three hundred, with pokers and all kinds of weapons of both offence and defence. This evening they have been as bad. I saw one poor Fellow pulled to safety into Mr. Barrett's - he looked almost dead - there were about 60 townsmen after him. One gownsman last night got his leg broken, and many others were very much hurt.

Ugly incidents sometimes occurred when the Proctors arrested a woman whom they suspected of being a prostitute. Such an offender was tried in the Vice-Chancellor's court, where she was allowed no legal aid and no witness to speak in her defence. Her punishment was, usually, a spell of imprisonment in the notorious Spinning House[54]. The townspeople bitterly resented these proctorial powers which, they argued, belonged more properly to the police; they usually, therefore, rushed to the aid of any woman whom they saw being arrested. One such rescue was seen by Josiah on 7 January 1847:

> There was a great row in the street this evening with the Proctors. They had taken up some girl, but the townsmen had rescued her and were hooting the Proctors.

The Royal Visit, 1847

On 5 July 1847 Queen Victoria came to Cambridge with the Prince Consort for the installation of the latter as Chancellor of the University. The town began to prepare at the end of June for the occasion by, as Josiah wrote, 'painting and washing the houses and so on'. Mr. Lilley's employees, on 2 July went to Downing College, where there was to be a Horticultural Fête, to 'cover the tents and tables with green baize', while on 3 July,

> A body of the 2nd Life Guards came in. The company are arriving fast, and an order is out from the Mayor for the suspension of business on Monday at 10 a.m. and on Tuesday at 11 a.m., but the drapers have agreed also to close on Wednesday.

The 4 July was a Sunday, and Josiah and William went to Great St. Mary's Church in the morning to hear Bishop Perry of Australia, 'late minister at St. Paul's Church, Hills Road', and in the evening to hear Dr. Wilberforce, Bishop of Oxford. Then the two boys walked through the courts of St. John's, Trinity and King's to see the crowds. 'It was really astonishing where they all came from. I never saw so many in my life before on a Sunday'.

On 5 July:

> We closed, as did all the shops in the town, at ten o'clock and people began to congregate towards the station to witness the arrival of Her Majesty. At eleven o'clock the Mayor and Corporation marched with the band of the Sappers and Miners attended by the Whittlesey Yeomanry and the Pensioners. The illustrious personage arrived at one o'clock; I had a good opportunity of seeing her from Downing wall. From there I ran the back way to Fitzwilliam Street and saw her opposite the Museum. I then made my way to St. Michael's Church where I had another good view of her and the Prince Consort . . . After tea William and I and G. Battell went down the water as far as Ditton in a boat, where we had a bottle of ginger beer each, after which I went to see the fireworks which certainly were splendid. They were preceded by a fire balloon and followed by a magnificent piece displaying Victoria and Albert in large letters surmounted by a crown. I heard part of the rehearsal of the concert and heard Signor Salvi and Mddle. Albonie, two beautiful singers.

On the following day Josiah rose early and walked along the Trumpington Road to meet his father and his sister Eliza, who were coming from Saffron Walden by pony and trap. They breakfasted together at the *Woolpack* and then went to the Senate House, Josiah having previously secured tickets, to hear the Prize Odes recited in the presence of the Queen and the Prince. In the afternoon they went to the Horticultural Fête in the grounds of Downing College. It was very crowded and 'infernally hot', as well it might be, for there were over 6,000 people there. In the evening Josiah, with his brother Tom from Saffron Walden, and some friends, went on the river, calling on their way back at the *Roebuck* Inn, Chesterton, for ginger beer, and biscuits. From the garden of the inn they had a good view of the 'grand Installation Balloon' which went up from Parker's Piece, the ascent being made by the aeronaut, Mr. Green, who was paid a fee of £60 16s. 8d.

On 7 July, when the shop closed at midday, Josiah went to hear part of the rehearsal of the *Messiah* by the Choral Society in the Town Hall, and then, after dinner, 'saw the Queen go out of the Town attended by her suite'. She and the Prince had, before leaving, attended the public breakfast in Neville's Court,

Trinity College, which followed a ball given in St. John's the
two colleges, as Josiah recorded, 'being connected by a temporary bridge costing £70'.

Fires

Disastrous fires were frequent occurrences in the 1840s. Many
of them broke out in neighbouring villages where the flames
spread rapidly through old timbered and thatched buildings. The
smoke and flames were often visible in Cambridge because of
the absence, at that time, of intervening buildings. So it was that,
on 10 September 1847 Josiah was able to see a large fire at
Cottenham where 16 houses and three farms were destroyed,
and a second one, 'over Swaffham way'.

On 13 June 1845 he wrote of wheat stacks on land in
Madingley Road, belonging to Jonathan Swan, a Cambridge
estate agent and auctioneer, catching fire. A man named Mays
was suspected of arson and was sent to the Town Gaol, but,

> when they went to him this morning they found him dead. He had
> hanged himself by his neck handkerchief. When he had been examined
> at the Town Hall he swore he would kill Mr. Swan the first time he got
> the chance.

On 30 March 1845 Josiah was awakened at half past three in
the morning by

> an alarm of fire in the street. So we got up directly and went out. We
> found it was at the *Red Bull,* just at the bottom of the row, which made
> us quite frightened, but it was soon put out.

Soon extinguished, too, was a fire at the Pitt Press in the evening
of 6 December 1846. It had been caused by burning soot which
ignited some boards which had, somewhat foolishly, been placed
on top of a chimney to prevent it smoking.

A more serious fire occurred on 21 February 1846 at Headly's
iron foundry on Market Hill. Josiah wrote on the 22nd:

> We had not been in bed last night half an hour when we heard the
> alarm of fire - it was between eleven and twelve. We got up immediately
> and found it to be at Headly's Iron Foundry. I have not learned how it
> originated, but at all events it burned down all the building and part of
> Warren and Baker's[55], and Hebblewhite's[56] and the *Chronicle* office. It
> was not three yards from Simpson and Basham's,[57] but they soon got
> their great warehouse cleared by carrying the goods over to the *Red
> Lion.* I carried the books, but happily the premises did not catch.
> Mr. Lilley came down and tied up our books, but I did not think there
> was any occasion for that. After we had done all we could, William and
> I walked behind the Hall and had a glass of lemonade each. I went to

bed about three o'clock, but Stephen and Hayes sat up all night. At
seven I got up and went to look at the ruins. It certainly was a
miraculous escape for Petty Cury, for had the wind been in the North
it must inevitably have come down, but fortunately it lay exactly to
blow the flames towards Trinity Church where there was a vacant space
with no houses.

The fire caused great consternation among the residents of
Market Hill, Market Street, Petty Cury and Sidney Street, for
it was a disaster that had long been feared. The *Cambridge
Chronicle*, on 28 February wrote of the 'exceeding impropriety
of having such premises on such a site. They extend backwards
from Market Hill as far as the corner of Trinity churchyard,
surrounded on all sides by valuable property, much of which is
built of wood'.

The foundry itself consisted mostly of 'a mass of wooden
beams and rafters, old, dry, and exceedingly inflammable'.
Moreover, as the *Chronicle* pointed out, next door was, on one
side, Warren and Baker's shop, 'filled with tallow, fat, turpentine,
oil, gunpowder and all sorts of combustibles', while nearby
were two spirit vaults, 'to say nothing of linen drapers, shops
and warehouses, and wooden stabling and hay lofts. In the very
midst of this sort of property, shut out from the street and
difficult of access, was placed the large iron foundry, a nuisance
at all times to those unlucky enough to live within earshot of
its steam engines, or reach of its "blacks", at all times a source
of danger'.

On 24 February Josiah referred to a letter which had been
sent to Messrs. Headly, 'praying them to desist from rebuilding
their foundry'. The Headlys wrote to the Chronicle denying that
their premises had ever been a source of danger or, indeed, that
they had been completely destroyed in the fire, and pointing
out that the expense of moving to another site would be
considerable. Eventually, however, the iron foundry did find
a new home in Mill Road[58]. Josiah went to see it on 26 April
1847 and found, 'they are getting quite a little town in that
part of the world'.

Market Hill was to be the scene of a still more spectacular
fire in September, 1849, and one which was to alter considerably the appearance of this central area of Cambridge. At that
time a block of shops, built back to back, with living accommodation above, occupied the centre of the market place where
the stalls now stand. Up against the east end of Great St. Mary's

Church, and separated from the central block by a narrow lane
known as Pump Lane, or Warwick Street, were yet more shops
and the *Grapes* Inn. The market stalls, in those days, were set
up on the opposite side of the Hill between Market Street and
Petty Cury, as well as on Peas Hill and under the arches of the
old Guildhall. Outside the last-named building stood Hobson's
Conduit from which the fire engines of the insurance companies
and of Trinity College drew water to fight the fire.

About a quarter to one on the morning of 16 September
Josiah was awakened by Miss Aikin who told him there was a
fire somewhere:

> I immediately jumped out of bed and looked out of the window and
> thought it appeared to be near Mill Lane. I dressed very hastily and
> bundled downstairs when, to my horror, I found it was on Market Hill
> at Lodge's, next door to Orridge the chemist. I ran at once to the engine
> and began pumping, then handed the buckets for a long time. After that
> I went to the *Chronicle* pump and helped to pump and hand the buckets
> for half an hour. All the time the flames were rapidly advancing to
> Orridge's shop. There were very soon 5 or 6 engines there, most of them
> not better than squirts[59]. After a while I went to Mr. Barret's and we got
> out on to the top of the house and watched . . . then we went round by
> the Cury and on to the Hill again . . . The fire raged till about six o'clock
> and burned down 8 houses and seriously damaged several more, all
> tradesmen's. I went home about seven, had a cold bath and went to bed
> and slept till ten. After church I went to look at the ruins, and surely it
> was dreadful - buildings that could have been seen only a few hours
> before, now lying nearly flat to the ground, all black and smoking. I
> must confess though, that while it was burning it was a glorious sight,
> and when the chemist's was on fire, every time a bottle cracked there
> was an explosion superior to fireworks.

Reports in the local newspapers described the terror caused
by the fire. Furniture and crockery were hurled through windows in an effort to save them, salvage carts arrived to take
away the ruined and inflammable contents of Moden's oil and
colour shop, while from Orridge the chemist's spurted a livid
flame from a broken gas pipe. Gas works officials had hastily to
be sent for to turn off the supply at the mains lest an explosion
should occur. As the flames spread it was feared that they might
reach the shops in St. Mary's Street, so Mr. Reed the silversmith
began to move his more valuable stock to Emerson's bakehouse
in Warwick Street. But the danger was averted by the men
handling the pumps, who drenched the walls of the houses in
St. Mary's Street with water, while the occupants placed wet
blankets on the roofs and hung others from the windows. In

the midst of the noise, heat and confusion, the Town Crier moved about the crowds announcing the loss of a gold watch.

Throughout Sunday the engines continued to drench the ruins with water, while the pitiful collection of householder's goods, saved from the fire, was placed at one end of the Hill under the protection of the police, who had a busy time seeing that nothing was looted. As news of the fire spread abroad, large crowds began to filter into Cambridge from nearby villages to look at the devastation. Miraculously, in view of the extent of the blaze and the confined space in which it occurred, there was no loss of life, though many people narrowly escaped being crushed under collapsing walls and beams.

On Monday, 17 September Josiah recorded,

> There has been an inquest held at the Town Hall on the fire, and it is adjourned to tomorrow at 6 o'clock.

The enquiry was held as a result of the many allegations that Mr. Lodge, the clothier on whose premises the fire had started, had deliberately caused it because he was in financial straits. The rumours reached his ears, and he immediately served writs for scandal on a number of persons. So many witnesses had to be examined that the inquest had, perforce, to be adjourned until the following day when, as Josiah wrote, 'the verdict was that the fire originated at Lodge's house, but there was no evidence of its origin'.

By 19 September the men had begun to clear away the rubble. The Corporation began to plan for the future, and after endless debates, discussions, arguments and negotiations, the new market place emerged in 1853. Pump Lane disappeared with the demolition of the property at the east end of Great St. Mary's, the central block of houses was never rebuilt, and Hobson's Conduit was moved to the present site at the junction of Trumpington Road and Lensfield Road.

Later in that same year, 1849, yet another fire occurred in central Cambridge, and once again Josiah helped to extinguish it.

On Sunday, 11 November:

> After coming from Sunday School this morning and on my way to church, I heard that St. Michael's Church was on fire, so away I cut. I reached there before the flames had broken out. As soon as I found out where it was I returned home and changed my clothes in order to work to better advantage, which I found a very wise plan, for in passing the buckets my feet became thoroughly wet. It began at a

quarter to eleven and was extinguished before one o'clock. Fortunately there were not many people in the church.

The water was obtained from the pump in Trinity College kitchen and when the supply began to fail, the double line of helpers, among whom was Josiah, was extended so that the buckets could be passed through the New Court to the river and back again. The fire began in the flue of the church's heating stove and spread to the roof of the south aisle.

Public Penance at Ditton

On Sunday, 6 May 1849 extraordinary scenes occurred in the village church of Fen Ditton near Cambridge. Edward Smith, a gardener and former parish sexton, had, two years before, when he had been over-indulging in the village inn, made libellous statements concerning the chastity of the Rector's wife, Mrs. James. These were later repeated to her and she brought a case against Smith in the Ecclesiastical Court. In 1849 this finally reached the Court of Arches which sentenced him to do penance and to pay costs amounting to £49 7s. 6d.

When the sentence became known, there was great excitement in the county, and on the day appointed for the performance of the penance, about 3,000 people went to Ditton in the hopes of seeing Smith wrapped in the traditional white sheet of the penitent. Among the crowds were respectable inhabitants of Cambridge and the neighbourhood who had applied for tickets for reserved seats, but on arriving at the church they found it already crammed with a noisy band of labourers from Barnwell and lightermen from the river barges. These had clambered on to the chancel screen and on to the capitals of the pillars, and had smashed several windows in their efforts to get through them.

The Rector pleaded in vain with his wife to call off the affair, and so, at eleven o'clock, the Rev. A.H. Small of Emmanuel College, followed by Mrs. James, her husband and her lawyer, entered the church to begin Matins. What followed almost exhausted the vocabulary of the newspaper reporters who had come to describe the event.

Josiah was not present, but in the afternoon,

William and I, Cook and Miss Aikin's nephew, walked over to Ditton to the church to see what sort of a wreck was left,, for during the morning service a man named Smith was to do penance in the church for having defamed the character of Mrs. James, the minister's wife, imputing to her the crime of adultery. Mrs. James carried it into the

Arches Court and got her accuser condemned in costs and to do
penance. Accordingly, this morning hundreds of people were wending
their way to Ditton to see the performance of one of the last monkish
institutions of popery. The service was performed by a Mr. Small of
Emmanuel College, Cambridge. As soon as he began he was saluted
with 'Speak up, old boy' and such-like exclamations. When the sermon
began the mob began to set up cries and yells and noises of all description
so that it was impossible to hear what was said, and about half past
twelve Smith, the culprit, made his appearance. He was received with
shouts and cheers quite deafening; the bells rang and the minister left
the pulpit to get nearer to him in order to hear him read his recantation;
but that was impossible, and the pulpit immediately filled with spectators. In the porch was a dog fight and in the church two men were
fighting, and others were smoking pipes of tobacco. But to crown the
affair, the basses[60] used for kneeling upon were used as missiles and
hurled from one end of the chancel to the other. One hit Mr. Small on
the head. The tops of the pews were all crowded and many of them
gave way from the crush. The pieces were taken to throw at the minister,
and an old broom that was found was used very effectively. The bells
were ringing the whole time, and after the service, which was obliged to
be ended prematurely, two men took Smith and carried him on their
shoulders to the *Plough*, and there they spent the rest of the day
drinking and smoking. I had my history from several eye-witnesses,
besides what I saw of the ruins. It was the most disgraceful affair ever
witnessed and the like can surely never happen again in England. The
people hooted and hissed parson James to his house and, it is said,
broke his windows with stones. Mrs. James was married to her husband
about two years ago; she had been his cook and the man Smith was his
gardener. Previous to her marriage she was ill for about a month, and
only her master tended her, and a very short time after their marriage
this man Smith, digging in' their garden, found a child's head severed
from its body, and its body in a pond close by, which was very sus-
picious. Bit it all passed off until when this man Smith, when he was
one day half drunk, called Mrs. James a w...e, which was communicated
to her, and this that I have related is the consequence. It is to be feared
the man had some cause for making such an assertion, but even if
erroneous, how absurd the punishment.

The allegations made by Smith were believed by very many
people but were never proved. He himself, though a collection
was made on that famous Sunday, and local farmers contributed
generously, never paid his costs, probably because the money
never reached him. In July, therefore, he was imprisoned in the
County Gaol for five months before being finally discharged as
an insolvent debtor.

British Association Meeting

In 1845, in Cambridge, the British Association for the Advancement of Science held its 15th annual meeting from 18-25 July. Josiah did not attend any of the lectures, but he does record that one of Mr. Lilley's employees, Mr. Best, spent the whole of one day putting green baize on tables in preparation for a Horticultural Fete on 20 June. Mr. Lilley did not come down to the shop in the evening of that day, so Josiah was able to leave just after eight o'clock and visit the flower show with William. There they met their cousin, John Chater of Haverhill, whose entry of pansies gained first prize; he afterwards gave the flowers to the boys.

The British Association meeting was a serious affair, with no excursions or outings; indeed, the *Cambridge Chronicle* described the Horticultural Fete as, 'the only little bit of relaxation from the more severe pursuits of science which has yet been afforded the visitors'.

Thefts and Burglaries

On Thursday, 2 October Josiah recorded,

> On Monday last, or Tuesday morning, someone broke into Peterhouse College and stole about £300 or £400 worth of plate out of the buttery. A £60 reward is offered this morning.

The *Cambridge Chronicle,* on 4 October, reported that thieves from London were suspected of the crime. Messengers had been sent to the capital, and to Yarmouth, Norwich and Bury St. Edmunds with a description of the stolen plate, but the time they had to spend in travelling gave ample opportunity for the criminals to get away. 'Had the electric telegraph been installed on our railways', declared the *Chronicle*, doubtless Peterhouse would have recovered its plate'.

In 1849 Josiah wrote of another burglary, this time at Grange Farm in Cambridge:

> On Saturday night a party of robbers broke into Mr. Toft's house at Grange Farm, went into a room where slept two ladies, and took two gold watches and £7. 10s. Tofts, hearing them, jumped out of his window and ran off to the police station without anything more on than his shirt and drawers. When he arrived there he was locked up for three hours as he was considered mad. Well might they think so, to leave his sister and another female to the mercy of three robbers and run all that way, nearly two miles; most absurd, seeing he had on his premises two other men, besides dogs.

Cholera Epidemic

In 1846 Josiah noted, on 4 August, 'the English Cholera is now raging in this town and several persons have died of it, one a waiter at the *Lion*. He died in a few hours'.

English Cholera, also known as Summer, British or Autumnal Cholera, was characterised by severe vomiting and diarrhoea which, especially where the disease was epidemic, could result in death. Alternatively, the symptoms could disappear in a day or two. Josiah himself, at the end of July, 1846, 'felt very queer' one day and thought that he had 'a slight attack of the English Cholera', but after dosing himself with a blue pill and half an ounce of salts, he had recovered by the following evening. On 5 and 6 August two of Mr. Lilley's employees went down with the complaint and were away from work for two days. As in Josiah's case, their symptoms were not severe enough for a doctor to be consulted.

In 1848 and 1849 an epidemic of the malignant Asiatic cholera reached Cambridge. Josiah noted the deaths from the disease, in these years, of several local inhabitants, and on one occasion he heard a sermon at St. Michael's Church in which the preacher attributed the outbreak to God's displeasure with the nation. The appalling sanitation of most English towns and villages at that time, and the drinking of sewage-polluted water were, however, more accurately to be blamed for it.

The epidemic, which had appeared in 1841 in India and China and had finally reached England in 1847, was even more deadly than an earlier one which had broken out in Bengal in 1823. This had spread to other parts of Asia and to Africa, reached Russia in 1830 and 1831, and thence to Britain by way of Germany, and to Ireland and across the Atlantic to North America. In Cambridge it had led to the establishment, in November 1831, of a Board of Health composed of the Vice-Chancellor, seven members of the University, the Mayor, seven inhabitants of the town, 14 surgeons and six physicians.

In 1848 the first Public Health Act was passed, which established the Central Board of Health. Early in the following year, over 600 Cambridge residents signed a petition to the Board requesting the application of the Act to the Cambridge district. The superintending Inspector of the Board made a general survey of the town - its water supply, sewage disposal and drainage - and published his report at the end of May.

On 18 June a public meeting was held in the Town Hall to discuss this report. Josiah attended the meeting and recorded,

> I went to the Sanitary Reform meeting this evening, which was a very poor affair, like all Cambridge meetings for the public benefit. No order - all uproar and confusion. A resolution was passed that they did not want any improvement.

Yet, in 1849, about a sixth of the population of Cambridge lived in unventilated houses tucked away in small courts and yards, with no drainage and no water supply. A large portion of the town was undrained, and the outfall of what sewers there were was into the river. The streets were dirty and many of them were unpaved. Many people relied for drinking water on pumps, some of which provided water which had travelled through graveyards and 'filtered through the corpses of our ancestors' as the Improvement Commissioners heard from their surveyor at a meeting in 1852. It was small wonder that the Inspector of the Central Board declared, in his report, 'the sanitary conditions of numerous courts and places is so wretched as to be a disgrace to humanity, and still more so to civilisation'.

To improve such a state of affairs was to be the work of the last half of the 19th century; but it was to take time, for Cambridge was notoriously slow to take kindly to change, even when such change was to benefit the health and well-being of its inhabitants. Even by the early years of the present century there were still houses built back-to-back, and cases of one tap being shared by 20 homes, even of homes which still had to use water from wells or pumps.

Seasonal Customs

Regularly, while he was living in Market Street, Josiah wrote of hearing the bells of Great St. Mary's Church being rung for a quarter of an hour to signal the ending of the old year and the beginning of the new.

On 1 January 1844 he recorded,

> The boys made such a row with their hot New Year's cakes this morning.

This is unfortunately, the only mention he makes of these cakes; indeed, this is the only known reference to them. The cakes may have been made by one of the bakers in Petty Cury, Market Street or Market Hill and their sale was, possibly, limited to this area of the town.

Twice he noted the presence of the Plough Monday dancers. On 13 January 1845:

> The first thing this morning was the morris dancers, it being Plough Monday. They did kick up such a row as I never heard before in all my life - all day long, men, women and the boys.

In the following year, however, he reported that there were 'Not so many ploughboys about today'.

Plough Monday was celebrated in Cambridge until the early years of this century, dancers coming in from nearby villages to perform on the market square. The omission from the diary of any reference to the day after 1846 is due, probably, to the serious-minded Josiah having but a poor opinion of such a custom.

He did, however, record regularly the pre-Christmas visits of the Waits. Thus, on 15 November 1844,

> Last night, about half past one or two o'clock, I heard the Waits, that is 3 or 4 persons who go about the streets from the middle of November to Christmas Day, playing on instruments which sound beautiful in the dead of night.

The Town Waits are first recorded in the year 1511, when four men were paid by the Corporation to perform not only at Christmas but on other occasions of rejoicing. By the 18th century their number had increased to 15. Records of payments made by the Town Treasurers in the 16th century show that russet or red material was, at that time, provided for the minstrels' cloaks and that the singers also wore silver collars or chains and silver arm badges. In the 19th century the Waits were often accompanied by groups of hand-bell ringers.

External Affairs

Throughout the diary Josiah's references to national and international events and affairs are few in number, but he did, in 1848, mention briefly the abdication of Louis Philippe and the civil unrest in France preceding the proclamation of a republic.

A believer in the doctrine of free trade, he was delighted when the Corn Laws were repealed in 1846. The diary shows that he had read, in the *Times* and other newspapers, reports of Sir Robert Peel's speeches, and that he had attended lectures delivered in Cambridge in support of the free trade movement. Once, in order to hear the other side of the question, he went to a Protectionists meeting held in the County Courts, but reported, 'there was such an uproar that some could not speak at all'.

On 6 August 1846 he and his brother went to the *Osbourn Arms* in Hills Road where, 'there was a grand display of fire-works, dancing and a balloon in commemoration of the Corn Law Repeal Bill'.

With the failure of the potato crop in Ireland in 1845, the resulting plight of the starving people of that country became a burden on the social conscience. Money was raised by public subscription and collections were made in churches and chapels to relieve the sufferings of the Irish.

In St. Andrew's Street Baptist Chapel, so Josiah recorded in 1846, a collection made on Sunday, 17 January, raised £236: 'an enormous sum for a small place like this'. A second collection on the following Sunday resulted in a further £264.

The chapel members, however, were less in sympathy with the Irish in the matter of the grant made by Sir Robert Peel to the Roman Catholic College of Maynooth in 1845. On 9 April Josiah noted that there was to be, that evening, a meeting at the Independent Chapel in Downing Place, 'to draw up a petition to oppose the intended grant to Maynooth College'. He himself did not attend the meeting but Mr. Lilley did so and he told his employees all about it.

The petition was placed, on the following Sunday, on a table in the chapel, to be signed by those attending the services; then it was taken to Simpson and Basham's shop in Petty Cury where, two days later, Josiah added his name to it.

Personal Affairs

The year 1849 - the year in which, on 12 November, he reached the age of 21 - was a period of worry and uncertainty for Josiah. In the first place he had, by then, realised that he was 'truly in love' with Agnes Barrett, whom he was eventually to marry. In 1849, however, his prospects of ever being able to propose to her were black indeed. Secondly, Mr. Lilley had, in March, suggested that, as his period of apprenticeship was nearing its end, he should, in order to gain experience, begin to look for employment elsewhere, though there was no question of his being dismissed until he had found a suitable post. So Josiah was applying for jobs, most of them outside Cambridge, although he had no great wish to leave the town and the many friends he had there and was, of course, reluctant to go away from the girl he loved.

Agnes Barrett is first mentioned in the diary on 1 May 1845 when Josiah recorded that, on the previous evening, he and two of his fellow apprentices had been running races with her in the yard. She was then a 12 year-old schoolgirl, living with her parents, Mr. and Mrs. John Barrett, and her elder brothers and sisters, above John Barrett's woollen drapery shop next door to Mr. Lilley's. It was inevitable that she and Josiah should see much of each other. They not only lived in the same street, but they met at lectures, at the Choral Society, at concerts and in the houses of the many friends they had in common.

Casual friendship ripened into affection. By the end of 1848 each knew the other's feelings, though they very sensibly agreed not to be seen too much together, so that no one would have occasion to gossip. Meanwhile, Josiah, nearly five years her senior, adopted an almost paternal attitude towards Agnes: he supervised her serious reading, brought books for her from the Mechanics' Institute, taught her to play chess, and interested himself in all she did at school, which she did not leave until she was 16 in 1849. From September, 1848, he was a welcome and frequent visitor to the Barrett household, especially after the sudden death of Agnes' mother in the early hours of 26 December of that year.

But although Josiah could find an outlet in his diary for all that he felt about Agnes, he knew that marriage was impossible until he had decided what his future was to be, and until his financial position was more secure. His salary, at the end of 1849, had risen from the £10 a year that he received on first coming to Cambridge, to the magnificent sum of £20. From the end of March, therefore, he worried a great deal about his future, although his uncle and all his friends, including Mr. Lilley and Miss Aikin, promised to do all they could for him.

By mid-September Josiah was thinking of going as a clerk in a surveyor's or builder's office - 'I should not like to be a draper' - although he realised that he would have to serve a further period of poorly-paid apprenticeship. A month later he was considering whether he ought not, perhaps, to return to Saffron Walden to help his father in the running of his seedsman's and landscape gardener's business. He went to London and was interviewed for office work, but was not really sorry when he failed to get a post. He became depressed and anxious, feeling that he was, 'starting life all over again, as it were'. Nor was his depression lessened by the death on 7 August after a short illness, of his uncle, William Adams.

William Adams was born in Haverhill, Suffolk, in 1776, and was educated in the Cambridgeshire village of Chesterton. While he was there, he used to visit a distant relation by marriage, a Mr. Simpson, who was a woollen draper in Cambridge. Eventually, William Adams became an employee, and later a partner in Mr. Simpson's business, married his daughter and became, in time, solely responsible for running the firm. He did this so successfully that he was able to retire fairly early in life and to devote himself to the numerous charities in which he was interested, and to his duties as deacon of St. Andrew's Street Baptist Chapel of which he had become a full member in 1806.

It was through their uncle that both Josiah and William Chater had come to Cambridge. He saw a great deal of them, had them to his house on Sundays and, as Josiah recorded in his diary, 'agreed to clothe us until we received a salary of £20 a year'. That he was a generous provider of clothes is evidenced by the many new jackets, coats, trousers, shoes and hats that the boys had. Doubtless Mr. Adams wished his nephews' appearance to do him credit, and only on one occasion did he remark to William that he thought they, 'had had too many clothes last year'.

Between the years 1844 and 1849 Josiah carefully recorded the items of dress that he acquired. He had arrived in Cambridge, as he wrote in a *resume* of his life on his 21st birthday,

> in jacket and lay-down collars, but of course, seeing lads of my own age aspiring to stick-ups and coats, I could not be long behind them, and was not easy until I had donned myself in that habit.

So, on 19 October 1845:

> I first began this morning to wear stick-up collars and I do feel queer in them. I put on one of my striped cravats, but I cannot tie them as I would like.

The collars had been made by his stepmother, and on the next day he wrote to her to ask her not to send him any more; however, in a little while he mastered the knack of tying the cravats and found that he, 'contrived to make the collars go somewhat better this day. It was the fault of the stiffening'.

Josiah's coats, trousers and waistcoats were made to measure at Smart's, the clothier in Petty Cury. On 9 April 1845, for example, he was measured for a new jacket and waistcoat of mulberry cloth and, two days later, for a pair of ash-coloured trousers; to wear with these he bought, 'a pair of braces and a pair of ends for them, all for 9d.'.

On Good Friday, 1847, Josiah went home for the day resplendent in 'a new suit, black and white check trousers, plaid waistcoat and olive green double-breasted jacket', in which he felt 'no little swell'. His brother was also elegantly attired that day, in trousers of similar check, 'but his coat and waistcoat different'. He was probably not wearing the new olive dress coat in which Josiah had seen him for the first time a few days before, and reported him as, 'looking slap'.

A blue plaid double-breasted waistcoat, costing 6s. 6d., blue and white doeskin trousers, light summer waistcoats, numerous jackets and a suit consisting of green trousers, 'with a border down on one side, blue silk velvet waistcoat and black dress coat', were among the items that joined Josiah's wardrobe between 1846 and 1848. With them were several hats, made to measure, and several pairs of hand-made Clarence boots[61] and 'Oxonian'[62] shoes. Small accessories such as gloves - lavender-coloured kid for summer at 1s. 0d. a pair, or Berlin wool, lined with wash-leather for winter, at 9½d. a pair - and scarves and handkerchiefs, Josiah seems to have purchased himself. On several occasions, when he went to see his brother at Simpson and Basham's, he would notice a piece of material - black and white, striped or plaid silk - which took his fancy. He would buy sufficient of this and send it home to be cut down the middle and sewn to make a scarf for himself and another for William.

William Adams died a wealthy man. Besides bequests to his widow - to whom was also left his house at No. 19 Fitzwilliam Street - and members of his family (he had no children), he gave, by his will, over £4,750 to charitable institutions in Cambridge and elsewhere. To each of his nephews, William and Josiah, he bequeathed the sum of £300. This legacy provided the answer to Josiah's doubts about his future, and was to enable him, with his brother, to set out on a completely new way of life in Cambridge.

NOTES TO PART I

1. John Purchas (1750); Hart & Ansell (1784); Hart & Howell (1793); Howell, Staples & Eaden (1798); Howell & Eaden (1808); William Eaden (1833). William Eaden was succeeded in 1839 by his nephew

William Eaden Lilley, great grandfather of the present directors of
W. Eaden Lilley & Co., Ltd.

2.   William Adams moved shortly before his death to 19 Fitzwilliam
Street. His widow bequeathed this house to Josiah and William
Chater.

3.   These plasters, made of Burgundy pitch or of tar resin and beeswax,
were a popular remedy for chest ailments.

4.   The warehouse in which sperm oil, used in lamps, was stored.

5.   Robert Sayle opened his drapery and silk merchant's business at 12
St. Andrew's Street in 1842. On 13 March 1847 Josiah visited the
shop to see its 'dashing new front'.

6.   He lived in Park Terrace near Parker's Piece. On his marriage in 1850
he moved to Hills Road but, by 1858, was settled in his new house
in West Road - then called New Road - which was to remain the
Lilley family's home for the next century.

7.   Granted by royal charter of *c.*1211 to the lepers of the Hospital of
St. Mary Magdalen, the fair, once one of the greatest in Europe,
was later acquired by the Corporation of Cambridge. It was proclaimed both by the Mayor and, until 1855, by the Vice-Chancellor
of the University, but its importance as a trade fair declined from the
late 17th century. It was last proclaimed in 1933.

8.   This spelling of Stourbridge was common until the mid-19th century.

9.   The horse fair was held separately from the main Stourbridge Fair.
A brisk business in the buying and selling of horses, saddles, harness
and other leather goods continued until the early 20th century.

10.   John Barrett's linen drapery shop adjoined Mr. Lilley's premises.

11.   This inn became the *Coach and Horses Dining Rooms* 1870-83. It
was on part of the site now occupied by the True Form Shoe Co.
on the corner of Petty Cury and Sidney Street.

12.   Pulled down in 1848. Its yard is now Market Passage.

13.   The Cambridge Guildhall was often called the Town Hall in the 19th
century.

14.   Congregationalists were formerly styled Independents.

15.   Such changes in title had less significance in those days than·they
would have today.

16.   *History, Gazetteer and Directory of Cambridgeshire,* 1851.

17.   This stood near the corner of Sidney Street and Hobson Street on
part of the present site of Lloyds Bank.

18.   At the corner of Petty Cury and St. Andrew's Street. It was pulled
down in 1884 and a new General Post Office, opened 1885, was
erected on its site. The Post Office moved to its present premises
in St. Andrew's Street in 1934; the earlier building, used in its last
years for the Civic Restaurant, was demolished in May 1972.

19. These were: *The Cambridge Chronicle and University Journal; The Cambridge Independent Press and Huntingdon Gazette; The Cambridge General Advertiser.* The last-named ceased publication in 1849.

20. Shorthand, known from ancient times, was revived in England in the early 17th century; several systems were in use in the 1840s. All however, were based on the letters of the alphabet and not, as was Pitman's, on phonetics.

21. Josiah occasionally, at this period, wrote a few words in his diary in William Mayor's system of shorthand.

22. George Pryme (1781-1868), Professor of Political Economy and several times M.P. for Cambridge.

23. Treatment of disease by means of hot and cold water baths, wet packs etc. became increasingly popular from the early years of the 19th century. Hydropathy was introduced into England by Captain Claridge in 1840; soon afterwards medical baths opened at Matlock and elsewhere.

24. Erected for the University in 1822 on the Madingley Road.

25. The existence of Neptune had been suspected, before it was actually observed, by reason of its action on the planet Uranus, discovered in 1781 by William Herschel. In 1843 John Couch Adams (later Lowndean Professor of Astronomy at Cambridge), then up at St. John's College, proved mathematically the existence of another planet which would account for the irregularities in the motion of Uranus. He left a record of his findings with Sir George Airy (later Astronomer Royal) who, with another Cambridge man, James Challis, Plumian Professor of Astronomy and Director of the Cambridge Observatory, had also worked on the problem. Soon afterwards the French astronomer, U.J.J. Leverrier, published similar conclusions, arrived at by independent study. A search for Neptune was begun on 9 July 1846 with the Northumberland telescope at Cambridge; its existence was finally established in September. J.C. Adams and Leverrier were awarded equal honours by the Royal Society.

26. The Duke of Northumberland, Chancellor of the University, not only presented the telescope in 1835 but defrayed the cost of the buildings in which it was housed.

27. Son of Edward Battell, tailor, 5 Market Street, Cambridge.

28. Established in 1847.

29. Popularly known as 'the Swedish nightingale', Jenny Lind (1820-87) was born in Stockholm and sang regularly in opera from 1837. She first visited England, which she later made her home, in 1847, when she sang in a number of towns and cities, including Norwich. In Norwich she made the acquaintance of the Bishop, Edward Stanley, and it was his influence, it is said, that led her to give up the stage as a career. She made her last appearance in opera in 1849; thereafter she sang only in concerts and oratorios.

30. Mrs. Pink's house was on the east side of Peas Hill where a row of shops stood until demolished, 1935-6, for the building of the present Guildhall.

31. Daughter of the Rev. Samuel Thodey, minister since 1820 of the Independent Chapel in Downing Place. He left Cambridge for London in 1848 because he was unwilling to accept a reduction in his stipend.

32. These processions were held from 1832 until 1892.

33. Then, as now, the nearest station for Saffron Walden.

34. The men who worked on the barges which brought goods to Cambridge in pre-railway days were noted for their distinctive dress. Many of them wore sleeved waistcoats of crimson or dark blue, fastened with glass buttons.

35. John Scrafield, baker, 20 Market Street.

36. Josiah was to remain friendly throughout his life with the Macintosh family. Alexander (Alex) Macintosh, who is so often mentioned in the diary, was the son of William Macintosh who, in 1816, began trading as a coppersmith at 23 Market Street. Alexander, after apprenticeship with an ironmonger, joined his father in 1845 and added ironmongery to the business. In 1884 Alexander bought the ironmongery business of Edward Beales, 14 Market Hill, and moved his own stock to the new premises. His sons William and, for a time, Charles, joined him and the firm was known as A. Macintosh & Sons Ltd. The business was continued by the family until 1962. No. 14 Market Hill, demolished soon afterwards in a redevelopment scheme, is known to have been an ironmonger's shop since 1688 when it was acquired by William Finch. Four generations of Finches succeeded him until 1847 when the business passed to a nephew, Swann Hurrell, who was succeeded in 1870 by his nephew Edward Beales. The iron foundry owned by the Finches stood near the site of St. John's College Chapel until *c.* 1862. It was replaced by one in Thompson's Lane which, with the Market Hill shop, was acquired by the Macintoshes who ran it until 1924 when it moved to Mill Road.

37. A bow and arrow maker with a shop in St. Edward's Passage.

38. This game, very popular in Cambridgeshire, was played with a small hard ball and a wooden trap. The last-named was 6-7 ins. long, solid but with a central groove in which was inserted a spoon-shaped wooden trigger mounted on a pivot, the handle extending over the toe of the 'shoe'. The trap was placed on the ground and two boundary lines were fixed to mark the area of play. The first player then put the ball on the 'bowl' of the spoon-shaped trigger, hit the handle with the bat, then struck the ball as it rose. The other players tried to catch the ball in flight or, failing that, to retrieve it from the ground and throw it to hit the trap. The striker, if caught or knocked out, gave way to the next player. Each striker aimed to stay in until he had scored 20 hits.

39. Elizabeth Woodcock, on 3 February 1799, had come in on horseback from Impington to do her weekly shopping in Cambridge.

She set out for home late in the afternoon, stopping, on her way along Castle Street, at the *Three Tuns* (a 17th-century inn demolished in 1936). Here she had a glass of gin, by no means the first she had taken that day. When she came out of the inn it was quite dark, and the snow, which had been falling intermittently all day, was coming down thickly and there was a bitter north-east wind blowing.

Though half-blinded by the swirling flakes, she managed to ride to within half a mile of her cottage and then, on a bridle path which she had taken as a short cut, her horse, frightened by the sudden flash of a falling meteor, reared, turned round and made for a ditch running alongside the path. Elizabeth was forced to dismount; she managed to catch the horse and lead it a little way, but the animal was still so alarmed that it tore itself from her grasp and bolted. Weighed down by her snow-sodden garments and by the basket of groceries on her arm, Elizabeth struggled on for a few yards and then, exhausted, sat down under the shelter of a hedge which grew on the top of a high bank.

The falling snow, blown by the high wind, piled up all around her as she sat, until she was finally enclosed in a kind of cave formed by the wall of snow in front of her and the hedge and bank behind. Here she stayed until, on the third or fourth day, she saw a gleam of light in the snow wall and managed to push through a twig to which she had tied her red handkerchief.

Meanwhile her family and friends, alarmed by the return of the riderless horse, had organised a search party, but it was not until the Sunday, 10 February, that a young farmer, William Muncey, caught sight of the handkerchief and, approaching the spot and peering through the snow wall, thought that he saw a human figure on the other side of it. He fetched help and Elizabeth was rescued and taken home, but she lived only until the following July, in great suffering from the frost bite which caused her toes and fingers to turn gangrenous and finally to drop off.

A stone to commemorate her extraordinary experience was erected soon after her death, on the site of her imprisonment, but this became so defaced by visitors who carved their initials on it, that it was replaced by a new one, set up in the middle of a field, though later, as it interfered with ploughing, it was moved to the hedge-side.

The dedication of this second monument was a great day in the neighbourhood and was celebrated by the party to which Josiah Chater was invited.

Towards the end of the last century the then owner of Impington Hall, on whose land the stone was placed, decided to move it to the site of the first one. The Histon builder, Merrington Christmas, who carried out the removal, found in the foundations a stone column, rather like a milestone. A faint inscription on it led him to believe that it was the first memorial stone, and this belief was endorsed by the then very old and bed-ridden son of William Muncey, who could remember its being erected. Christmas sold the stone to Mr. W. Harding of Histon Manor who, in 1904, gave it to the Sedgwick Museum of

Geology in Cambridge which, in 1937, transferred it to the Cambridge Folk Museum.

40. The office of Yeoman Bedell was abolished in 1858.

41. 2 August 1845.

42. These were supplied by S.P. Widnall, florist and seedsman. He wrote three books on Cambridgeshire which he printed on his private press at his home, The Old Vicarage in Grantchester. Josiah Chater's father supplied the floral decorations for Great Chesterford station.

43. 6 September 1845.

44. A steam coach (Handcock's), built to travel between London and Cambridge, had made its first journey on 30 September 1839 when it arrived at the *University Arms* hotel 4½ hours after leaving *The Four Swans* in Bishopsgate Street. One afternoon, when travelling along Trumpington Road, it swerved and landed on the marshy ground of Empty Common. A number of blacksmiths took several hours to get it back on the road. On the following day it set off for Newmarket races and seems never to have re-appeared in Cambridge.

45. 16 October 1845.

46. These were erected on the part of the Piece lying towards Clarendon Street. A long pole divided the structure into two so that Conservatives and Liberals were separated lest, presumably, bodily contact might lead to bodily harm.

47. From 1295-1885, except for a brief period in the Commonwealth, Cambridge returned two members of Parliament. The Redistribution of Seats Act 1885 limited boroughs of less than 50,000 inhabitants to one member.

48. The men engaged in constructing the railway.

49. The Whig headquarters in Bridge Street; the inn closed in 1911. The Tories met at the *Eagle* in Benet Street.

50. 19 July 1845.

51. These were: vote by ballot, manhood suffrage, annual Parliaments, payment of M.Ps., abolition of the property qualification for M.Ps., equal electoral districts.

52. Daughter of Thomas Reed, jeweller of Market Hill.

53. The American midget Charles Sherwood Stratton (1838-83). At maturity he was 3ft. 4ins. tall.

54. Founded in 1628 on property given by Thomas Hobson, carrier, to provide shelter and employment for the poor and to serve as a house of correction. By the end of the 18th century the house was used almost entirely as a prison for prostitutes who were sent there following arrest by the University Proctors. In 1891, after a long legal battle following a case of wrongful arrest, the University ceded its rights to the town, which had always resented the Proctors' authority over town girls. The Spinning House was pulled down in

1901 and the Police Station, now in new buildings on Parkside, was built on its site.

55.   Grocers at 4 Market Hill.

56.   Frederick Hebblewhite, linen and woollen draper of 5 Market Hill.

57.   Woollen drapers and tailors of Petty Cury.

58.   The *Eagle* Foundry on Market Hill had been founded in the late 18th century by Robert Headly, father of James and Edward Headly who owned the business at the time of the fire. The new premises in Mill Road were also named the *Eagle* Foundry; in 1849 the *Eagle* locomotive engine was built there for the E. Counties Railway. In *c.* 1852 the brothers dissolved partnership. James remained in Mill Road (in partnership with John Manning 1853-9); Edward set up an ironmongery business in Corn Exchange Street. This was carried on by his sons, who built a foundry in Newmarket Road. In 1885 the firm became Headly & Edwards; it ceased business in 1934. The names of J. Headly, Headly & Manning and Headly & Edwards can still be seen on ironwork in Cambridge.

59.   The water supply of the Conduit was limited. A chain of helpers passed buckets to and from the river by way of Garrett Hostel Lane.

60.   *Bass* . . . A fibre obtained from certain palms, used for brushes, ropes etc. a mat or hassock made of this. *O.E.D.*

61.   Boots with a triangular gusset of soft folded leather and eyelet holes for lacing across.

62.   Probably Oxford shoes with tongue, eyelet holes and laces, or more probably at that date, short lace-up boots.

II

1850 to 1855

EARLY YEARS IN BUSINESS

Last Months in Market Street

In the first two months of 1850 Josiah continued working in Market Street, his future still undetermined. Mr. Lilley, much preoccupied, probably, with his own forthcoming marriage, seems, indeed, to have given no indication of when he wanted him to leave, though from time to time he promised to speak for him to some of his business acquaintances in London and the North. The indecision worried Josiah:

> I should like to have a clear understanding so as to get settled some-where. This is a miserable state of affairs to be in, not knowing what is before me, not even for a month ahead. I cannot endure it much longer.

Meanwhile his daily routine of counting house work, serving in the shop, stock-taking in January had to go on, relieved by leisure-hour activities of church and lecture-going, visits to the Mechanics' Institute and attendance at the Mutual Improvement Society and, occasionally, at the Church of England Young Men's Society[1]. On most days, too, he managed to see Agnes and was sometimes invited to her home.

In January there was the usual round of New Year parties, including one at Mr. Basham's on the 16th, 'with plenty of singing and country dancing', and a somewhat grander affair on the 22nd given by Mr. Metcalfe, the Green Street printer. The latter coincided with stocktaking, so Josiah was unable to get to the house until half past nine, when

> I found them dancing a Spanish dance. It was a large party, many of them strangers. After an introduction to Mr and Mrs Metcalfe, I went about seeking my own pleasure. The first was to join in the first set of quadrilles, which I managed decently, then I chatted away to the ladies till supper. We escorted them into the supper room and found there a famous spread comprised of tipsy cake, trifles, custards, jellies, tarts, patties, fruit and numberless other knick-knacks which we offered to the fair ones. When they were satisfied we returned them to the drawing room and left them there to amuse themselves as best they might, while we ascended upstairs to regale ourselves with the rich dainties

provided for us . . . Then we rejoined the ladies below and played Family Coach and danced Sir Roger de Coverley, which brought us to one o'clock when we parted.

On 1 and 2 March 1850 Josiah travelled to London and was interviewed by several firms - wholesale drapers and shipbrokers - to whom he had been recommended as a clerk, but received no definite news of whether he was accepted by any of them. Then on 14 March he was paid the legacy from his late uncle and recorded in his diary:

> Mr Basham has been recommending William and me to begin business as soon as we can - he says there is an opening and we ought to try.

It is probable that William and his employer, Mr. Basham, had already discussed the question of the two brothers setting up on their own as woollen drapers, for from then on events moved quickly.

Josiah spoke, on the following day, to Mr. Lilley, who, though surprised at the news, was not discouraging, although, 'he was awkwardly situated and my leaving him suddenly might seriously inconvenience him'. Josiah wrote, too, to his father to get his opinion, while Mrs. Adams, who was also consulted, gave her approval to the plan.

The first step was to find suitable premises. After looking over two or three, which proved unsatisfactory, Josiah and William, on 17 April, went to inspect a property at No. 20 Sidney Street[2], owned by John Swan, auctioneer and cabinet maker who lived next door. Situated on the corner of Hobson's Passage, No. 20 had previously been the offices of the *General Advertiser,* a local newspaper which had ceased publication in 1849. The brothers found the place rather large but decided to 'risk the affair'. On 4 May they went home to Saffron Walden to consult their father, who advised them to take the premises, provided that the rent was not too high. He himself came over, in the following fortnight, to look over them and, recorded Josiah, 'seemed quite decided that we ought to make a move at once; the only thing is the rent is too high'.

After some bargaining with Mr. Swan, a rent of £70 a year was finally agreed upon, and on 15 July the lease was signed. But the brothers could not yet move into the building, for a number of repairs and alterations had first to be made. These were set in hand at once, however, and on 1 August William left Mr. Basham's shop and on 20 August Josiah ceased his employment with Mr. Lilley, who had, all this time, been most encouraging and helpful. He continued, though, to sleep in Market Street while the builders, Quinsee and Attack, were working in Sidney Street. On the 28th Josiah was able to report,

> They are progressing rapidly, having lowered the floor and cut away the chimney. Mr. Quinsee has promised to get it all completed by the 22nd, so we can have possession by then.

2 September

> We decided on our cards today - they are very neat and plain, and also saw a proof of our bill-heads . . . Our premises are progressing and we shall be able to have the key by Saturday, the 21st. They have cut away ten inches more of the chimney than we expected, which has increased the size of the shop and so made it all the better for us. After tea we saw about the gas fittings and arranged to have 8 burners in the shop; 2 in each window and 2 over each counter - bronze pendants with a relief in blue glass - very neat. The estimate for them was about £4. 10s.; we had thought it would be £10.

9 September

> I saw Mr. Lilley this morning and, after thanking him for all his kindness towards me whilst I have been with him, shook hands and bade him goodbye. He very kindly offered to answer any letters that might be addressed to him in reference to our respectability. He wished us every success and was willing to trust us for a while for any linens we had of him.

Next day, Josiah and William set out to buy stock for their new shop. They travelled by the half-past six Parliamentary train[3] from Cambridge, reached Huddersfield at half past nine in the evening and put up at *Browker's Temperance* Hotel in Church Street. In the morning they visited several wholesale warehouses, buying black and fancy doeskins[4], broadcloth[5] and woollen cord[6] before going on, by train in the afternoon, to Leeds. Here, on the following morning, they purchased more goods from a firm which had been recommended to them by one of Mr. Lilley's suppliers, and were delighted to be able to obtain 'some short lengths, which is a great advantage; so we shall be able to make a much better assortment for the same amount of outlay'.

Their next call was at Manchester, which Josiah found 'far superior to Leeds in the laying out of the town; it is really well built and has some good public buildings'. After a night spent at the *Albert Temperance* Hotel, and a morning devoted to purchasing at warehouses where they were 'treated very civilly', they travelled to London to buy buttons, fancy vestings and more doeskins at three warehouses. They were, however, not 'prepossessed with Londoners' manner in business; Manchester and Yorkshire are far more pleasant'.

On 16 September, leaving William in London for another night, Josiah returned to Cambridge, called at the shop to see how the builders were getting on, and on Agnes where 'I was very happy to spend an hour with her and her sisters, reciting my adventures in the North and giving an account of our successful buying'. He then journeyed, in the evening, to 'Saffron Walden for a brief rest before returning, on the 18th, to find that a quantity of the goods they had ordered had already been delivered to the shop. Some of these were unpacked late that night, but the real task of settling in began on the following day.

At No. 20 Sidney Street

When Josiah wrote his diary, late on 19 September 1850, he was able to record,

> We have worked uncommonly hard today, and between us have unpacked, measured and boarded[7] about 50 lots of doeskins and broads. The goods generally turn out very well. Have a good many friends to see how we are getting on. We locked the place up and left it last night, but tonight William is sleeping there, not deeming it safe to be left alone. We bought some crockery just to go on with. Everyone seems well satisfied with the place and I am more and more pleased with it, but sorry it will not after all, be ready by the 24th. However, we intend beginning somehow or other in the warehouse, if we cannot get into the shop.

20 September:

> Finished boarding our doeskins and broads, also marked up and boarded some vestings, and this evening we unpacked all our Manchester goods - were at it till nearly ten. William went to a sale at Swan's and bought a desk for 30/s.

William went home on the following day, so Josiah slept in the warehouse, as he called the room at the back of the shop. This store place was to be the temporary shop until the builders had finished work, and although it had windows facing on to Hobson's Passage, these were not so visible to the public as those of the main shop which fronted on to Sidney Street. Josiah's night in the warehouse was an uncomfortable one:

> I did not get to bed till half past twelve o'clock, for I had to make up my bed and clear up, which took a long time, tying up string, smoothing

papers, &c. I made my bed on the counter, with two pieces of calico for my bolster - very hard indeed!

22 September:

I have slept in some queer places in my life, but I think never in such a one as last night. When I awoke I wondered where I was: however I slept tolerably, got up at half past eight and went to Miss Aikin's for breakfast, and then on to Sunday School.

Next day, Monday, the rest of the goods which the brothers had purchased arrived and were unpacked; the warehouse was cleaned and a bench was set up to serve as a temporary counter. On Thursday, 24 September, the new firm of W.G. & J. Chater began business:

Before breakfast this morning we got our doeskins packed very nicely on our bench, ready to show, when down they came with a bang! So we had to make it stronger. Then we cleaned our little back room and made the window smart with waistcoats, and built large piles of goods about the place. One of our new counters came, so that altogether we were tolerably shipshape when we opened. Henry Lilley was our first customer - he bought a waistcoat and William measured him for it. Our takings today have been about 35s. - not bad considering our out-of-the-way situation. We have several tailors to look round, who promise us their patronage.

25 September:

Have had more people in today and took 43s. There is a great variety of opinion about the policy of our having started so early, but although things are in a great deal of confusion, it will be getting us into the way of the place. Our shop progresses; we expect to be quite closed in to-morrow. Being Stourbridge Fair day we might have done well if we had been in the front of the premises, but we must not complain. We take enough to pay our sundry expenses.

The brothers continued to sleep, somewhat uncomfortably, at the back of their premises, although they had, by now, bought bedsteads and other odds and ends of furniture. Parents of their many friends invited them to supper and sometimes took them in a meal at midday, but at the end of their first week in business, Josiah and William had a quiet 'celebration' on their own:

We made tea and enjoyed it very much in our little back room. Felt quite jolly. I bought a kettle, made tea and washed up, but we only had one spoon, which obliged us to take turns with it. For supper we were determined to have a treat, in search of which, after nine o'clock, when we closed, I sallied forth and bought of Mr Clayton[8] two Yarmouth bloaters, brought them home and, on a small apparatus bought of

Macintosh for the purpose, I managed to cook them, admirably, and we made a first rate supper. I feel persuaded no king could have been happier than we were.

By 30 September the front of the shop had been glazed and some of the fittings been installed; business improved daily and new stock had to be ordered. Josiah felt 'almost too elated, I fear, for should success meet with corresponding reverses where should we be'.

On 4 October William went to London by an early morning train to order more cloth, leaving Josiah to discover that carrying on a business and, at the same time, coping with domestic affairs single-handed, is not always easy:

> I got into a rare muddle this morning. At breakfast I had just got my milk on the fire when in came a customer and, on going back to look at the milk, I found it boiling over and more than half of it gone. I had no butter and could not leave the shop to get any, so tried to make a piece of dry toast but had to leave it to serve a customer, and it was burnt to a cinder. So I cut another round of bread, but that served me the same, so after that I contented myself with a small piece off the wrecks of the two rounds, and drank my coffee very miserably. Oh, the blessings of a bachelor's life!

However, he found consolation in the fact that, at last, the carpenters had finished one side of the front shop, so early next morning:

> We cleaned our plate glass windows for the first time and brought a good many goods to dress the windows, though the carpenters are still at work. But we have waited so long that we are positively tired of it and are determined to make a show·today, and a very nice one it was. The public seemed quite astonished and gave us great praise.

The carefully-arranged window display had to be taken down in the evening and packed away in the back room, for not until a week later were the alterations finally completed so that the whole of the front shop could be used.

After 13 October the brothers no longer had to look after themselves, for on that day, to their great relief, their elder sister, Eliza[9], came over from Saffron Walden to be their house-keeper, as Josiah thankfully recorded:

> Eliza cooked our dinner for the first time - boiled ham and apple tarts she brought with her - and in the afternoon she and I went shopping, to grocers, bakers, butchers, ironmongers and one or two other places. She has set us up in crockery.

16 October

> We are getting the place cleared up and it makes us quite comfortable.

What a famous thing it is to have someone to get our meals ready.

He probably appreciated this even more when, three days later, he was left in the shop on his own while William made his first journey into the country, for travelling was to be his main share of work in the partnership. On this occasion he went to Milton, Waterbeach and Cottenham 'and did very well, too; about £10 worth of orders'. Occasionally Josiah made one of the journeys, travelling, as William did, by train or, until the brothers acquired one of their own, by hired pony and trap. He recorded in his diary his enjoyment of these excursions into the country, which provided a change from his normal routine of serving in the shop and keeping the books.

In March, 1851, William and Josiah were joined by another brother, Alfred, who came from Saffron Walden to assist in the running of the shop in which another young assistant had also, by then, been engaged. The business was, on the whole, prospering although, in common with other Cambridge shops, it had its seasonal declines in trade in December and in July when the Colleges were closed. Josiah kept in his diary a careful note of the firm's accounts, and recorded his jubilation when trade was good and his fears and despondency when it was bad, or when wholesaler's accounts had to be paid. On 24 September 1852, the second anniversary of the opening of the shop, he recalled,

> two years have elapsed since we commenced selling woollen cloths at No. 20 Sidney Street, and we have been calling it to mind today. What is our position? Why, that we have kept ourselves and Eliza and Alfred and two servants[10] and increased our £300 each to about £500 each in two years. Well, that is something, most decidedly, and our business is still increasing.

He and William, still only 23 and 25 years old respectively, could certainly congratulate themselves on their enterprise, on which they had expended so much hard work and initiative. Nor did their will to succeed grow less. Almost exactly a year later they decided to go into the tailoring business,

> We have engaged a young man named Osbourn, late cutter for Hodson[11], and have taken part of the counting house for him as a cutting room. Today we have ordered a lot of circulars to send to our friends. We have bought about £1,400 worth of goods.

Diary entries show that the new venture was successful, and it was even planned to start making up goods for sale to London tailors. On 18 October 1853 Osbourn went to London, 'to get

patterns from his brother, a tailor there, and to learn the prices
they pay for making up'. But, on the following day:

> Osbourn returned this afternoon; he found London and the export
> trade very dull indeed, cargoes of goods returning from Australia as
> there is no market for them.

So the project was abandoned and tailoring was done only for
local residents. That the four young men - James Osbourn,
William, Josiah and Alfred - were prepared to work hard to
make it a success is proved by an incident which occurred in
December 1853. One Wednesday Josiah took an order from a
Mr. Wood for a dress coat to be delivered at seven o'clock on
the next evening. The man who usually did the coat work in his
own home was 'on the drink', so Osbourn and the assistant in
the shop set to to make it themselves, in spite of having plenty
of work already in hand. By 10 minutes past seven, on the
following evening, the garment was finished and delivered at
the customer's house. 'I must say Osbourn is a brick', wrote
Josiah.

Marriage

Even in the midst of settling in at No. 20 Sidney Street in
1850, Josiah continued to see as much of Agnes Barrett as he
could, in her own home and at friends' houses. They went to
church and chapel together, for Agnes, although a member of
the Church of England and a fairly regular attendant at Holy
Trinity Church, did not object to going also to St. Andrew's
Street Chapel or to the Independent Chapel in Downing Place.

On 13 May 1851 Josiah approached Mr. Barrett for permission
to become engaged to Agnes. 'I fancy', he wrote, 'that I made
a pretty tolerable impression on him', but he had to wait a
fortnight before he was given an answer. On 29 May, however,
a month before Agnes's 18th birthday, the young couple were
told that they might consider themselves officially engaged.

In March 1853 Josiah felt himself in a sufficiently secure
financial position to begin to make plans for the wedding, so he
and Agnes began to look for a house. They went over one or
two that were for sale or to let in various parts of the town, but
Josiah was particularly attracted by one in St. George's Terrace,
a row of houses which formed part of Chesterton Road. On
2 May he took his future father-in-law to see it:

> he was very much pleased with it, complaining only of the distance;

but we walked it in 12 minutes. Then I came back and went over again with Alfred and Eliza; the latter is delighted with it and recommends our having it.

On 5 May he told the owner, George Shippey the iron-monger that he would take the house on lease, and very soon began to get the garden in order, to fix new roller blinds and to arrange for workmen to whitewash and paper the rooms. The early part of June was spent in buying furniture: six chairs for £1 10s., a table for £4 15s., a bedstead and mattress for five guineas are among the various purchases which he noted in his diary.

Agnes would consent only to a marriage in church, so on 25 June 1853 the Rev. C. Clayton, Vicar of Holy Trinity, was asked to perform the ceremony. Two days later Josiah bought the wedding ring, which cost him 10s., and a marriage licence, considerably more expensive at £2 6s.

On 6 July:

The long looked-for day arrived at last and now it seems to have come all at once somehow. I did not get much sleep last night . . . After some slight refreshment we all met at Mr. Barrett's and punctually at half past ten the march to church commenced - I with Harriet Barrett, William with Eliza Barrett, Fred Barrett with Eliza, Father and Mr. Barrett with Agnes. The service was conducted with much decorum and after it we assembled at Mr. Dixon's[12] for breakfast. 26 sat down, among them three clergymen: Mr. Charles Clayton, who married us, Mr. Ralph Clutton, who came over from Saffron Walden especially, and Mr. Frederick Whitehead, the curate of Holy Trinity. Before breakfast commenced, Mr. Clayton read from St. John the account of the miracle at Cana and made some exceedingly appropriate remarks thereon, and afterwards engaged in prayer. We then commenced breakfast, which was certainly a very neat and elegant turnout . . . Mr Clayton proposed the health of the bride and bridegroom . . . We chatted the afternoon away till half past four o'clock, then Agnes and I bade adieu and William and Mrs Dixon went to the station with us. We got to Slough on the Great Western to stay the first night.

The 10-day honeymoon was spent in Bath, Bristol and Chepstow, ending in a weekend at Saffron Walden where, on the young couple's arrival, 'the bells struck up a jolly peal on our account and made us feel quite proud'.

It was not long after their return to Cambridge that Agnes began to find her new house in Chesterton Road too far from the centre of the town, where all her friends were, and from her old home in Market Street. True, Josiah could cover the distance to Sidney Street in 12 minutes, but Agnes, hampered by the long skirts of her day, would doubtless have been unable to walk so briskly. By November she was asking her husband whether they might move, although he pointed out to her the advantages of the 'country air' which they breathed, and the fact that their lease did not expire until the following March. So they stayed on until after the birth of their first child, Ethel, on the anniversary of their wedding day, 6 July 1854. In the following month they went to live over the shop in Sidney Street, where the living accommodation had been improved. The problem of the lease of the Chesterton Road house was solved by William taking it over, he having by this time become engaged to Mary Ann Hutton of London, whom he married on 17 August.

A New Business Venture

At the end of 1854, a tailor's shop at No. 65 Bridge Street went out of business. It had been opened in 1845 by the James Hodson for whom James Osbourn, employed by William and Josiah since 1853, had worked as a cutter. In 1850 it had been taken over by another tailor, George Field, whose stock was put up for sale on 29 November 1854. Josiah and William discussed the possibility of the premises being acquired for their brother Alfred and for James Osbourn. Negotiations began for a 14-year lease at £70 a year, and matters were finally settled on 2 December when Josiah wrote,

> Alfred Chater and James Osbourn are now in full possession . . . we immediately had posters printed and put about the place: 'To be opened in a few days'.

Two days later, William and Osbourn went to London to buy goods for the new stock, Alfred stayed to look after No. 20 Sidney Street, and Josiah kept an eye on the workmen who were carrying out several improvements to No. 65 Bridge Street.

> We all set to in clearing up and preparing for tomorrow. I fitted the cutting room, and the others dressed the windows. Al seems in his element and Osbourn hardly knows how to contain himself.

9 December

> Well, the day has arrived. They opened this morning with a blazing show, and very nice indeed the place looked. The weather, too, seems to have come to their assistance, it being very cold. They have taken £8 or £9 and several good orders.

The enterprising William and Josiah had, therefore, a

satisfactory year in 1854, and at the end of the following year they expanded their business still further by taking over a shop in Royston which they had been supplying with cloth. The owner of the business was in financial difficulties and, wrote Josiah,

> wanted us to do something for him. So I went over and took stock, made out a balance sheet for him and we agreed that the business should be ours and he should be our servant. I have given him a set of new books and started him off afresh. We sold his bad stock, took what was good, in payment of our debt, and made the affair entirely ours.

The keeping of the books at Royston was, therefore, added to Josiah's work in Sidney Street and Bridge Street. But with all his business affairs, and his responsibilities as a married man and a father, he still took an active part in the affairs of St. Andrew's Street Chapel and of the Independent Chapel, and still taught in the Sunday School and served as librarian. He continued to keep himself fit by swimming in summer and by skating whenever this was possible, and his zeal for self-improvement grew no less. In the years 1850 to 1855 he became involved with two new cultural institutions[13] established in Cambridge, yet all these interests did not prevent him from keeping up his written record not only of his personal life but of all that went on in the town about him.

EVENTS IN CAMBRIDGE 1850-55

A Public Hanging

On 13 April 1850 Elias Lucas and Mary Reader of Castle Camps in Cambridgeshire were hanged at the gaol on Castle Hill, Cambridge, for the murder of Mary's sister, Susan Lucas. The execution took place in public, and although Josiah did not witness the event,

> I went up at nine o'clock this morning to see the gallows prepared for the two poor souls condemned to die at twelve. They were hung at that time, and thousands of people were there to witness the sight. The town has been full all day and hundreds have been rolling about Market Street drunk, proving what a demoralizing effect public executions have upon the people.

The last public hanging in Cambridge was in 1864; but even after the passing of the law which ensured that executions should, in future, be carried out in strict privacy, people gathered in large crowds, on those grim occasions, hoping for a sight of the black flag being hoisted, and to hear the solemn tolling of the execution bell. Thus, when a murderer was hanged in 1910, in the execution shed in the exercise yard of the County Gaol, several hundred people clustered on the roadway and pavement opposite the Shirehall. They left disappointed, however, for no flag was flown and no bell was tolled.

The 20-year-old Mary Reader, hanged in 1850, had been a servant in Cambridge before going to work in Castle Camps for a farmer by whom her brother-in-law, Elias Lucas, was also employed. In January, 1850, she left the farmhouse and went to live with Mr. and Mrs. Lucas and, it was said at the trial, commited adultery with her brother-in-law. On 22 February her sister died after eating some gruel which, a post-mortem examination proved, had contained arsenic. Although both the accused, at their trial, maintained that they were innocent, they both subsequently confessed, although Mary Reader declared that she alone had administered the poison[14].

Ragged School Bazaar

In June 1852 a bazaar was held in the Town Hall in aid of the undenominational school which had been founded, in 1846 in New Street, Cambridge, and which was commonly known as the Ragged School because the area which it served was then an extremely poor one. The School relied, for many years, on voluntary subscriptions and fund-raising activities for its maintenance.

Josiah was asked to take the bookstall at the bazaar; accordingly, on 2 June:

> At half past nine I took my place with Jonathan Cook, draper, at the bookstall in the Town Hall. We had a capital day and took £7. 10s. Altogether, the cash taken was £160, and although the weather was very unpropitious, we had a famous attendance all day. All the nobs of the town were there. Refreshments were provided for the waiters.

3 June:

> I went to the Hall and set our stall out, and then came home and sent William down until nearly three o'clock. Then I went, and stayed till the close, and fine fun we made of it. I took to hawking and went about the room selling penny bottles of ink, and penny pencils and pictures.

We closed at nine, having sold nearly all the articles. The takings amounted to nearly £240. We took at our bookstall £18.

Flood and Fire

On 10 November 1852 Josiah noted in his diary that business in the shop at No. 20 Sidney Street was very dull indeed as 'it has been raining nearly all day'. The rain continued to fall on the following day, while on the 11th, 'It still continues raining heavily and the river is very much swollen'. On 12 November:

> We hear this morning of two persons having been drowned; one of them I know — Mr. N. Clark of Bourn. I went to look at the floods. The Common is a complete sea, and boats are sailing about like fun from Park Street, along by Jesus Grove to the farther end of the Common, while all the Backs of the Colleges are flooded. I have never seen so much water out since I have been in Cambridge. But the rain is now ceased and business in the town has been a little more brisk today.

Only one fire in Cambridge is recorded in the diary between 1830 and 1855, but it was one which must have been somewhat alarming to Josiah and William because it occurred near their newly-acquired shop, not long after they had moved into it. On 22 November 1850:

> About 20 minutes to six this morning we were alarmed by a cry of fire, and I tumbled out of bed immediately and looked out of the window. I saw that the smoke and flames were quite close by, so I went down and found the fire was in our street, on the other side of the way, at Mr. Whitaker's. He is a dealer in old curiosities, &c. and has been moving his things, these last few days, to a house next door to the back of our premises. He was examined at the Town Hall this evening, and he says the fire arose from an explosion of gas; the inquest is adjourned until next Tuesday. Suspicions are rife in the town that he set fire to the place himself.

27 November

> A verdict was given last night upon the cause of Whitaker's fire. It is rather an open one and throws a great deal of suspicion on Whitaker. It is to the effect that the house was destroyed by fire and the unanimous opinion of the jury was that it was not effected by an explosion of gas. This is the cause Whitaker assigns to it. He says it knocked him down and blackened his face, but it was found that his hair was never even singed, and a sufficient quantity of gas to knock him down would have blown out the front of the house, and this did not happen.

Earlier in that same year had occurred one of the village fires which were so common in the last century, and which were so often visible from Cambridge. On 5 April Josiah wrote,

> Last night there was a very dreadful fire at Cottenham - between 30 and 40 houses burnt down. It was burning at eight o'clock and I could still see it distinctly at eleven.

Cottenham had several serious fires in the 19th century - Josiah had already recorded one on 9 September 1847. Twenty years before that, in June 1827, some premises on the village green were set alight by an incendiary, and a great deal of adjoining property was destroyed, while in 1848 and 1849, fires were again deliberately caused, the man responsible for the one of 1848 being discovered and sentenced to transportation. The fire of 1850 was, however, the worst of the century, destroying as it did over 40 farms and cottages as well as a quantity of corn and poultry. A high wind was blowing at the time and this helped the flames to spread, while only a limited amount of water was available to extinguish them.

Funeral of the Duke of Wellington

On 17 November 1852 Josiah recorded in his diary:

> The Mayor has issued a notice requesting the shops to be closed to-morrow, that being the day fixed for burying the Duke of Wellington. Many people are going from Cambridge to see the funeral pageant.

Josiah himself was not among these. Although he and William did not open their shop, they worked in the morning, preparing orders, and then Josiah walked with Agnes as far as Trumpington returned to dinner with her and her family and then went to King's College Chapel where they heard the 'Dead March' in *Saul* and an anthem. In the evening they attended St. Andrew's Street Chapel where a special service was held in memory of the Duke. All day, from 10 o'clock in the morning until four o'clock in the afternoon, they had heard the bells of the various churches slowly being tolled.

Elections and Bribery of Voters

At a general election in 1852, the Conservative candidates for Cambridge were Kenneth Macaulay, Q.C., and John Harvey Astell; their Liberal opponents, whom they defeated, were Robert Adair and Francis Mowatt. Josiah Chater, busy with his new shop, made only one brief reference to this election, which was the first in which, as a householder, he was qualified to vote. On 8 July,

> I marched off to Parker's Piece and there recorded my vote for the two Members of Parliament, Adair and Mowatt; the first time I ever voted in my life. I was not on the Piece more than ten minutes.

He was anxious not to stay longer because, later that day, he was leaving Cambridge with Agnes and his sister Eliza for a week's holiday in the Isle of Wight.

In March, 1853, this election was declared void by a resolution of a Select Committee of the House of Commons which had been appointed to enquire into complaints that the agents of the successful candidates had offered bribes to voters.

Three months later a Royal Commission enquired into the whole matter of corrupt practices at Cambridge elections. The Commissioners met 15 times in June, in the Town Hall, and four times in August, and examined nearly 300 witnesses. They reviewed all the elections held in the borough since 1832, although it was only in those of 1839 to 1852 that any detailed evidence could be obtained. This evidence, however, was sufficient to lead the Commission to the conclusion, 'bribery, treating and other corrupt practices have for a long period systematically prevailed at elections'. The candidates, though, were proved to be ignorant of the illegal methods employed by their agents to secure votes.

The most notorious of these agents was Samuel Long who, having previously acted as a general messenger and payer of tavern bills, was, after 1839, employed by the Conservatives as their chief briber, although he never actually met any of the candidates. He received a fee of £50 for each election, together with other payments for acting as registration agent, and he was also given the sum of £200 in compensation for his imprisonment, in 1839, following a conviction for bribery. He did not, however, work alone, for the inquiry revealed the names of several leading Cambridge citizens who secured votes for the Conservative candidates by corrupt methods.

Long's method was to inspect the rate books, discover the names of those who were in arrears, and then offer them payment in return for a vote, payment being made from sums provided by well-to-do Cambridge residents. The publication, in the report, of the names of both the bribed and the bribers, caused no little stir in the town.

Josiah Chater, at the time of the inquiry, was much pre-occupied with his approaching marriage, and his diary entries for June 1853 are mainly concerned with his business affairs and with the furnishing and decorating of his new home. However, he did note, on 5 June, the arrival of the Commissioners in Cambridge, and on 7 June that they had,

> found out a great deal more money was spent than was suspected. Hazard was examined today; he had, so he said, advanced £1,200 from his own pocket, but I cannot believe it.

But the statement was true. Hazard was a local corn merchant and a member of the Conservative committee. The Commissioners found that he had been approached, in 1852, by C.W. Naylor, proprietor of the *Cambridge Chronicle,* for money to be used in bribing voters. He paid over, in all, the sum of £1,250.

On June 9 Josiah reported that the Commissioners were 'going into the whole matter of bribery very thoroughly, and making the Tories look very black indeed'. Nine days later he went himself to the inquiry and 'found it very interesting. No case has been made against the Whigs at present'.

On 22 June

> I went to the Court of Inquiry today and heard the famous briber Jones examined - a mysterious affair altogether. I also heard Stearn examined - (one of the blackest looking rascals I ever saw) - It seems Jones was employed by Coppock, but he is to be examined again tomorrow, and no doubt more will be solicited.

Jones, whose real name was Hart, had figured in the general election of 1841. He was sent to Cambridge by the Parliamentary agent, Coppock, at the request of a local solicitor, Francis Gunning, who paid him £100 to be used for bribing voters to support the Liberal candidate. Hart, *alias* Jones, paid out only one bribe of £10, to a man who took the money so that he could inform against the giver of it, with the result that Hart was arrested and sentenced to 12 months' imprisonment. Coppock paid for his defence and, later, gave him £100 from a fund raised by the Liberals to pay for electioneering expenses. The Commissioners, in their report, gave this case as, 'the only act of direct bribery proved before us to have been committed at any election on the Liberal side'.

They reported that one witness, Joseph Stearn (the black-looking rascal of Josiah's diary), told them that he had learned from Hart that the latter had been sent to Cambridge by a Mr. Burcham, a barrister-at-law then living in the town. Hart denied this, and although Burcham was requested to appear at the inquiry he sent a doctor's certificate, on 6 August, stating that he was not well enough to attend. The Commissioners asked him again, five days later, but learned that he had left for the Continent. His absence, the Commissioners reported, was not thought sufficient justification for postponing the publication of their findings.

Joseph Stearn, with Samuel Long, was also found guilty of offering bribes during the election of 1845. In that year it seemed that the Liberal candidate, Robert Adair, would be returned; Josiah Chater had recorded in his diary, on 14 July, 'the show of hands was certainly 3 to 1 in favour of the Whigs'. But, almost at the last moment Kelly, the Conservative, was victorious by the narrow margin of 77 votes. The Commissioner's inquiry disclosed how this sudden swing had been brought about.

A number of voters had assembled at the *Star and Garter* Inn[15] in Petty Cury and refused to vote unless they were paid to do so. So Samuel Long settled his assistant, Stearn, inside the inn by a window in which a hole had been cut in the pane. The blind was then pulled down and, as each voter was called in turn and came up to the window, a hand came through the hole in the pane and passed over £10, though in one case this sum was increased to £12. These bribes were given just before the closing of the poll, so that some of the voters did not have time to reach the bustings, which accounted for Kelly's low majority. That this affair was known in Cambridge before the inquiry began is evidenced by Josiah's diary entry for 15 July 1845 when he noted that 'they say the last 40 that voted for him [Kelly] cost him one thousand pounds'. The Commissioners verified this figure, and named the Cambridge business men who had supplied the money to Long for distribution, but the Report declared Kelly himself to have been guiltless of any actual participation in the bribery.

After the Royal Commission of 1853, the privilege to elect

two Members of Parliament for Cambridge was suspended for nearly 18 months. In August, 1854, a new Writ was issued and an election was held on the 15th, the candidates being Robert Adair, Francis Mowatt, George Hatton (commonly known as Viscount Maidstone) and Frederick Slade. The Liberals, Adair and Mowatt, were duly returned. On 16 August Josiah wrote,

> Cambridge is all agog, for this has been nomination day. Mowatt and Adair gained the show of hands - the former made a glorious speech and trimmed up my Lord Maidstone in fine style. I heard all but Adair and Lord M. speak. The town is all life. Mowatt spoke at the Hoop Inn from half past eight till ten this morning; Slade and Maidstone at the Lion.

The next morning he recorded his vote on Parker's Piece for Mowatt and Adair then went off to London for the day to attend his brother William's wedding. Returning in the evening he heard, 'Mowatt and Adair were both returned as Members for the borough, and the town has, apparently, been wonderfully excited all day. Most people shut up their shops'.
On the 18th,

> I went on to the Piece to hear the Poll declared and the returned members speak. Mowatt spoke most admirably; Adair was washy in comparison. The Liberals are wonderfully elated.

Anti-smoking Lecture

The years 1850 to 1855 seem to have been comparatively free from Town *v.* Gown disturbances. However, on 3 November, 1854 Josiah wrote,

> A man intended to give a lecture at the Town Hall against tobacco smoking this evening, but a lot of gownsmen went up and interrupted him and made an uproar, upon which the Mayor went in and dissolved the meeting, which was not effected without blows and three of the gentry being taken into custody.

The lecturer was a London man, Thomas Reynolds, and no sooner had he begun to speak than the undergraduates in the audience lit cigars and pipes and began to shout him down. This so enraged him that he hurled abuse back at his interrupters, and soon the hall became a scene of great confusion. The Mayor intervened and, with the help of the Proctors and the police, the room was cleared. Two members of St. John's College were, on the following day, each fined £5 by the magistrates for assaulting the police.

Visit of C.H. Spurgeon[16] to Cambridge

On Friday, 6 April 1855 Josiah recorded, 'Mr. Spurgeon, the great man from London', had been preaching that day to packed congregations in St. Andrew's Street Baptist Chapel. 'He is a wonder; used to preach in our Sunday School'. The famous preacher came a second time to Cambridge that year, on 8 August:

> Mr Spurgeon has been preaching today at St Andrew's Street for the Sunday School Union. Agnes and I heard him and liked him very much indeed; he gave an excellent sermon.

The Cambridge Young Men's Christian Association

Had Josiah Chater been asked to name, of the many organisations with which he was connected, the one that gave him the most satisfaction, he would doubtless have replied that it was the C.Y.M.C.A. - the Cambridge Young Men's Christian Association.

The Y.M.C.A., with its red triangular emblem, is now known all over the world for its social and religious work. It owes its existence to a Mr. (later Sir) George Williams (1821-1905) of Dulverton. After serving an apprenticeship in Bridgwater, he went to work in London as a young draper and, on 6 June 1844, formed a group of 12 young men - Anglicans, Methodists, Baptists and Congregationalists - who gathered regularly for prayer meetings and Bible study. The group called itself the London Young Men's Christian Association, and soon other groups were established, each of them autonomous but with the same principles and motives as the first. The movement spread rapidly from 1851 onwards, for the Great Exhibition, held in London that year, was used as a medium of publicity, and before long branches of the Association were founded outside Great Britain, and the first International Congress was held in Paris in 1855.

In Cambridge, the idea of forming a Christian Association for young men came, in 1851, from the minister of the Independent Chapel, the Rev. George Bubier. Josiah Chater, who often attended the chapel and had joined the Bible Class held there, wrote on 6 January 1851,

This evening I went to a prayer meeting at Mr Bubier's and after it a
Bible Class . . . Mr Bubier spent the time in suggesting the possibility
of forming a Christian Young Men's Association, and I fancy we shall
carry it out.

20 January:

After eight o'clock I went to Mr Bubier's Bible Class. He again
mentioned the subject of a Christian Young Men's Association and
appointed a committee to carry it into effect.

27 February:

I went to Mr Bubier's to the first meeting of the Christian Young Men's
Association. They have chosen me as secretary.

4 March

I went to a committee meeting of the Young Men's Christian Association and proposed that we make an effort to enlarge our society, to
excite the sympathy of young men and other friends, that we may have
a good reading room for periodicals and newspapers. I made a suggestion to raise a sum of £36, hire a room for a reading room at £16 per
annum, and spend what it did not take in expenses on reading matter.
Objections were raised to my plan, which was to have two rates of subscription; 4s. a year and 10s. Some thought that a person paying only
4s. would object to receive the benefit of another's ten shillings . . . the
point was reached that I should get up a circular to address to such as
we might think would help us.

In the next few months no reference to the Association occurs
in the diary. But from one made on 16 June 1851 it would
appear that, in the intervening period, suggestions had been
made to bring the Association more into line with that already
established in London by George Williams. It would appear, too,
that Mr. Bubier was not wholly in agreement with this plan;
Josiah Chater, however, who had visited the London Association
was very enthusiastic about it. On 16 June 1851 he recorded,

In the afternoon I had an interview with Mr Bubier respecting the
Christian Association, but he does not enter into it with spirit, and
we merely agreed that whatever part any of the old committee should
take in the new society, there should be no misunderstanding about
it. At half past eight I went to Mr James Vinter's[17] house and the
others soon followed: Mr. W. Bond[18], G. Shippey[19], S. Mansfield[20]
&c., and after some conversation they agreed that Mr Bond and I
should draw up a sort of report and adjourn the meeting until such
report should be prepared.

2 July:

Had a provisional meeting at our house; a full meeting. We agreed a
report to the effect that a Society should be formed.

So came into being the Cambridge Y.M.C.A. with which

Josiah, with his brother William, was to be so deeply involved for many years.

The first written records of the Association date from 13 July 1852 and are the minutes of a meeting held that day in the vestry of St. Andrew's Street Chapel of the Sunday School Teacher's Institute and the members of Mr. Bubier's original Christian Young Men's Association. At this meeting it was proposed that the Institute and the Christian Association combine to form one Society, 'perfectly catholic in its basis, seeking the best interest of the members on the broadest Christian principles'. These ideals were to be achieved by the provision of a library and reading room where classes could be held and lectures delivered. The meeting, at which Josiah was not present, elected him on to the committee and appointed Henry Eaden Lilley as secretary.

On his return from the holiday in the Isle of Wight which had prevented him from attending the meeting, Josiah at once took up his duties as a committee member. On 9 August he spent an hour with William Bond, 'discussing a code of rules', based on those of the London Association, from whose secretary a good deal of information had been obtained. The rules, approved at a committee meeting held on 24 August, gave the aims of the Association as, 'the mental and religious improvement of young men', to further which a library, reading room and class room were to be provided. Membership subscription was to be 5s. a year and upwards, payable yearly or half-yearly in advance, and women were to be admitted to the lectures and, on one evening a week, to the library on payment of 3s. a year.

The first step, of course, was to find suitable premises, and on 16 September Josiah wrote,

> Had a committee meeting of our Association and fixed on having Finch's rooms for 12 months. Have gathered about £80 in donations. Appointed a committee to buy tables &c.

The rooms, at No. 22 Sidney Street, proved unsuitable, so on 5 October it was decided to lease two at No. 14 Rose Crescent for a period of six months at £15. On the 11th of that month Josiah was able to report,

> Our reading room is open and a very comfortable place it is, well matted and with a good supply of periodicals and papers.

On 24 March 1853 a move was made to larger premises, four

rooms at No. 5 Sidney Street: here the Association was to stay
for six years.

Public lectures, debates, prayer meetings and classes in French
and German all formed part of the first year's programme of the
Y.M.C.A. Josiah attended and took part in many of them,
although he resigned from the committee, for a short while, in
November 1851 so that a Wesleyan might temporarily replace
him.

The first public lecture was delivered in the Town Hall on 26
November by the Rev. H. Allin who spoke on, 'Individualism,
or the moral laws and limits of Association'. Josiah went with
Agnes Barrett to hear it; 'a capital lecture and I believe she enjoyed it'. He certainly saw to it that his future wife's education
was not neglected, for only four days later he took her to hear
another public lecture, not arranged by the Association, on,
'The Queen's Supremacy, Papal Aggression and Tractarianism',
which both found 'very interesting and instructive', and probably
long, for it lasted nearly three hours.

On 1 December 1852 Josiah 'met several members at the
room in the Crescent and four of us formed a German class'. He
was thus able to continue the study of the language which he
had already begun under the tuition of a young German to
whom he gave, in return, lessons in English conversation.

The debates and discussions, the latter usually termed 'conversation evenings', which were arranged by the Association
ranged over a wide variety of subject, religious and secular.
Often a debate was not concluded in one evening and was adjourned to a second or even third. Thus, on 3 May 1853 Josiah,

> went at half past eight to our Association to hear the discussion on the
> opening of the Crystal Palace on Sundays. Three Wesleyans made
> tremendous speeches, one of them named Long, son of the notorious
> Long, the briber at the Cambridge elections. But this man is an excellent,
> good sort and a very clever fellow. I enjoyed the debate very much and
> seconded the adjournment, intending to say a word next time, if I dare.
> There were between 90 and 100 present.

At the adjourned meeting he spoke, 'and got on quite well, but
I feel I require much more practice'.

An important event in the early years of the Cambridge
Y.M.C.A. was the annual Conversazione in the Town Hall. This
was, usually, a lengthly affair, lasting from half past six in the
evening,to half past ten, and consisted of musical items and short

lectures with, half way through the programme, a pause for refreshments.

The first Conversazione was held on 21 September 1853. It began with the singing of the *Old Hundredth* and the reading of *Psalm 32.* Then came an address by the President on, 'Adapting our movements to the general movements and wants of the time', followed by the reading, by the secretary, of the first Annual Report. An anthem, *Praise the Lord O Jerusalem,* was sung and another address was given, on the theme, 'The cultivation of mental talent is not incompatible with true religion'. At a quarter to eight, after another anthem, an interval of one hour allowed refreshments to be served before the audience sang *Psalm 104* and then settled down to hear the Hon. Secretary of the London Y.M.C.A. address 'the young men of Cambridge'. The singing of another anthem concluded the evening which, declared Josiah, 'went off first rate'.

The second Conversazione, held on 13 December 1854, was equally long. Josiah was asked by the *Cambridge Chronicle* to send in a report of it, and although he was, at that time, extremely busy with the opening of Chater and Osbourn's new shop in Bridge Street, he managed to find time not only to write the report, but to spend 13 December, 'running about all day after our conversazione'. When he went to the Town Hall in the evening he took with him his

> electrifying machine and some instruments to entertain the people. We had one end of the alderman's parlour for it, and fine fun we had. It was a glorious evening - the speaking was good, the music exquisite and the provisions first rate.

Foundation of the Working Men's College

In May 1855, replacing the now-defunct Mechanics' Institute, a Working Men's College was established in Cambridge. The institution was inspired by the one founded in London in 1854 by the Rev. Frederick Denison Maurice[21] who, until deprived of office in 1853, had been Professor of English History and Literature and of Divinity at King's College, London. In 1866, he was to become Professor of Moral Philosophy in Cambridge and, from 1870 until his death in 1872, Vicar of St. Edward's Church

Cambridge.

The idea of forming the Cambridge college came from an undergraduate, Henry Montagu Butler, later Master of Trinity, from the brothers Daniel and Alexander Macmillan, booksellers and publishers of Trinity Street, and from Francis Gerald Vesey of Trinity Hall. The Vicar of St. Edward's Church, the Rev. Harvey Goodwin, subsequently Dean of Ely and Bishop of Carlisle, became the college's first principal.

The founders rented rooms at No. 6 Market Hill, over a gymnasium recently opened by Mr. Fenner, which was used by the students for gymnastics and boxing, and classes began. College dons acted as tutors, and in the few years of its existence the College promoted a very friendly relationship between Town and Gown, its students going often to their tutor's rooms for social gatherings as well as for instruction. Making his report, at the end of the first year, to an audience of over 200 members of the college and their tutors, the Rev. Harvey Goodwin was able to say how grateful he was, 'so many young men were coming forward and paying for instruction after a day's work'.

Josiah Chater, with his zeal for learning, was not long in availing himself of the opportunities offered by the new college, in spite of his business activities and his involvement with the Y.M.C.A. On 24 October 1855 he recorded,

> This evening all the members of the Working Men's College attended at the rooms for a preliminary examination. I have entered for Latin and German; Alfred and Osbourn for French and Mathematics.

30 October
> We had out first lesson in German of Mr Lightfoot, Fellow of Trinity College, and in order to get us on he has promised us two.lessons a week.

1 November
> We had our first lesson in Latin from Mr Hort[22] but have been put into two divisions. I am in the first and Mr Mayor[23] will be our teacher.

External Affairs

In 1851 was held, in London's Hyde Park, the first great International Exhibition. Organised by the Society of Arts, under the presidency of the Prince Consort, it was open for just over five months and was visited by six million people.

Having noted, on 25 April 1851, that the price of season

tickets for the Exhibition had been raised from three guineas to four, Josiah Chater recorded, on 1 May,

> This is the day for the opening of the Great Exhibition of Industry and all nations, and the Queen intends opening it in person. Various and gloomy have been some of the conjectures as to the success of this noble enterprise; some people have even been conjuring in their minds all sorts of dangerous and evil consequences that must, they say, inevitably flow from it, but more noble-minded souls have rejoiced and hailed with gratitude the day that should see the binding together of all the working classes of the world in one common bond of mutual dependence on one another . . .

Josiah visited the Exhibition in July. On Sunday, the 22nd, he went home to Saffron Walden so that he could travel to London on the following day with his younger brother, Jabez. The visit also gave him the opportunity of seeing his older brother, Tom, who was then seriously ill and was to die in October.

On the Monday morning Josiah and Jabez went to Audley End station and there,

> A tremendous train came in, with Agnes and Harriet on it. They made room for me and Jabez in their carriage and we had a very pleasant run to London. At the Shoreditch station Charles met us, whereupon he, Agnes, Harriet, Jabez and I went to Pimlico where we deposited Agnes and Harriet at their cousin's and then we started in search of quarters for the night. We enquired of a man whether he knew of a comfortable lodging house, and he directed us to 'The Working Men's Home for 1851', and introduced us to the proprietor, who showed us over the place. It was prepared for 200 men and was fitted up with ship's bunks, which I did not altogether like. So I enquired for private rooms but those, we found, were not to be had. So after a little conversation with Mr Castle, the man who had taken us there, he said he would do what he could for us. We followed him to his own house, saw Mrs Castle and in the end we were accommodated with bed, good breakfast and supper until Saturday for £2 for the three of us. Our Landlord is a ship's broker and his house is situated just at the foot of Vauxhall Bridge, about a mile from the Exhibition, which suits us well.

26 June
> After breakfast we went off to the Crystal Palace at the Exhibition . . . had not been there for a quarter of an hour when we lost Jabez, who had gone off to get a look at the Queen. We all saw her; it was quite delightful to see her walking up the noble building between two walls of human beings. After a couple of hours we went to the refreshment room and there we found Agnes and Harriet and their two cousins, so I kept with them for the remainder of the day. It is wholly impossible for me to attempt a description of the magnificence of the place, or of the beauty of the productions exhibited. I was thoroughly delighted

and pleased. We saw the products of all nations and the people of all nations, and all working in peace . . .

On the following day Josiah's father came to London and with his sons visited the Exhibition, where they again met Agnes and her sister and a number of people from Cambridge whom they knew. On 21 September, Josiah paid for the maid servant who helped his sister Eliza in the house at No. 20 Sidney Street, to go to the Exhibition in the company of his brother Alfred. 'This is her very first visit to London' he wrote, 'but she has been a very good girl and had worked well and been very attentive, so that I am sure she deserves it'. Had he not paid her expenses, the girl would, doubtless, have been unable to go to London because, as Josiah had noted in his diary when he engaged her, soon after Eliza had come to keep house for him and Alfred, her wages were only one shilling a week.

The diary tells us little of the Crimean War of 1854-6, although Josiah recorded, on 11 April 1854, that the Duke of Cambridge and Lord Raglan had set out for the East. On 25 April he wrote,

> This day has been appointed by the government to be observed as a day of humiliation and prayer on account of the war. In the morning I went to hear Mr Robinson[24] preach at St Andrew's Street, and in the evening went to Trinity Church. The afternoon Agnes and I spent at home - a delightful day, so quiet and calm and peaceful.

Two days later he reported the war 'to have begun in earnest'. Otherwise, apart from brief references to the battle of the Alma in September 1854, to the defeat of the Russians at Inkermann in November and to the first bombardment of Sebastopol in 1855, Josiah chose to continue his diary as a record of his own affairs and of events nearer home.

NOTES TO PART II

1. The Cambridge branch was formed in 1848.

2. 20 Sidney Street now forms part of Waring & Gillow's furniture shop. John Swan's former premises are now part of W. Heffer & Sons' stationery shop at 18-19 Sidney Street.

3. By the Cheap Trains Act 1844 all railway companies had to run one train daily, in each direction, calling at all stations if required, at a fare of 1d. a mile. The normal range of third class fares was based on 1½d. a mile. The importance of Parliamentary trains continued until

third class fares were generally reduced to 1d. a mile. This reduction was first made by the Midland Railway Co. in 1872; the other companies then followed the example.

4. *Doeskin:* A closely-cut thick black cloth, twilled, but dressed so as to show little of the twill. *O.E.D.*

5. *Broadcloth:* Fine, plain-woven black cloth. *O.E.D.*

6. A fine ribbed cloth.

7. The bales of cloth were unrolled, checked, then folded round thin wooden boards. Modern tailors usually call this *blocking* the cloth.

8. Robert Clayton, fishmonger, 11 Peas Hill.

9. She died in Saffron Walden, 13 April 1855, aged 30.

10. They were paid 1s. a week.

11. James Hodson, tailor, 65 Bridge Street.

12. Probably Thomas Dixon, stationer and bookseller, later of 9 Market Street.

13. The Young Men's Christian Association and the Working Men's College. See below.

14. A broadsheet, sold on the day of the execution, is in the Cambridge Folk Museum. It gives an account of the trial and of the events which led up to it.

15. This inn, closed 1910, is now occupied by Dewhurst Ltd., butchers.

16. Charles Haddon Spurgeon was born in Kelvedon, Essex, in 1834, the son of an Independent minister. Going as an usher to a school in Newmarket, he there became a follower of the Baptists, and was baptised on 3 May 1850 by total immersion in the river near Isleham ferry in Cambridgeshire. Very soon afterwards he became an usher in a school in Cambridge and preached his first sermon in a small cottage in the nearby village of Teversham. This sermon, which first revealed his great powers of oratory, was preached almost by accident. A local preacher had asked him to accompany another young man to Teversham, and as they walked along together to the village, each gained the impression that the other was going to address the meeting. Arrived at the cottage, Spurgeon, whose conversation had much impressed his companion, was prevailed upon to preach, and so, with no notes and totally unprepared for the occasion, he held his small audience spellbound.

In 1852, aged only 18, he became the pastor of the Cambridgeshire village of Waterbeach, receiving a salary of £45 a year. But his fame as a speaker soon spread, and in the following year he went to the New Park Street Chapel in Southwark. At the age of 22 he had become the most popular preacher of his day, and when he went to the Metropolitan Tabernacle in London, which opened in 1861, large congregations flocked to hear him, as they had done in 1857 when an estimated crowd of 24,000 heard him preach at the Crystal Palace on the day ordered by the government to be observed as one of national humiliation for the Indian Mutiny. On several occasions, before his death in 1892, Spurgeon returned to Cambridge to preach or lecture.

17.   A well-known corn merchant in Cambridge.

18.   William Bond, grocer, of the firm of Brimley & Bond, later Brimley & Whibley, 32 Market Hill.

19.   George Shippey, ironmonger, 52 Sidney Street.

20.   Stephen Mansfield, draper, Fitzroy Street.

21.   Maurice (1805-72) entered Trinity College, Cambridge in 1832 but migrated to Trinity Hall where he obtained a degree in civil law in 1827. He later took a classics degree at Exeter College, Oxford before being ordained in 1834. In 1848 he helped to found the Queen's College in London, for the education of women. Interested in Christian Socialism, his teachings had a great influence on the growth of the Co-operative movement. His alleged sceptical leanings led to the loss of his professorship at King's College, London.

22.   Rev. F.J.A. Hort (1828-92). Lady Margaret Professor of Divinity 1887-92.

23.   J.B. Mayor (1828-1916). Fellow of St. John's College; Professor of Classics at King's College, London 1870-9.

24.   Rev. William Robinson, minister of St. Andrew's Street Baptist Chapel 1852-73.

III

1856 to 1866

ON MARKET HILL

The Move to Market Hill

At the beginning of the year 1856 Josiah Chater, by then aged 27, was still living with his wife and baby daughter over the woollen drapery shop in Sidney Street. His brother, William, now married, had taken Josiah's former house in St George's Terrace,[1] while the third Chater brother, Alfred, in business with James Osbourn in Bridge Street and, previously living with his partner, moved, early in January 1856, to live with Agnes and Josiah. The two shops of W.G. & J. Chater and of Chater & Osbourn were quietly increasing their trade, while the woollen and drapery shop in Royston was still being managed for the Chaters by the man who had transferred the business to them in payment of his debts.

Josiah, always interested in new labour-saving devices that came on to the market, ordered from London, in August 1856, a new pattern cutter. He received delivery of it only two days later, and on 28 August wrote,

> I have been all day at work on the Engine, our new pattern cutting machine. We have found out the go of it and it works famously. I like it very much; it is very exact and easy in all its movements.

The shop of No. 65 Bridge Street, at the corner of St. John's Street, owned by Alfred Chater and James Osbourn, was enlarged in the October of the same year by the renting of adjoining premises, as Josiah recorded on 8 October,

> I brought over from Royston a nice blind to put in Alfred's new window, *i.e.* their new shop. They have hired a room next door in St. John's Street for a cutting and private room away from the shop, and I think it will answer very well in time. They have had it new papered and have enlarged Osbourn's cutting board. In the shop Al has had the

counter widened and the fixtures put back, which makes a first-rate looking shop of it now.

But the major extension to the Chaters' business was made in 1857. On 4 April Josiah wrote,

> We heard that Mr Bonnett wished to dispose of his stock and that Lincolne[2] had been after his house. I went to Lincolne and asked if he had indeed taken it, and he told me that he had given it up, so I determined I would go and see Mr Bonnett, thinking, probably, there might be a chance for us to take his stock, which we could do very comfortably if he would give us the time to pay it off. I saw him after tea and he was very polite, and thought we might come to some arrangement, so we fixed for a meeting at 12 o'clock on Wednesday. We thought perhaps the house might do for Alfred for a ready-made shop, but Bonnett thought it might be better for us, but we shall see.

John Bonnett was a woollen draper who, since the early 1840s had carried on, on his own, the former business of Baker, Bonnett & Clayton at No. 1 Market Hill, at the corner of Petty Cury. It was here that on Wednesday 7 April, the pre-arranged meeting was held between Josiah, William, Alfred and Mr. Bonnett. The last-named,

> showed us over the place and answered fairly every question we proposed. He supposed there would be about £1,700 worth of stock; he would be willing to give us two years to pay it off and would give us the lease, which has 7 years to run. He would also recommend his connections to us. He would require a little for the good will, but that we rather demurred at . . . In the evening we went to Mrs Adams and asked her opinion. She is much opposed to either Al or ourselves moving, but she thinks the matter is worth our consideration . . . We again went to Mr Bonnett and asked him the amount of his returns, which he gave us for the past few years. In 1850 I think it was about £5,000; last year he did £2,040; he also showed me his stock book and the stock itself, so that we can have a good idea of what it is. His tailoring must be about £66 a year, as he paid last year £182 in wages. He seems, so far as we can judge, to be quite fair and square with us, and I do think we may make a very good thing of it.

On 13 April William discussed with John Bonnett the securities which the latter was willing to accept in payment for his stock. These matters were arranged satisfactorily, and when, later in the day Josiah saw Mr. Bonnett he was able to record that 'he is quite willing, if we agree on other points, to accept us as purchasers'.

On the following day, Josiah and James Osbourn went to look over the house and shop at No. 1 Market Hill. Osbourn 'expressed himself delighted with the place and pleased to move from 65 Bridge Street, feeling quite certain of being able to do better trade there'. Josiah's father also looked over the premises and 'was very pleased with the place for Alfred's business'. At 10 o'clock on 20 April:

> William and I went to Mr. Bonnett's and began valuing the stock . . . as far as we have got we have bought the things at pretty well our own price and have no reason to complain.

21 April
> We have been busy valuing the doeskins today . . . About 4 o'clock Mr Bonnett, who had been busy with Town Council meetings, asked us into the parlour to have a glass of wine, and then we discussed the affair. We told him we would give him £100 for rent up to next Michaelmas, and the good will, but he stuck out and would have the £100 for good will. After a little arguing we settled to pay him £130 for rent, good will and everything - rates, gas and taxes up to Michaelmas, and to take what furniture we wanted and the fixtures at a valuation by an appraiser, so that soon we may consider the stock is ours, to be paid for £800 by January, 1858, and the remainder by January 1859, with licence of 2 or 3 months beyond for £200 or £300, we paying 5% per annum.

By 24 April arrangements had been made for a valuation of the fixtures and furniture, and it was becoming public knowledge that Mr. Bonnett's business had changed hands; 'the trade is all agog with our moving and are quite excited about it'.

An advertisement appeared in the local newspapers on 25 April announcing that W.G. & J. Chater, woollen merchants and Manchester warehousemen of No. 20 Sidney Street, respectfully informed their friends and the public that they had purchased, 'Mr Bonnett's woollen drapery and tailoring business, with his extensive and select stock', and would be carrying on the business on and after Saturday, 2 May, when they hoped, 'to receive that share of patronage hitherto so liberally bestowed upon their predecessor'.

On 2 May Josiah recorded that he and William spent all day on Market Hill:

> We have sold about £25 worth of goods, £10 of which is retail and paid. We have not been very busy at No. 20 or in Bridge Street, the weather being very cold. It is just one month today since I walked in to speak to Mr Bonnett to ask him if he wished to dispose of his business and place. I had asked William to go first as he knew him well, and he said he would, but afterwards he drew back and said I might go if I liked. So, being determined the opportunity should not be lost, I went at once and now, just one month after, here we are, fully installed and had one day's trade. That is the way to knock off business; there is nothing like

dispatch. Everything seemed very opportune for us. Only that week, Mr Bonnett had just taken a farm and was, in consequence, much more anxious to dispose of his business when I stepped in.

6 May

Had an order at No. 1 for someone to go to Gog Magog to measure the brother of Lord Godolphin[3] for some clothes. I propose driving Osbourn there on Friday morning.

8 May

I drove Osbourn up to Gog Magog this morning to measure the Hon. William Osborne, brother of Lord Godolphin, for a suit of clothes. We had our new pony, which I like very well... I settled with my workmen who have made one suit for us at No. 1 Market Hill. The public generally speak well of our opportunity and think we shall make it answer well.

The Chater brothers and James Osbourn did, indeed, make their new venture answer well, and trade at No. 1 Market Hill continued to expand alongside that carried on in Sidney Street and in Bridge Street[4]. The success was no small credit to the young men's energy and enthusiasm, for the year 1857 was not the best one in which to start such an enterprise. Trade, generally, was bad, as Josiah recorded on 13 November:

Alarming failures are taking place all over the country, and very frightful in America where trade is almost at a standstill.

But there were some more troubles to be faced in the first two years on Market Hill. In the autumn of 1858, an Act of Parliament was obtained by the Corporation of Cambridge for the improvement of the Hill, and No. 1 had to be re-fronted. Josiah and William applied for a grant[5] towards the cost of this, hoping to receive at least £60, but on 7 December were told that the Market Committee would agree to give only 50 guineas, a sum which, Josiah wrote, 'all I have mentioned is to say take, and be thankful'.

The alterations began in January 1858, and business had to be carried on as best it could amidst all the confusion. On several occasions, because the front of the shop was not closed in, James Osbourn, with one of the brothers, had to sit up all night to keep watch on their stock. On 25 January, Josiah recorded,

They are getting on very slowly; have been putting an iron pillar under one corner of the huge stack of chimneys in the little shop . . . it is wonderful how the old place has held up as long as it has - all the storey pots were decayed and some were completely gone at the bottoms.

On 25 February Alfred Chater, 'dressed one of our new

windows and it really looks very nice indeed', but not until 7 March could Josiah thankfully record, 'I think we are now almost complete'.

No. 1 Market Hill was, indeed, old property. Many years later, in October 1889, by which time it was occupied by a music and pianoforte seller, it was pulled down[6] and new premises erected on the site. Demolition revealed that the whole building dated from the 16th century, having been built in 1538 by a grocer named Veysey whose arms, and those of the Grocers' Company, were carved on fireplaces[7] in various rooms.

There were a few difficult periods in the Chaters' early years on Market Hill, when Josiah recorded in his diary his anxiety concerning their financial position, for there were always bad debts to be faced besides the delays in payment for goods supplied to both wholesale and retail customers. In September 1859, Josiah had to drive over to Chatteris to see a tailor and outfitter who, he suspected, had forged a receipt:

In March 1857, this man bought a parcel of goods which we omitted to enter on our books. I only found this out at the beginning of this year, but I sent him notice of it two or three times. He has, however, evaded payment, and when William went over there last Monday he (the man) showed him a receipt bearing his (William's) signature. But my brother said it did not look like his writing, so after getting a lawyer's opinion of how to act, I went over and found my gentleman at home and asked him to let me look at the receipt as we could not quite make the account right, and our clerk had left us. As soon as I saw the receipt I asked if he had paid my brother on the journey, and he said yes, in the shop. Immediately I folded up the bill and the receipt and placed them in my pocket, whereupon he flew to the door and said I should not leave until I gave them up. But I took out a statement of the account and presented it to him, telling him I did not mean to go until it was paid. The forged amount was £3. 5s. 10s.; the whole bill was £7; and after a little conversation . . . he asked me to call in half an hour and I did so, when he took me to his sister, a very respectable lady, a milliner, who promised to see me paid. He must have taken the stamp[8] off an old bill and put it on this one, which he finally acknowledged to have done.

In November 1861, Josiah asked the building firm of Quinsee & Attack to submit an estimate for altering No. 1 Market Hill so that the Sidney Street business could, perhaps, be transferred there. He makes no further reference to this plan until 23 March 1862 when he wrote, after a period of some weeks during which he did not make any entries in his journal:

During the past two months I have been very busy with a variety of matters. First and foremost: 5 weeks ago we began our alterations at

No. 1 Market Hill preparatory to moving our woollen trade from Sidney Street, and have had a lot of men at work ever since. We have gone on very nicely up to the present, no serious obstacles interfering to stay our progress, and I hope we are in a fair way of getting nicely clear of our premises in Sidney Street by the 1st of May. We are now in treaty with a man named Savidge[9] to take them for an ironmonger's business and I hope it will be settled tomorrow.

The diary was kept so irregularly at this busy period in Josiah's life that there is no record of the day on which the Sidney Street shop was given up, or on which the business of W.G. & J. Chater moved to No. 1A Market Hill, occupying part of the premises of Chater & Osbourn. The living accommodation in Sidney Street had, in any case, not been required for the previous two years because, by October 1860, Josiah, Agnes and their three children, Ethel, Elizabeth and Mary (Polly), had moved to No. 19 Fitzwilliam Street, left to them on the death of William Adams's widow.

At No. 19 Fitzwilliam Street

It was in July 1859 that Mrs. Adams, then in her 70s and often ailing, told Josiah that she was going to leave her house to him and William[10], though she hoped it would be Josiah and Agnes who would live in it after her death. Like many elderly Victorian widows of substance, she devoted much care and thought to the making of her will and spent many hours thinking about her death and making arrangements for her burial. On several occasions she gave Josiah instructions concerning small legacies which she intended to make to various poor old women whom she had always befriended, and then, on 27 October 1859,

She asked me to go up in the afternoon and take my pencil and paper. When I went, the old lady, who was in bed and looking very queer, ordered me to make a list of the furniture she intended to give to an old woman named Solomon, and I was to see she had it within a week of Mrs Adams' death. She also went into very minute descriptions of sundry chests and cupboards in her house, with the fittings, fixings and arrangements, that I may be enabled, when I go to live there, to have everything as clean and comfortable as she has them herself. She impresses on me her wish, each time I go to see her, that I shall conform in her ways of management. One old maxim I pencilled down just as she said it, not because it was new to me but because of her quaint way of putting it. In giving her reasons for recommending some little plan about moving out the chairs from the kitchen, that they might not be scratched when workmen came in, she said, 'Because you know, Josiah,

one ounce of prevention is better than a pound of cure'. She says she is
giving away most of her things and means to give away all she can before
her death because she says she will not have a sale in the house after her
death.

In January 1860 Mrs. Adams again issued Josiah with a list of
instructions:

> The old lady related to me again how she wished me to manage her
> house when she is gone, and that I am to have all the furniture left after
> she has given those things away that I have on paper. Her best bedroom
> and the front parlour are to be left as they are except for three little
> things which I have down.

The death of Mrs. Adams's sister, Harriet Simpson, which
occurred on 16 January, doubtless led to the old lady's continuing preoccupation with her own end. Josiah attended Miss
Simpson's funeral having taken the opportunity, on the preceding day, to visit the family vault, opened for the occasion, in
the cemetery in Histon Road, and to

> look at Uncle Adams' coffin. It is in an excellent state of preservation,
> the brass plate scarcely tarnished and the cloth quite fresh, although it
> has been there 10½ years.

In April 1861 Josiah received from Mrs. Adams meticulous
directions as to,

> how her funeral is to be managed: cloths and plumes for the horses and
> the hearse; the men who do down the leaden coffin to have a shilling
> each, and I am to be sure and have it done in the day and not at night,
> and in the back parlour if possible. At the cemetery the corpse is not to
> be taken out of the hearse while the mourners go into the chapel, as it
> is all nonsense to take the corpse all that way down to the chapel,
> because the dead cannot hear and there is not much room for the living.

A month later, on 10 May,

> Mrs Adams held me that she should like to be buried between 11 and 12
> in the morning, that the bearers were to be good-sized men, Marshall at
> the chapel to be one of them, and a man named Freeman, in Hobson
> Street, another, Jonathan Swan is to make the coffin, but she has not
> decided yet between Ellis and Dee to make the lead coffin.

It was not until 7 August 1861 that Mrs. Adams died. On the
following day her body was placed in the lead shell and, 'laid at
the foot of the bed exactly according to her wish'. The funeral
took place on 13 August, the ceremony being conducted
according to her instructions.

From that day, until 8 October, there are several blank pages
in the diary which, presumably, Josiah intended to fill when he

had sufficient time. During this interval, with Agnes and his four
little daughters (the youngest was born early in 1861), he moved
into their new home in Fitzwilliam Street where, on 1 January
1862, Agnes gave a New Year's children's party:

> She said there were to be 10 or 12, and I said I warranted there would
> be a dozen, and sure enough there were 24, and a pretty cram we had.
> But I think they all enjoyed themselves. We had a Christmas tree, a
> magic lantern, which I hired from Nichols the photographer for 2/6d.,
> and snap dragons which employed the time well until half past ten.

The removal of the Sidney Street business to Market Hill and
the move to Fitzwilliam Street made the years 1861 and 1862
very busy ones for Josiah. In addition, his younger brother,
Jabez, came to Cambridge in November 1862 to open a nursery
garden in Gonville Place, and Josiah helped him a great deal to
settle in, and also assisted and advised him in the keeping of
his accounts. For these reasons the diary was kept erratically in
those two years, while from 1863 until 1 January 1866 it was
not kept at all. This may have been because Josiah was too busy
or because of personal bereavement, for it was during this
period that his little daughter, Polly, died.

Leisure Activities
The Working Men's College

His many preoccupations at home and in business did not
deter Josiah from continuing to attend Latin and German classes
at the Working Men's College, and from joining classes in History
and Mechanical Drawing. On 21 May 1856, after attending a
Flower show in St. John's College, for which he had been sent
tickets by his cousin, Jonathan Chater, he,

> adjourned to a tea meeting given by the Council of Teachers to the
> Working Men's College, which indeed was a slap-up affair. Harvey
> Goodwin[11] presided, and Mr Maurice of London, famous as the
> originator of Working Men's Colleges, attended, with another gentleman
> from town, and addressed the meeting. There were in all about 300
> present, amongst whom were about 80 University men. After tea several
> addressed us, and at the close Mr Kingsley, of Sidney College, gave us
> some splendid experiments on the microscope, and showed us the hydro-
> oxygen light. Between these experiments and the addresses, and before
> we retired from the Hall, I took occasion to thank the Chairman and
> Council of Teachers, on behalf of myself and the students, for their
> kindness and the trouble they had taken to instruct us. I had not
> prepared anything, but got up on the spur of the moment and spoke

out very boldly, and as the newspapers afterwards reported, the
company were very boisterous in their applause. I was glad afterwards
that I did it.

22 October [1857]:
I attended a meeting of the Working Men's College and was elected a
member of the Council of Students which, it is thought, may be a
means of giving fresh life and vigour[12] to the College. There are 12 of
us and we have our first meeting tomorrow.

23 October:
Attended our committee meeting and made a few laws for our guidance.
Macmillan[13] is on the Committee; he has the opportunity for seeking
such men to speak as we could otherwise have no chance with.

A tea meeting was held at the College on 26 March 1858, the
management of it falling on Josiah's shoulders:

Everything was ready by a quarter past eight; all the waiters were at
their posts, the tables set in three rows down the centre of the gymnasium and covered with green baize. At the end was a huge Union Jack
and this, with a few other flags, were all the decorations we had, for we
had little time to make preparations. Mr Goodwin took the Chair at a
quarter past eight, accompanied by Mr Maurice and several of the
Council of Teachers. After he had pronounced a blessing, we set to and
everything went as merry as marriage bells. The eatables were served up
in good style, and the drinkables, also, left nothing to be desired. That
part of the performance completed, Mr Goodwin gave a short account
of past, present and future proceedings and then called in Mr Maurice,
who gave a splendid speech. He began by expressing his satisfaction at
our having assumed the name of College[14], and then explained at some
length the proceedings of the Working Men's College of London. He
went on to the duties of men in their different stations, and of the
different classes of society, and the duties of each man for the general
good, not only of his own town and country but for the whole world.
It was a wonderful speech, and at the conclusion it seemed to have a
most potent effect on all present and, apparently, on no one more than
on the Principal, Mr Goodwin. When the Council had retired, the
students spread themselves about and began to practice gymnastics,
some fencing with foils, some boxing, and others climbing. We are
promised a class in gymnastics.

Another tea meeting was held that year, on 16 December,
Josiah being largely responsible for making the preparations:

I got Mrs Braddle and Mrs Osbourne to make the coffee, cut bread and
butter, &c., and they boiled the water in our copper at No. 1 Market
Hill. I lent crimson baize for the tables and we made a screen for the
door. Mr Vesey and Mr Gray helped decorate our lecture room which,
when lighted up, looked quite cheery and comfortable. We gave them a

good tea and charged 6d. each, which quite amused our tutors, and they seemed very pleased and satisfied with the arrangements. The business of the evening was transacted, a new Committee elected, and Mr Vesey gave a good description of his visit to an Arab sheikh.

On 6 June 1859 members of the College visited Ely:

> We went by excursion train to visit the Dean[15] and to see the cathedral. About 36 students went and a nice treat we had. We went to the top of the tower and into the roof, which is being completely restored by a gentleman, Mr L'Estrange, who is giving his time and talents *gratis*. He has been at it now about two years and it will take him three more to complete. Dr Goodwin showed us about the cathedral and gave us a nice little lecture on it, and then we all walked down to the Angel where a capital dinner was provided. After dinner about 20 of us had a game of bat and trap on the Green, and so amused ourselves until 6 o'clock; others went to the service at the cathedral. We reached home about 8 o'clock.

Immediately it was formed, early in 1858, Josiah joined the gymnastics class at the College. This class did more, probably than all the others to promote friendly intercourse between University men and townspeople, for the former acted as instructors in fencing, boxing, and gymnastics. Often they invited their pupils to their rooms, as on 8 June 1859 when Josiah, with 10 members of the class, went,

> to our boxing master's (Mr. J.S. Hughes') rooms at Trinity Hall to tea, and a very pleasant little party it was. After tea we adjourned to his brother's rooms where was a piano and a big bowl of punch, and several of Mr Hughes' friends coming in we set to some singing; Mr Gray played, and one chap, a Mr Ainger, amused us till nearly 12 o'clock with some comic pieces, and kept us roaring with laughter.

The 8th Cambridgeshire Volunteers

It was because Josiah Chater was a member of the Working Men's College that he became a member, too, of the 8th Cambridgeshire Rifle Corps, which was raised, in 1859, among inhabitants of the town, the majority of them attending the College.

In the April of that year it had been proposed that an association be formed for men who wished to acquire skill in rifle shooting, and that from such an association a corps might be raised of members who would be willing to submit a military discipline and to use their skill in defence of their country, should this be needed. After a meeting between the Mayor of Cambridge and representatives of the town and the University, the University Member of Parliament, the Rt. Hon. Spencer Walpole, was approached. He communicated the proposal to the government and, on the following day, the Home Secretary announced the willingness of Parliament, 'to afford countenance and good will', to any 'gallant spirits ready to enrol themselves in Rifle Corps and similar Volunteer Bodies'.

The Cambridge Rifle Club, the first in the country, was accordingly established in May 1859, and a number of others were soon formed in other parts of Britain. From the Cambridge Club two corps were set up: the Cambridge University Rifle Volunteers[16], whose uniform was light grey in colour, and the 1st Cambridgeshire Rifle Volunteers, with a green uniform. Later in the same year the 8th Cambridgeshire Rifle Volunteers were established, the members - townspeople and members of the Working Men's College - wearing light grey. The three corps were maintained from the funds of the Rifle Club and used a shooting range on Mill Road.

Josiah Chater, when it was first proposed to form the 8th Cambridgeshire Corps, was not wholly in agreement, as he recorded on 16 December 1859:

> This evening I attended a meeting of the Working Men's College for the purpose of raising a Volunteer Company. Resolutions to that effect were passed, and Page and I took upon ourselves to oppose the movement. We each made a speech on the occasion, he considering it as costly, I as impolitic, but I think very likely they will be able to muster 60.

His next reference to the Volunteers was recorded on 27 September 1860, the entry being the first that Josiah had made in his diary since 19 January of that year. He had by then, apparently, changed his mind about joining the Volunteers, for he,

> met the whole Corps at the Working Men's College. The Chairman, proposed Dr Leapingwell[17] to be Captain; this was carried unanimously, also C.J. Clay[18] to be a lieutenant. Then I proposed Mr H. Gotobed[19] as Ensign, but he being present, got up and objected, and although he was seconded and would have been unanimously elected, he persisted in refusing office. As no other name had been thought of we were in a fix, but whilst waiting for a solution of our difficulty, up jumped Flack[20] and proposed Mr Josiah Chater as Ensign, which I protested against and wished them to look out for another. But Mr Turner[21] got up and seconded my name, and they asked me point blank whether I would serve if elected. I said I was not ambitious for the office, yet felt it to be a great honour, and if they were willing to accept me I would do my best.

Josiah was duly elected, and on 13 October, 'attended at the

Working Men's College to receive Club fees and subscriptions for
uniforms of the 8th. Cambs. Rifles'.

1 November:
> Had a good muster. I took my place as a commissioned officer, but as a
> Lieutenant, Mr Clay having left.

2 November
> Squad drill this evening - had 10 new recruits, making the numbers up
> to 86 and 4 officers.

3 November:
> At 9 o'clock this evening we had a meeting of the Corps and decided on
> the dress: a grey trimmed with scarlet, with stiff cap. We also decided
> that Chater & Osbourn should be the regimental tailors. Just after tea I
> had an invitation to luncheon with the Mayor to meet the Lord
> Lieutenant of the county on Tuesday next on the occasion of the
> inspection of the 1st Cambridgeshires.

By 5 November 18 of the corps had been measured for their
uniforms and Josiah was having a suit made for him to wear at
the review and luncheon on 6 November, a date which proved
to be, 'a grand red-letter day' in his life:

> The 1st Cambridgeshire Rifle Volunteers assembled on the Market Hill
> at 12 o'clock and from thence they marched up to Fenner's ground to
> be inspected by the Lord Lieutenant of the County, the Earl of
> Hardwicke. I went up to the ground for half an hour and saw some of
> the performance, then ran home to dress for luncheon. I had had a suit
> knocked up quickly, and got a pair of stars for the collar of my coat as
> the Ensign's badge. Unfortunately I could not get a sword down in time,
> but perhaps it was just as well as I should have scarcely known where to
> put it; so I went with a plain belt. The suit looks very nice and I like it.
> I arrived at the Mayor's house on Parker's Piece about 5 minutes past
> three and was ushered into the dining room where about 20 gentlemen
> sat at table, having finished the first course. But I soon caught up with
> them and made a jolly good meal; the sherry and champagne were both
> excellent, and so too was everything else. I quickly made myself at home,
> notwithstanding it was a formidable affair, and I detected the company
> quizzing my uniform very closely. Elliot Smith, the Mayor, presided; on
> his right were the Lord Lieutenant; Captain Prest; Thomas St. Quintin,
> Esq., deputy lieutenant; Colonel Baker, Captain Fryer, Hall the surgeon,
> and Crosse the chaplain of the 1st Cambridgeshires, then I and the Clerk
> to the Lieutenancy, Mr Samuel Peed. On the Mayor's right were Colonel
> Wall, E. Ball, Esq., M.P., Captain Pemberton of the Mounted Rifles,
> Captain Leapingwell, Lieutenant Clay, Mr Ficklin, Mr Fawcett. The
> officers of the 1st and the Sergeant and Chaplain of the 8th came in
> after me. Lunch being over, Mr Mayor proposed the Queen and the rest
> of the toasts, and at half past four we left. In the evening I went to drill

in my uniform and pleased the Corps amazingly; I am the first who has
appeared in it.

On the evening of 8 November Josiah, his senior officers not
being present, had to take command of the drill practice for the
first time. Two days later:

> At our Working Men's College this evening I proposed 4 members to
> a committee to provide coffee at our room on Saturday and any other
> evening convenient, for the members of the Rifle Corps to drop in and
> have a little chat. I named it the Union Coffee Club; the plan was carried
> and next Saturday we are to begin.

The first meeting of the club proved very successful; two
officers came to it and stayed for 20 minutes talking to the men
for whose entertainment chess, draughts and newspapers were
provided. Josiah attended several subsequent meetings of the
Coffee Club at which he, and other members, sang or recited.
On 24 November:

> The Captain came and we had a regular swearing-in; had 80 who took
> the oath, amongst them our chaplain and doctor; the Captain has
> ordered a parade next Thursday in uniform.

The corps, however, were unable to appear in uniform owing
to, 'some mistake about the buttons, which have not yet come'.
But on 5 December about 50 men paraded in their new outfits,
looking 'very first rate'. Josiah was, however, obliged to turn
out in undress uniform as he still had no sword belt.

Drills and parades occupied many of his evenings. On 11
December he attended a drill with arms in the Corn Exchange,
taking his position as Ensign but feeling 'rather odd' because he
was still without a sword. After the drill, he heard that the 1st
Cambridgeshire wanted the 8th to go with them on a march on
24 December and to dine afterwards at the *Lion* Hotel.

> But our men do not relish the idea; the Captain has no objection, but he
> will not be there, nor will the Lieutenant, so I do not think it worth the
> Ensign's while to spend 5/- or 6/- to placate the 1st, therefore I shall
> not go.

The decision to go on the march was, however, reversed, and
Josiah had some anxious moments because a supply of belts and
caps, ordered from London, had not arrived. On 22 December
he telegraphed three times to London about them, and learned
that the goods had been sent off the previous afternoon. So he

met the mail train in the evening, but succeeded in getting only one bandsman's cap and could get no news of the rest.

On Monday, 24 December:

> At 7.30 I got up and went to Market Hill. The caps, &c. did not arrive till a quarter to nine, and then we were beseiged by those of the Corps who wanted to go on the march. We just managed to get them all equipped by 10 o'clock and then we mustered on the Hill, upwards of 70 in all. We marched down Market Street, Sidney Street, Trumpington Street, St Andrew's Street and Petty Cury back on to the Hill, preceded by the University Band. At eleven we joined the 1st and marched up Hills Road to Shelford. It was a lovely morning and I enjoyed it, although marching over the snow was rather hard going. We halted at Shelford for about half an hour and got some lunch, and returned home via Trumpington. I went off to Walden by the 5 o'clock train, and the others went to dinner at the Lion.

Prince Albert visited Cambridge on Monday, 31 December, and the station master asked the 8th Corps to provide a guard of honour, but early on the Monday morning the Captain was told that, as the visit was a strictly private one, no Volunteers were to assemble. However, as Josiah recorded,

> So many of our men were dressed and ready that about ten went to the station and had the honour of forming a guard whilst his Royal Highness passed by.

Josiah's membership of the 8th Volunteer Corps did not please his aunt, Mrs. Adams, who on 21 February 1861 told him,

> she had got one thing to ask me, and that was whether any of us who belonged to the Rifles, as someone had told her I did and she would not believe it. I told her that both Alfred and I belonged, and then she told me she was very sorry and wished I had asked her about it first. She felt grieved, because she had heard of their goings-on, the drinking and the spending of their time and money to such bad purposes. But I told her that our Company did not do that; we had never been out in the day and I never allowed it to take me away from business. The evil practices she had heard about were committed by the 1st; ours was the 8th, and we were under very different management. Our officers, Dr Leapingwell and Mr Clay, would not countenance such proceedings. She was glad to hear this and said she knew both gentlemen. I brought her round in the end by explaining the true state of the case.

So Josiah continued his regular attendances at evening, and occasionally early morning, drill, shooting practices at the Mill Road butts, and at the Saturday evening meetings of the Union Coffee Club. On 11 April 1861 the 8th made their first attempt at singing while they marched:

> We got about 20 or 30 men up at the Working Men's College and marked time to the tune of the *Red, White and Blue.*

Occasionally the parades of the 1st and 8th Cambridgeshires through the town attracted unwelcome attention from passers-by, as on 23 April 1861, when Josiah recorded,

> We had uniform drill at the Corn Exchange this evening; then, coming on to the Market Hill to dismiss, the Captain got a lemon thrown at his head on King's parade, and several others were hit too.

On 30 October 1861 the Prince of Wales opened the new University Rifle Ground in Grange Road, Cambridge, which had been acquired by the University Rifle Volunteers earlier in the year, when the corps withdrew from the Rifle Club. To mark the opening,

> At 2.15 o'clock the 8th Cambs. Rifle Volunteer Corps assembled at the Corn Exchange and marched to the University Rifle ground which was opened by H.R.H. the Prince of Wales. The 1st assembled on the Hill at 1.45 and were on the ground first, but quite out of the way, as we had the receiving of his Royal Highness. He passed between our front and rear ranks, the front being faced about, then left the 1st and went to the University Corps. Some little ceremony was gone through of his presenting a Challenge Cup to the University, and the ladies presented the electric targets to the Corps. We then marched to the other end of the ground and Ross, the Champion of England, fired five shots at 800 yards, which constituted the opening of the ground. We had a famous place close against Ross, and the 1st Cambs. were all behind, so that we had the laugh of them all through the piece - and they innocently thought they were going to have the best of it.

Josiah's diary indicates, on several occasions, that the 1st and 8th Volunteer Corps regarded themselves as rivals although, from 31 May 1861, the two had amalgamated on withdrawal of the 1st from the Rifle Club, both corps paying the Club an annual rent for the use of the rifle range.

On 14 December 1861 the Prince Consort died. His funeral was held on the 23rd, and on that day, in Cambridge,

> The Corps assembled on the Market Hill for divine service at St Mary the Great to hear Dr Jeremie[22] preach a sermon to the University. The 1st Cambs. also mustered on the Hill and thought we were going to march with them, but Mr Clay would not, they having formed in column; we formed in line. But in order to be first in church they cut off, whilst our band played the Dead March from *Saul,* and then we quietly walked into church; the 1st having very unceremoniously taken

all the front seats of the gallery, of course we sat behind. As it was, we managed as good a muster as they did. At 9.15 we mustered again in the Corn Exchange where I caused to be conveyed 4 dozen torches, and at half past nine we marched out in Indian file, with these torches alight, down Pembroke Street, King's Parade and into the Square opposite the University Library where, on the steps of the Senate House, the Band of the University Rifles played the Dead March by torchlight, and a most solemn effect it had coming just after the dumb peal. I was in full command of our Company. We did it out of compliment to the Band of the University who had, on several occasions, shown us kindness, and they were very pleased; the 1st had nothing to do with it. All our men were delighted. There were thousands of people to witness the scene.

The, 'cocky little 8th', as Josiah said his corps was often called, together with about half a dozen of the 1st and a few friends, assembled at the *Hoop* Inn in Bridge Street, on 14 January 1862:

> We sat down to supper at half past 8; had hot and cold meats, pies and pastry and everything proper, with ale and waiters included for 2/6d. each. It was a very jolly affair, uncommonly well served. After the captain was gone, I took the chair for about half an hour, then left. I only saw one man a little the worse for the punch, 19 bowls of which the officers put upon the table.

George Wallman, a member of the 8th Volunteers, died in hospital on 18 January 1862, and as his was the first death that had occurred since the formation of the corps, many of the members expressed a wish to attend the funeral. So, in the evening of 20 January Josiah,

> went on the Hill and mustered the men and then marched them off to the Corn Exchange where I put them through the funeral exercise and rehearsed what we intend doing tomorrow.

On the following day,

> At 12 the firing party met at the Corn Exchange just to have half an hour's drill, and at 1.30 the Corps met and we marched down to Flack's in Bridge Street where the mortal remains of poor George Wallman lay. On getting into position the procession, to the sound of a muffled drum roll, marched off to the cemetery on Mill Road where we congregated 3 or 4 hundred people. The afternoon was very fine and there was a tremendous lot of lookers-on. Our chaplain, Mr Hadley, officiated, and a very solemn ceremony it was. At the conclusion 12 men fired 3 volleys over the grave, and after leaving the ground we marched home by Regent Street, playing a variety of lively tunes, and dismissed on the Hill. I was the only officer there.

With Josiah's failure to keep his diary during the years 1863 to 1866, the affairs of the 1st and 8th Volunteer Corps are not recorded. Presumably, however, he continued to take an active part in them.

The Y.M.C.A.

Throughout the period 1856 to 1866, Josiah was actively involved in the Young Men's Christian Association on whose committee he still served, and of which he was elected secretary in 1857. On 26 May he recorded,

> We are to have another Soiree and Mr Wetenhall[23] wants me to read a piece of poetry, so I have chosen two pieces from Cullan Bryant! *The Forest Hymn* and *The Old Man's Grave*.

On the following day,

> This evening our Soiree came off; it was a pleasant affair. The eatables consisted of biscuits, with lemonade as substitute for coffee, which was far the best drink, the weather being warm . . . I read my piece and I hope it is not vain conceit if I write here my belief that it was as well as any there, and better than some.

As secretary, Josiah had much to do with the annual Conversazione of 1857. On 14 December he wrote,

> We had a grand rehearsal this evening at 9 o'clock. I had collected and reckoned up the number of tickets, which is upwards of 300, and tomorrow I only have the selling of them. Great numbers are anticipated at the meeting.

5 December:

> At 8 o'clock I was at the Town Hall expecting the carpenters, but they did not come till half past nine. We then began in earnest. I had a line of evergreens running round the Hall at the bottom of the windows, and a festoon from the caps of the pillars of the gallery. The pictures on the walls were hung with evergreens; there were ten or eleven oil paintings lent by Mr Roe[24], and three or four very fine engravings. Between them were 30 or 40 photographs lent by Mr Nichols[25]. and three beauties from Mr Vesey[26]. The refreshments were in the Council Chamber as before, but in addition we had the Aldermen's Parlour. At 5 o'clock everything was complete and I went home to dress. We began punctually at 6.30 and everything went famously to the close, without a hitch or break in any way to mar the affair. Everyone I spoke to said they had never seen the old Hall look better in their lives. The music was excellent the lectures and experiments all that could be wished. We had about 460 there.

On the following day, Josiah was down early at the Town Hall to see that everything was cleared by midday. He then spent the morning preparing for the tea meeting of the Working Men's College, for which event, as for the Conversazione, the tea and coffee were made at No. 1 Market Hill and then carried in urns over to the Town Hall.

At a committee meeting held on 7 August 1858, it was decided that Josiah Chater and Alexander Macintosh should represent Cambridge at the second International Conference[27] of the Y.M.C.A. to be held, later in the month, in Geneva. The two delegates decided to join up with Josiah's brother, Alfred, and four friends - Henry Wallis,[28] Owen Jones,[29] Fred Barrett,[30] and Edwin Barrett[31] - and to have a few day's holiday on the Continent before the Conference began. Josiah recorded, in great detail, the events of this trip, together with those of two earlier holidays[32], in a separate quarto notebook, at the end of which he pasted all their hotel bills, his passport and a list of their expenses.

The seven men travelled, on 13 August 1858, to Le Havre and then on, by steamer, to Rouen where they spent a day exploring the town before taking the train, on 15 August for Paris. Here they had an exhausting day seeing as much as they possibly could, for although the 15th was a Sunday, and they found everything so different from, 'a homely English Sunday', they managed, as Josiah wrote, 'to quieten our, I am afraid, not too sensitive consciences'. They visited the Madeleine, the Louvre, the Tuileries, ascended the Arc de Triomphe, and thoroughly enjoyed a fair that was being held in the Place des Invalides, and all this before catching the night train to Macon, which they reached at 11 o'clock on the following morning.

At Macon, feeling tired and travel-stained, they went to the public baths, but found,

> the hours for gentlemen's bathing had passed and the Bath was now occupied by ladies. But I would not understand and said that I must bathe as I had not washed since yesterday and had been travelling all night . . . At last they consented. Our whole party had made up their minds to bathe, but when we looked in we found there were two women already bathing; but I was not going to be frightened, especially as they provide you with pants. Edwin was the only one who dared to venture with me . . . In the bath there was plenty of room to dive and swim about and the two fat old ladies did not in the least molest us but seemed rather pleased at seeing us disport ourselves. They remained in the water up to their necks.

After dining at Macon the friends travelled on to Geneva, arriving there at half past 10 that night. They asked for rooms

at the *Hotel du Grand Aigle*, where the landlord assured them
he could accommodate them. Jones and Wallis, Edwin Barrett
and Alfred Chater were given tolerably comfortable bedrooms,
but Alex Macintosh was put into 'a sort of closet without a
window', while for Fred Barrett and Josiah

> the landlord turned a large lumber room about and hastily put up beds.
> At one end were large windows and glass doors, but all dark and
> curtained. Presently, two or three female voices were heard giggling
> and laughing, which seemed anything but pleasant to us, as we had no
> keys to the doors, and in a place so utterly strange.

The two men, however, managed to sleep soundly until five
o'clock when,

> suddenly those ominous glass doors opened and through our room
> stalked a great woman. Half an hour later another came stealthily forth,
> and a third shortly after. Then we understood why we could not fasten
> our doors; it was the servants' bedroom.

The next day was spent in exploring Geneva. In the evening,
Josiah and Alexander Macintosh went to the local Y.M.C.A. and
accompanied about 30 of its members on a 'singing meeting' on
the lake, in candle-lit boats.

On 18 August the seven men went by diligence up into the
mountains, stopping for dinner at St. Martin where they were
given chamois to eat, which they found, 'a little too high'. At
the hotel they changed the diligence,

> for a lighter conveyance called a *char a banc*, a low, four-wheeled vehicle
> built expressly for mountain travelling, with two horses or mules, but
> generally the latter.

They left this vehicle at the hamlet of Chede, preferring to
let it continue to Chamonix with their luggage while they walked
along mountainous paths bordered with alpine plants, and to
the accompaniment of 'millions of grasshoppers'. They finally
reached Chamonix at 5 o'clock in the evening and put up at the
Hotel de la Couronne.

Next day they went on an excursion into the mountains and
over the Mer de Glace, 'which looks to rest so quietly within its
rocky barrier yet is, really, incessantly moving downwards at the
rate of 400 to 500 feet annually'. Wide fissures had to be crossed

by means of ladders with boards laid over them, an experience which Josiah found, 'really frightful'.

Returning to their Chamonix hotel that evening, the friends were just thinking of going to bed when,

> Jones called me and said he wanted to buy some writing paper with pictures on, if I would go with him. We tried all the shops, but could not procure what he wanted; then he said we might as well get some cigars for tomorrow.

A policeman directed them to a tobacconist's shop, and as they were walking towards it, they encountered a group of mountain guides talking together at a corner. Josiah, to make sure that he and Jones were going the right way, enquired of one of the men, in his best French, if the tobacconist's was far away. The man, learning that they wanted to buy cigars, said there was no need for them to go to the shop; he had some in his pocket which he had bought that day in Martigny. As the cigars that he produced looked satisfactory, and the price he asked for them seemed a fair one, Jones and Josiah decided to buy them. Neither, however, had the right money, so Josiah offered the smallest coin he had - a half napoleon. This the man took, saying he would get change from a nearby shop, but instead of so doing he disappeared into the darkness. Jones dashed off in pursuit, but failed to find him so. With the linguistic assistance of a Swiss whose acquaintance they had made in the hotel, the matter was reported to the police. This done, Jones and the Swiss went off to bed, leaving Josiah to face what followed.

Two policemen, 'uncommonly well got up in dark green dress, white belts, long swords and cocked hats, and with great blue cloaks with one corner thrown over their shoulders', first conducted him all round Chamonix and into inns and bars and lodging houses, but in none of them could Josiah see anyone who resembled the thief. Then, though it was raining hard and he was wearing his thin-soled boots, Josiah was taken to a house at the foot of the Glacier du Bussons. Here they were ushered into a room which seemed 'to serve as dining room, parlour, kitchen, scullery and dormitory for the entire household'. A long discussion in rapid French, which Josiah could not follow, took place between the police and the middle-aged couple who occupied the house, before the husband accompanied them to 'an out of the way sort of chalet', where the police stood guard under the windows while the man knocked on the door.

> This was opened in the dark and immediately one of the police stepped in, struck a lucifer and beckoned me to follow, and there was presented to my view a poor fellow just awakened out of his first sleep.

At once Josiah saw that he was not the wanted man, and having convinced the police of this, with some difficulty, they all, to his relief, returned to Chamonix, the time being now nearly midnight.

At half past five on the following morning, as he was dressing, Josiah was summoned to go once more to the police station. From there he was taken, on foot and still in pouring rain, to the village of Bains, two miles away, and into a 'low-looking, miserable sort of house' where a young man sat writing at a table. Josiah instantly recognised him as the object of their search. Questioned by the police, however, the man swore that he had never seen Josiah before, but when the latter said that he had a friend who could identify him as a thief, he produced the half napoleon and confessed that he had run off with it. His wife and mother, meanwhile, had been standing in the room, sobbing bitterly, which so moved Josiah that he told the police he was prepared to forgive the culprit[33]; but the young man was marched off to the police station. Here, later in the morning, Jones swore to his identity and both he and Josiah signed a statement. The stolen coin, however, was not given back to them; it would, they were told, have to go to the police head-quarters at Bonneville and they would get it, eventually, either in Geneva or through the Sardinian Consul. So they decided to have no more bother with it - a decision which might well, perhaps, have been taken on the night before - and gave instructions that it was to be given to the poor of Chamonix.

The remainder of that day, as it continued to rain heavily, was spent in the hotel, Josiah being glad to rest after all this excitement. On the following day, a last excursion was made into the mountains before Alexander Macintosh and Josiah left Chamonix, on Sunday 22 August, for Geneva to attend the Y.M.C.A. conference. They arrived too late for the opening service in the cathedral, but went, in the afternoon, to the Palais Eynard where they met the other delegates. In the evening they attended a meeting at which the President of the Geneva Association, M. Perrot, delivered the inaugural lecture.

The morning of 23 August was spent by Josiah and his companion at the Conference, where they listened to, but did not entirely follow, the discussions in French on the future development of the Y.M.C.A. In the evening, all the delegates were taken in boats across Lake Geneva to the gardens of the Count de Gasparin where they had supper. It was an excellent meal and,

> the only two things wanting to the full enjoyment of the feast was, first, a knife and fork to eat the meat with, for they never use these necessary articles, it seems, at parties, and second the presence of any ladies.

After supper, the guests returned to their boats and, with an accompanying choir, were rowed over the lake to the sound of music and singing and the occasional firing of Roman candles.

Josiah and Alexander made a brief visit to the meeting of the following morning, then went off on a sight-seeing tour of Geneva. At 4 o'clock they met up with the other delegates and walked with them to the local President's house in Chamysses, four miles away. Here, after strolling for an hour about the gardens, the party were entertained to supper at tables set under the trees, after which, 'in a grove hung with variegated lamps', many of the delegates spoke of the work of the Y.M.C.A. in their own countries.

The Conference ended on 26 August with a breakfast on Mont Saleve, at which votes of thanks were made by the foreign delegates to their hosts, Josiah speaking on behalf of the Cambridge Association. In the afternoon, he and Alexander, and their five holiday companions, who had arrived in Geneva the previous evening, left for Macon, dined there and, travelling on through the night to Paris, reached England by way of Dieppe and Newhaven.

Josiah seems to have acted as treasurer for all the party, excluding Jones and Wallis. The statement of accounts which accompanies the 160 pages he wrote describing this memorable fortnight, shows that the expenses for himself, his brother, Alex Macintosh and the two Barretts, including fares and hotel accommodation, amounted to £63 10s.

In September 1858 the Cambridge Y.M.C.A. moved into new rooms at No. 1 Hobson's Place[34]. On the 28th:

> Held our first meeting in the new rooms, a Consecration meeting. We had about 30 present . . . not so many as might have been there. Our new gas fittings look very nice and everybody appears well pleased with the rooms.

29 September:
> At a committee meeting this evening I presented my Report, also the Treasurer's. We have a balance of £10. 12. 1d. The annual meeting was held in the large room and we mustered about 50 members.

4 October:
> We held our first monthly Prayer Meeting in our new rooms this evening. Had 18 members present.

5 October:
> William has been busy today preparing for our Soiree which is to be held tomorrow. We have secured 12 ladies to send trays of provisions *gratis*, and have sent circulars round to members to say that ladies are allowed to come.

6 October:
> We have had a very lovely evening; quite successful. About 90 present and plenty of room. The worst feature was the sending of so many provisions, we scarcely knew what to do with them. We cleared £2. 2s. 0d. I lent the use of my piano.

At the Annual General Meeting of the Association held in September 1859 Josiah relinquished the office of secretary, which he had held for two years, feeling it to be more than he could manage with all his other commitments. He was succeeded by Mr. Eaden Lilley, Jun., but remained on the committee.

The records of the Cambridge Y.M.C.A. reveal that, during the years 1859 to 1866, there were long discussions on whether it was worthwhile for the Association to continue. It was passing through a difficult period financially, and the year 1865-6 began with a deficit of £15, which is not recorded by Josiah Chater because he had then temporarily ceased his diary-keeping. From 1866 to 1869 there is a gap in the Association's records, but this is filled, to some extent, by entries in Josiah's diary which he resumed in January 1866.

The Savings Bank[35]

On 11 December 1860 Josiah recorded that he had attended 'a committee meeting of the Penny Bank'. Whether this was for the first time is not clear, but from then onwards he took his turn, usually on one evening in the week, in taking deposits at the Bank. These evenings were often busy ones; he recorded, for example, on 10 November 1861, 'We took nearly £23 tonight and had 300 depositors'. He noted, on that same date, that the Post Office Savings Bank had opened on the preceding Monday.

With the hours that he spent at the Y.M.C.A., the Working Men's College, the Penny Bank and with the Volunteers, it is not surprising that Josiah seldom spent an evening at home. His wife, therefore, was much on her own, although Josiah wrote, somewhat ruefully, on 4 February 1859,

> I did not go out this evening but sat quietly at home with Agnes, a rare thing for me; but however she could scarcely appreciate it, I think, for she went fast asleep!

He continued to attend St. Andrew's Street Chapel and to teach in the Sunday School there, and occasionally went to a concert, as on 20 February 1856 when he heard 'the Organophonic Band at the Town Hall: men imitating with their mouths different musical instruments'.

In the summer of 1856 he and his brother Alfred had a week's holiday in Scotland with Alex Macintosh, while Agnes went, with the two children, to stay in Huntingdon. In 1857 the three Chater brothers, Josiah, Alfred and Jabez, with Edwin Barrett and Alex Macintosh, spent a fortnight touring in Holland and Germany, the events of this trip, with those of the Scottish one, being carefully recorded in a separate notebook.

Although Josiah and Agnes entertained at home from time to time, they seem to have attended fewer parties, in this period, than in their single days. Doubtless their contemporaries, as in their own case, were increasingly occupied with furthering their careers and with the responsibilities of parenthood. However, in February 1858 Agnes decided to invite a few friends to a dance and supper. The party was held in Sidney Street, where she and Josiah were then living, part of the shop premises being used for the occasion:

> About 3 o'clock I began to get the warehouse ready, moved the counter to one end, borrowed Mr Barrett's piano and placed that. Then we draped the fixtures and walls all round with red padding, and the beams we ornamented with evergreens, covering the counters with green baize

and making the old place look quite comfortable. At 8 o'clock we went to it in fine style; danced till 11 o'clock when we had supper - a roomful, 24 or 25 in all, the most we have had in this house. I got John Thurlborn to give us *Those Good Old Days*. I hired a wig at Dimmock's and he dressed up in character and came to the stage in fine style - breeches, glasses, &c., and sang the song most characteristically, after which we danced again at intervals until one o'clock.

In the summer of 1859 Josiah took up photography as a hobby, inspired to do so, it seems, by his two friends, Owen Jones and George Norman. On 22 June he wrote,

Yesterday morning George Norman brought his camera and chemicals and we are going right in to photography. He knows a little of it and we can just manage to get a picture. It is a very interesting art.

7 July:
We got on capitally with our likenesses, and I took one of George: first rate, with Fred Barrett at his side in our passage.

In September Josiah went, on business, to Leeds, Huddersfield, Berwick and Hawick, and took the opportunity to take photographs of some of the places he visited. On his return to Cambridge these were printed by Owen Jones and, 'the stereoscopic pictures sent to· London to be printed'. On 5 October, Josiah and Jones spent a day in Saffron Walden, travelling,

in a pony and dog cart and taking with us the large camera and the stereoscopic camera. Got there to breakfast and immediately set to work; we took a view of the church, then two of Father's greenhouse and frames, then the cemetery, and last the Sun Inn and the interior of the church.

On the following day he reported that the stereoscopic pictures had been developed by Jones, 'and only one appears to be bad'. The large ones cost 6s. and the 25 small ones 4d. each.

When in London for the day, on business, a fortnight later, Josiah purchased for 2s. 9d. a stereoscope through which to view his pictures. In 1858 he had been lent one by Owen Jones, together with the stereoscopic pictures which the latter had taken in Switzerland at the time of the Y.M.C.A. Conference. Jones does not seem to have taken photographs of his holiday companions, however, for soon after their return to Cambridge the friends decided to go to a professional photographer and, 'have our seven likenesses taken in a group, with alpine stocks in hand and in travelling costume'.

EVENTS IN CAMBRIDGE 1856-63

The Peace Celebrations

The treaty of Paris, which ended the Crimean War in 1856, was celebrated in Cambridge by a general holiday and by a dinner for school and Sunday school children. Josiah, at that date, was still living above his Sidney Street shop, and on Monday, 2 June, he

> attended a meeting of the Committee for giving all Sunday Schools in the town a treat on Parker's Piece on Thursday next on the occasion of the Peace rejoicings. The clergy had all been invited to join, but refused until this morning, when they consented.

4 June:

> We are busy preparing to decorate our house with flags, &c. I propose to have an arch to form a rainbow and from it a Dove alighting on a Globe suspended, and have got Windridge,[36] our opposite neighbour, to consent. I had some iron from Macintosh's to form the arch and some hoops to make the globe, and I think it will do well.

5 June:

> We were up until 2 o'clock this morning and up again at five to make our display. We finished it by ten; certainly it was the best design[37] in the town, and did us credit, although we could not manage the Dove. The Dove was to have been between the arch and the globe. At one o'clock I went to the School [St. Andrew's], where the children were assembled, and with them marched to the Market Hill. All the schools marched to that spot and a glorious sight it was. The day was cool, but bright and very pleasant - a nice air just to enliven the flags and banners. The Hill was crammed. The Mayor addressed the children for a few minutes, and they sang God Save the Queen. At two o'clock they commenced marching to the Piece by way of Sidney Street, Trinity Street, Trumpington Street and Downing Terrace. An orchestra was build in the centre of the Piece, with tables radiating from it, which formed a pleasing figure. Nearly 7,000 children had tea, but only about 6,000 were provided for, this making a foolish job of it, but those who came short were regaled at their respective chapels and schools, so they got it somehow. In the evening, at half past nine, several balloons were sent up, and there was a display of fireworks, considered by some as very grand. They were, perhaps, all very well, but very expensive. The town was partially illuminated; we had a light in our Globe. Thurston[38] had V.R. and a Crown; Stanley Swan,[39] next door, a crown, and Sadd[40] on the Parade an extensive display of Chinese lanterns. Joseph Bond[41] was about the best of all, and Dr Bond[42] about the worst - his display was beggarly. About twelve o'clock I took all ours in and thus ended the Peace Rejoicing. May we never know another such occasion to rejoice.

Elections

The Parliamentary elections of 1857 and 1859 seem to have been fairly quiet in Cambridge; at any rate, Josiah did not record any particularly lively scenes. In 1857 some of the local Whigs were pressing for an enquiry into the question of the disestablishment of the Irish Church, and on 18 March Josiah attended a meeting of the party:

> It was resolved that if 50 could be got together they could throw the election and might dictate terms to Adair[43] and Hibbert[43]; if they would not support or vote for an inquiry into the Irish Church then the 50 would not vote for them.

This 'Radical declaration', he recorded three days later, 'has made a grand stir amongst the Whigs'.

On 24 March,

> The Whigs are highly exasperated with our sticking out and have made up all manner of stories about the triviality of our decision . . .

Josiah polled his vote on 29 March, reluctantly, but not liking to forego his right to do so,

> at 4 o'clock, and rather contrary to my expectation, Macaulay and Steuart, the Tory candidates, were both returned. I did a little expect Adair would have gone with Macaulay, but in consequence of Adair's adherence to Palmerston, the Radicals were so exasperated that many of them abstained from voting and scarcely one gave his services. Poor Adair must have felt it very much, as Steuart was only about 5 or 6 in the majority.

The Tory candidates, Kenneth Macaulay and Andrew Steuart, were returned again at the 1859 election. Josiah was very disappointed, because he and his brother William had both worked hard as members of a committee pledged to see that the two Liberals were elected. On 29 April, after casting his vote, he

> went down to the Hoop and commenced work by going round to the voters and getting them to the poll. We worked hard till 2 o'clock. At 9 this morning we were 80 ahead; at one o'clock we were a few behind, and at the close all behind. A sad job, but I am quite sure there was an immense deal of corruption on the Tory side or they would never have got in. Our party was wonderfully cast down. At 6 o'clock I went to the Piece and heard the poll declared.

In April 1858 Josiah had been summoned to appear before the Mayor to qualify as an Assessor for the Trinity Ward of Cambridge:

> I was called upon to sign a paper stating that I was worth £1,000 when

all my debts were paid which I refused to do as I am not sure about it.

Later entries in the diary, however, indicate that he was accepted.

Eclipse of the Sun
On 15 March Josiah recorded,

All excitement, everybody procuring coloured glass to view the Eclipse. It was predicted to commence at 11.42 a.m., and sure enough, just at that time, the moon began quietly to creep on to the face of the sun and put out his light. Alex Macintosh, Mr Buxton and I went on to Madingley Hill where we had a good view, and a pretty sight it was. The greatest obscuration was at one o'clock and just then it was tolerably clear so we had an excellent opportunity of witnessing the various changes assumed by the sun. I did not perceive a perfect ring but I saw quite ¾. The atmosphere was quite dull, not approaching to darkness, and all at once got very cold, as cold as just before sunrise.

Fire
The only outbreak of fire recorded by Josiah in the years 1856 to 1863, occurred on 15 September 1858, in Magdalene Street:

At a quarter to one this morning we were awakened by cries of Fire. I dressed myself and went out and found a house opposite Magdalene College in flames, and next door to Ingle's[44] whose stock, I know, Alex Macintosh has just bought. So I lent a hand at once to help clear out the goods, and that done I hurried off to Alex and called him up. We then went to Mrs Banks' house, which adjoins the burning property, and took out a few things, but fortunately the fire did not seem to touch it.

Telegraph Office
On 24 February 1859 Josiah wrote in his diary,

The Electric Telegraph Company have been busy preparing one of those compartments[45] under the Town Hall for an office. Being just opposite our corner I am rather pleased to see it, as it will bring a few people there.

Two years before, in October 1857, a special meeting of the Town Council had been held to decide on the matter of encouraging the Electric Telegraph Company to continue to have an office in the centre of the town. The Company had, apparently announced its intention of vacating its premises on Market Hill, and this, it was stressed at the meeting, would greatly inconvenience Cambridge people, who would be obliged to go to the station to send messages.

One of the aldermen proposed that, as the Council was on the point of getting rid of one of the public houses under the Town Hall, 'which were such a nuisance in the locality', these premises might be offered to the Telegraph Company at a nominal rent of five shillings a year.

The Company declined this offer, but in December 1858 it was reported to the Town Council that, following an application for the Town Hall archway premises made by the British & Irish Magnetic Telegraph Company, the first company had changed its mind and was now willing to take them at an annual rent of £12 10s. The British and Irish Company had asked for permission to erect posts to carry their wires from London by way of Newnham and the Backs of the Colleges, but without the help of the Electric Telegraph Company, already installed in Cambridge, they could not transmit messages to Ely or to any intermediate stations. The Town Council, therefore, agreed to accept the offer made by the Electric Telegraph Company.

Royal Albert Benevolent Society - Stone-laying Ceremony

The Royal Albert Benevolent Society for Decayed Tradesmen and Others, was established in March 1846 to provide homes for its aged and infirm poor members. The annual membership subscription was 5s.,[46] and the Society planned to erect its homes on any suitable freehold building land, within two miles of Great St. Mary's Church, which might become available, or to purchase or rent any suitable house within that distance.

For 13 years funds were accumulated through donations and subscriptions and by such fund-raising activities as benefit performances at the Barnwell Theatre or the holding of bazaars. One of the last-named took place in the Town Hall on 26 and 27 May 1858, when Josiah went to look at the stalls but not, it would seem, to buy anything from them. 'The things looked very nice', he wrote, 'but the place is so very small that scores of people were turned away and many others could not get near the stalls'.

The *Cambridge Chronicle*[47] reporter, in his account of the bazaar, was even more critical of the facilities offered by the Town Hall for such a function:

That wretched Town Hall! First and last, that was the cry. Long has it

been a disgrace to Cambridge, but never did it make one blush so much
for the mean spirit of the town as during the present week. It was no
mere work of amusement to which it was devoted . . . but an effort of
charity of which it was the scene. And charity has been baulked of its
full fruition because Cambridge, with its wealth of collegiate architecture,
is content with a municipal building which makes it the butt and laugh-
ing stock of every little trumpery borough in the kingdom.

Let it not be concluded from this grumbling introduction that the
Albert Society Bazaar was a failure . . . it was a very great success . . .

In 1859 a suitable site was found in Hills Road and the present
buildings[48] were erected. The foundation stone of the homes
was laid on 28 June 1859, a day chosen specially as being the
anniversary of the Queen's coronation. It was a gala day in
Cambridge; the streets were decorated with flags, the shops
were closed, and at ten o'clock in the morning the Committee
of the Society and their friends, officials of the Corporation,
and members of the Oddfellows and other Friendly Societies,
formed a procession at the Town Hall, the Trustees and Directors
carrying wands of office and wearing white rosettes.

The procession marched to Great St. Mary's Church where a
choral service was held, the sermon being preached by the Dean
of Ely. After the service, the procession re-formed and proceeded to the Hills Road site where the foundation stone was
laid by the Mayor, hymns were sung, prayers were recited, and
the Cambridge Amateur Musical Society sang the *Hallelujah
Chorus*. At five o'clock a dinner, described by the local newspapers as a 'cold collation', was held in the Town Hall.

Josiah Chater's diary entry on that day reads:

A grand day for some of the Cambridge people, it being appointed for
the laying of the Foundation Stone of the Royal Albert Benevolent
Society's new building. The Mayor, Mr Charles Balls, laid it; the Dean
of Ely, Dr Goodwin, preached a sermon in St Mary's Church, and the
Amateur Musical sang the Coronation Anthem, &c. I did not go to the
grounds or join the procession but quietly stayed at home and prepared
a new bath for my Collodion process.

He was then in the grip of his enthusiasm for photography.

Scene in St. Andrew's Street Chapel

On Sunday 18 May 1861 the congregation at the morning
service in St. Andrew's Street Baptist Chapel were somewhat
startled when, as Josiah recorded in the following week,

A University man, drunk, came into our chapel in the gallery opposite
me and, taking off his cap, said in a loud voice to our minister,

Mr Robinson, Oh, you venerable old heretic, for which offence he was duly incarcerated in the lock-up and hauled before the magistrate on the Monday following. He was liberated on the understanding he should see Mr Robinson alone, and apologise. Two others were with him and had to do the same penance.

NOTES TO PART III

1. Not long afterwards he moved to Maids Causeway and later to Hills Road.

2. Lincolne & Co. were grocers and wine merchants of 35 Sidney Street.

3. Lord Francis Godolphin Osbourne, 2nd son of the 5th Duke of Leeds, created Baron Godolphin 1832. M.P. for Cambridgeshire 1810-31; High Steward for Cambridge 1836-50. He built and lived in Gog Magog House, now demolished, near the Iron Age fort of Wandlebury on the Gog Magog hills in the parish of Stapleford. The stable block of the house remains; in the yard is a monument to *Godolphin*, one of the first Arab horses imported into England for the improvement of thoroughbred stock. The Gog Magog estate, with Wandlebury, is now owned by the Cambridge Preservation Society and is open to the public.

4. The Bridge Street shop was sold at the end of November 1857.

5. This was applied for as compensation for the loss of a market stall, the rent of which had previously been paid to Mr. Bonnett. The lease of the stall had been acquired, with 1 Market Hill, by Chater & Osbourne.

6. An account of the demolished premises is in the Cambridge Antiquarian Society's *Proceedings* No. XXXII (1891). The whole corner site of the old Veysy house, including 1 Market Hill and a portion of the north side of Petty Cury, was rebuilt. It was occupied 1893-1926 by Hallack & Bond, grocers. Since 1928 the premises have been those of Montague Burton, Ltd., tailors.

7. One of these fireplaces is in the Cambridge City Library.

8. Josiah had noted in his diary on Thursday, 13 October 1853, 'On Monday the new Stamp Act comes into force, i.e. a penny receipt stamp for all amounts over £2'.

9. The arrangements with Savidge came to nothing; the premises were eventually occupied by John Pigott, ironmonger and tool-maker.

10. William gave up his share in the house.

11. Rev. Harvey Goodwin, vicar of St. Edward's Church and Principal of the College.

12. The opening of the Borough Free Library in 1855 had led to a decline in membership of the College.

13. Alexander Macmillan who, with his brother Daniel (d. 1857), had taken over Richard Newby's bookshop at 17 Trinity Street in 1843.

In 1845 they acquired Thomas Stevenson's bookshop at 1 Trinity Street where the two businesses were combined, with Edward Barclay as partner, under the name of Macmillan, Barclay & Macmillan. In July 1846 the Macmillans' young nephew, Robert Bowes, came from Scotland to help in the business which from 1850 became Macmillan & Co. In 1858 an office was opened in London to which, in 1863 the publishing side of the business was transferred under Alexander Macmillan. Robert Bowes was left at 1 Trinity Street where the bookselling continued, from 1881 under the name of Macmillan & Bowes and of Bowes & Bowes from 1909 until the present day. Booksellers have occupied the premises since 1581.

14. When the College was first proposed in 1855, it was suggested that the scheme be called 'Education for Working Men'. The name Working Men's College was, however, attached to the classes from the outset and came to be adopted as the official title.

15. Rev. Harvey Goodwin had, by this date, been appointed Dean of Ely.

16. Their official title was The 3rd Cambridgeshire Rifle Volunteers. In 1887 the Corps became the 4th (Cambridge University) Volunteer Battalion of the Suffolk Regiment.

17. M.A. of Corpus Christi College; Deputy Recorder of Cambridge and Deputy Judge of the Borough Court of Pleas.

18. The University Printer.

19. Solicitor of 13 Hills Road.

20. Boot and shoe maker of 9 Bridge Street.

21. James Hovell Turner, Postmaster of Cambridge 1847-91.

22. James Amiraux Jeremie, Fellow of Trinity College 1826-50; Regius Professor of Divinity 1850-70; Dean of Lincoln Cathedral 1864-72.

23. H.J. Wetenhall, hop merchant of St. Andrew's Hill.

24. Robert Roe, engraver and printseller, 14 King's Parade.

25. William Nichols, photographer, St. Mary's Passage.

26. Rev. Francis Vesey, then curate of Great St. Mary's Church.

27. The first had been held in Paris in 1855.

28. Bookseller and stationer of 24 Sidney Street.

29. He is described in Craven & Co.'s *Commercial Directory of the County of Huntingdon and Town of Cambridge* (1855) as, 'cook to St John's College'. He lived at 8 St. John's Street in one of the houses which formed the Pensionary of St. John's College. The Selwyn Divinity School, erected 1878-9, occupies their site. A skilled amateur photographer, in 1862 Owen Jones took the photographs, now in St. John's College, of St. John's Street before it was altered for the erection of the new College Chapel 1863-9.

30. Josiah's brother-in-law.

31. Agnes Chater's second cousin. Edwin Barrett succeeded his father Robert Barrett (1808-91) in the family china and earthenware

business which had been founded, on Market Hill, by Simon Barrett (Robert's grandfather) in 1792. Simon had three sons of whom two - Robert senior and George - followed him in the business while John, Agnes Chater's father, set up as a linen draper.

32. In Scotland in 1856 and in Holland and Germany in 1857.

33. Josiah was assured that, if he did so, no action would be taken against the thief, although the man would have to go to the police station for a report to be made. On writing to Chamonix after his return to England, however, Josiah learned that the man had been sentenced to a term of imprisonment.

34. Now called Hobson's Passage.

35. This Penny Savings Bank had recently been established in Post Office Terrace, by a group of Trustees composed of leading Cambridge residents, to encourage working people and others to save small weekly sums from their wages. When the Post Office Savings Banks opened in 1861 they were empowered to accept deposits from Penny Banks whose Trustees deposited, in a collective account, the small savings of work-people, children and members of various social organisations for later re-imbursement to the individual savers when the need arose. Penny Banks were later established in Cambridge by the Co-operative Stores and by the Working Men's Institutes in East Road and Russell Street.

36. John Windridge, hat manufacturer of 62 Sidney Street.

37. Josiah drew a rough sketch of the arch in his diary.

38. William Thurston, wholesale and retail confectioner of Hobson's Passage and 14 Market Street.

39. Son of John Swan the cabinet maker and auctioneer whose suicide Josiah was to record on 26 February 1857.

40. Robert Sadd, jeweller and optician of 7 King's Parade.

41. Grocer of 55 Sidney Street.

42. Henry Bond, M.D., 3 Regent Street.

43. The Liberal candidates.

44. William Ingle, ironmonger.

45. The Shire House, erected 1747 in front of the Guildhall, stood on pillars which formed a space for market stalls. In 1835 this space was enclosed, forming the 'compartments'· to which the diary refers. A register, now in the Cambridge Folk Museum, of 470 local inns used 1841-95 as soldiers' billets, gives the address of the *Boar's Head*, the *Crown and Anchor* and the *Rose* as 'Under the Hall' up to 1859.

46. Now increased to 10s.

47. 29 May 1858.

48. The interiors of these were modernized 1969-70, but their Victorian exterior remains unaltered.

IV

1867 to 1876

END OF THE PARTNERSHIP

Life in Fitzwilliam Street

Leaving only one blank page after the last entry he had written on 27 January 1863, Josiah Chater resumed the regular keeping of his diary on 1 January 1866.

By then, he and Agnes had five children: Ethel, aged 12; Elizabeth, usually known as Lizzy, two years her junior; Millicent (Milly), aged five; Ernest, aged four, and two-year old Junia. Their little girl Polly, born on 22 March 1859, had died between 1863 and 1865.

On 11 January 1866 Josiah recorded that he had had a fire lit, for the first time, in his new greenhouse which,

> I began to build about 22 November last year and got it all finished and glazed by 22 December, and all by myself, save what little help (and I would not despise it) our groom, Cooper,[1] gave me by holding the light and doing a little of the heavy work. I only had my garden since Michaelmas; had a hole knocked through the wall which divides me from Mrs Brewis, and made a way across her garden, for which I gave her ten shillings.

From the end of the garden[2] a gate gave access to the yard of the *Little Rose* Inn.

The new greenhouse and the garden, in which he kept bees and poultry and in which grew a very fruitful walnut tree, gave Josiah a great deal of pleasure. He nearly lost the greenhouse, though, on 31 December 1870:

> At about eleven o'clock I sat smoking my pipe when a ring came to the door and a servant called to say that the greenhouse was on fire. I quickly slipped into my boots and pea jacket[3] and got some water, and soon managed to master it; it had broken out about the chimney and got on to the ridge of the roof and was flaring away furiously outside. Peck[4] and the *Little Rose* ostlers came in to help. We got it so far under that no sparks could be seen anywhere, so I went in to watch for the rockets from the nursery window. I heard one go up, but the fog being so thick I could not see it. Then, looking down to the greenhouse, I noticed puffs of smoke, so went down to look, and lo and behold, the fire was making its way through the lath and plaster wall into the

summer house. I broke a lot of the plaster off and then got on to the roof and took off a tile preparatory to pouring water down. Just as I had hold of the bucket my foot slipped and down I went - not quite to the ground, as luck would have it, but I gave Sarah, our servant, who was standing below, an awful crack with the waterpot on her fore-head. By one o'clock I had succeeded in quenching entirely the fire.

The rockets, of which Josiah heard only one on this occasion, were fired every New Year's Eve in the open space at the entrance to King's College. One was let off at the first stroke of midnight, the second immediately the twelfth stroke ceased. The custom was begun in 1815 by Isaiah Deck, the chemist of No. 9, King's Parade[5], to celebrate the victory of Waterloo, and was continued by three generations of his family, until 1914, to mark the passing of each old year and the beginning of the new. This is the first time that Josiah refers to the rockets, although he is to mention them on several subsequent New Year's Eves.

In 1867 a number of alterations were made to No. 19 Fitzwilliam Street to make the house larger and so better able to accommodate Josiah's ever-increasing family. The rooms at the back were extended, a cellar was made and the roof was raised so that three attic bedrooms could be added. The work, which was carried out by Charles Taylor of Tennis Court Road at a cost of £150, began on 20 May and ended on 1 July. Josiah continued to sleep in the house, despite the inevitable dis-comfort, but Agnes, who was expecting another child, went, with the other children, to stay with her father, sister and brother in her old home in Market Street.

The entries in the diary at this time throw an interesting light on the working conditions of builders at that period; they show, too, that the same set-backs and difficulties were encountered then as are met today by a house-owner having substantial alterations made to his home. Josiah had to deal with neighbours who complained that their drains or their roofs were being affected by the rebuilding, and with workmen who were slow, unpunctual or who, sometimes, failed to appear at all.

On Saturdays they worked a, 'short day', although this did not end until four o'clock in the afternoon. On most days they began work at six o'clock in the morning, sometimes earlier, and continued until seven o'clock or later in the evening. As the work progressed the number of tradesmen in the house in-creased; so, on 29 May 1867 Josiah

had 8 men at work . . . they have raised the roof to the first floor. Agnes and Junia each laid a brick this morning, and in the evening Ethel, Milly and Ernest each laid one.

Two days later Sophia, the baby of the family who had been born on 11 July 1866, was assisted in the laying of 'her brick',

3 July:

The men got on very well this morning, but in the afternoon the rain came on, and instead of their going to work indoors they all struck work and so lost half a day, which made me very angry.

To 'punish' them for this, Josiah refused, on the next day, to give them any beer to drink, 'which had a good effect on them'.

On 7 June there were 10 men at work, but three days later several of these got very drunk while, on 11 June two of them went on strike. On 13 June, however, things improved and the carpenters, plasterers, bricklayers, slaters and tinmen - a dozen in all - were reported to be working well.

19 June:

The carpenters and plasterers and two labourers came this morning at 5 o'clock, and I had ready for them, by half past, half a pint of coffee each and a slice of bread and butter, with which they appeared well pleased. I am sure they have worked uncommonly well all day.

Thinking, possibly, that his little *douceur* encouraged greater effort, Josiah provided coffee and bread on the two following days but on 24 June, was obliged to record:

Our men all came at 6 o'clock this morning, but the carpenters struck at 11 o'clock and, I suppose, went to the Fair, it being Midsummer Fair Day. But the plasterers kept on until half past seven this evening.

The next day Agnes was able to begin the formidable task of restoring the house to order, assisted by Josiah and the servants so that on 1 July she could return from Market Street and sleep for the first time in her newly-enlarged home where, 10 days later, her baby, Rowena, was born.

The additional rooms in Fitzwilliam Street were certainly needed, for in the period 1867 to 1876, six more children[6] were born. The diary for these years contains many references to the young Chaters: their childish sayings, their behaviour and their educational progress. Their many illnesses, too, are detailed. The youngest children suffered often from croup and bronchitis, while coughs, colds, sore throats, measles, whooping cough and scarlatina spread from one child to another, so that it was not uncommon for Agnes to have four or five invalids in bed at once.

True she had a nursemaid, a cook and one or two servants to help her but finding, and keeping, such assistance was one of her greatest problems, as it seems to have been that of many of her friends. On more than one occasion Josiah recorded that they had had 'no servant at all' for the past few days, while he had to report, several times, Agnes's anxiety because the maids she was employing did not get on amongst themselves.

The year 1871 seems to have been a particularly difficult one. On 13 February Agnes went to the Market Hill shop at midday in great agitation, to tell her husband that her servant Emma had smallpox. Josiah at once sent for Dr. Carter to examine the girl but, as he recorded in the diary, 'he says it is not smallpox but very probably measles and he recommends to get her away at once'. So the poor girl was sent home by train that afternoon, the thought that she might infect her fellow travellers occurring, it seems, to no-one. Later in that same year two servants, 'had the itch', so Agnes, terrified lest her children should catch the complaint, spent several days anointing the youngest ones with salves recommended by Mr. Peck, the Trumpington Street chemist, and giving them frequent warm baths.

In the autumn of 1874 she engaged as nursemaid a young, unmarried girl named Hannah, whose home was in Bishop's Stortford. The day after her arrival Agnes told Josiah that she was sure that the girl was pregnant. After some discussion, however, it was decided to allow her to remain, Agnes feeling sorry for her and grateful, doubtless, for help with the children.
On 20 October, when Josiah returned home at nine o'clock in the evening, he was met by a distressed wife with the news that Hannah

> had been confined; she kept up and did all her work till 4 o'clock and was then obliged to go and lie down, and in a few minutes a child was born and packed away in a box. When Agnes got up[7] and went to look for her she was in a deplorable state, but Agnes made her confess and bring out the baby. Then the girl dressed herself and wanted to go down and get on with her work, but Agnes sent for a nurse and the doctor made her go to bed. She says it is a beautiful little boy. Poor Agnes is in a dreadful way . . .

Two days later Hannah was reported to be making good progress, but on 24 October,

> Our nursemaid is not so well today so we have written to her mother.

Agnes is quite knocked up and has been in bed all day until this evening.
Ethel and Lizzie are doing much to help with our servant Ann.

On 29 October Hannah was so ill that the doctor came three
times to see her, and Josiah had to telegraph twice to her mother
who eventually arrived, in the late evening, to take care of her
daughter. Two days later the girl died. Her mother returned, the
same night, to Bishop's Stortford and, next morning, Josiah
followed by a very early train, to see Hannah's father and to
arrange with him how his daughter's baby was to be brought
from Cambridge. Josiah then travelled home and, before midday,
had ordered a coffin to be sent to Fitzwilliam Street. At seven
o'clock that evening Agnes and a friend, taking Hannah's baby
with them to be brought up by his grandparents, accompanied
the unfortunate girl's body by rail to Bishop's Stortford.

We have had a dreadful time of it; the whole house in upset . . . and we
can scarcely realise the fact, it seems so like a dream.

This tragic incident was not the only one of its kind to have
occurred in Cambridge within the period of the diary. On several
occasions Josiah referred to friends and acquaintances who had
engaged girls and then, finding them to be in an advanced state
of pregnancy, had promptly dismissed them with no thought of
whether they had any place to which to go. Agnes and her
husband certainly had more compassion than some of their
contemporaries.

Once, in his early married days, Josiah had recorded the sad
case of a Cambridge servant who, one night, gave birth to an
illegitimate child and suffocated it by placing it in a drawer
where it was found, the following day, by her mistress who
vowed that she was completely ignorant of the girl's condition.

Sometimes the stigma of bearing an illegitimate child could
not be faced. On 3 January 1873 Josiah recorded,

The poor girl assistant in Jackson's in the Cury, toy seller, was found in
the river this morning just below the Great Bridge. An inquest was held
this morning. M.[8] was summoned but did not appear; she left a note
stating that if he had done as he ought to have done he would not now
be answerable for her death and that friends were to apply to him to
bury her.

At the adjourned inquest a week later, a verdict of 'found
drowned in an unsound state of mind caused by her seducer',
was returned. The man whom the girl had accused in her letter
was present in court and was named by one of the jury. 'He had
a fearful reception', wrote Josiah.

Bereavement

In 1871 Agnes's father, John Barrett the linen draper, died at the age of 87. Following Victorian custom, the four youngest Chater children, their ages ranging from four to seven, were taken to see their dead grandfather. 'Junia could not stand it and ran off at first sight; the others did not mind a bit'.

The Barrett house and shop were taken over by W.H.C. Smith, a draper, to the great sorrow of Agnes and the children who,

> will not know what to do, they say, when they go down Market Street and are not able to go into the old house whenever they like.

John Barrett, though, was an old and ailing man, so his death was less of a shock than was that, at the age of 38, of Jabez, the youngest of the four Chater brothers who were established in Cambridge. He died suddenly, in his sleep, in the early hours of 19 March 1873.

In 1862 Jabez had purchased the Gonville Nursery[9] in West Road, Cambridge, having previously worked with his father in Saffron Walden.

Josiah had always taken an interest in his brother's business and had recorded, in his diary, the many occasions on which he used to visit the nursery to see how the plants and fruit trees were progressing. He had helped Jabez, too, by looking after his accounts and by encouraging him to take a shop on Peas Hill for the sale of his produce. He was always pleased when he could record that things were going well, and when Jabez was asked to undertake the floral decorations for important functions in the town. Now, in 1873, he devoted much time and energy to helping his widowed sister-in-law and her children and to finding a purchaser[10] for the nursery. On 27 September he wrote,

> I walked round the nursery for the last time. I was obliged to have a good cry at seeing the beautiful place all in good order and yet so desolate. Every walk and bush reminded me of the many events in poor Jay's life . . . and the house on which I had expended so much thought[11] to make it convenient and comfortable for him, now empty of all its furniture and waiting to be tenanted by a stranger. I walked down the garden and locked the gate, but could not say much to Harriet and Arthur[12] as we walked to her new home in Pembroke Street.

Business Affairs: The End of the Partnership

The woollen drapery business carried on by Josiah and his brother William at No. 1A Market Hill, and the tailoring firm conducted by Alfred Chater and James Osbourn next door, continued uneventfully for the first few years of the period 1866-76. William was still responsible for most of the whole-sale buying for W.G. & J. Chater, and for making the journeys to take orders and to collect debts; Josiah still kept the books and supervised affairs in Cambridge, making occasional visits to London and the North to buy goods or equipment.

He kept a detailed record in his diary of the progress of the business, expressing his satisfaction when trade was good and his anxiety when the bills had to be met and customers' accounts had not been paid. He was by nature prone to worry[13], so his occasional fears that he might not be able to pay for the goods that William had ordered were by no means justified.

Business was always slack from mid-July until September, with many of the well-to-do townspeople away on holiday, the undergraduates gone down and the modern tourist trade a thing of the future. Many tailor's shops closed in these months and the centre of the town was quiet and almost empty. Indeed, on 16 July 1874 Josiah, walking along King's Parade one afternoon, came across,

> Mr Greef[14] and almost a dozen ladies and gentlemen sitting out on the pavement cooling themselves, the weather being so very hot.

In 1871 Josiah decided to branch out into the ready-made tailoring trade. Accordingly, on 23 February, he engaged a man and set him to work cutting out coats and trousers. These, of course, had to be sewn, so on 14 March Josiah went to London to look at various makes of machines; he selected two which were delivered at the shop two days later. Part of Alfred Chater's kitchen at No. 1 was partitioned off to house the machines and on Good Friday, 7 April:

> Our new machinist, a Miss Goodship from Shelford, came and I set her to clean the machines. She is young but I fancy will do for us.

A male machinist was engaged, later in the month, to assist Miss Goodship in the garment making.

On 20 April two more Singer machines were ordered, at a cost of £4 12s. 0d. each, and three days later work was reported to be 'going well; we have sold a good deal of clothing'.

In June 1871 Josiah began to plan alterations to Nos. 1 and 1A Market Hill so as to utilise the brewhouse[15] and stables, at the northern end of the building, and to provide a new cutting room, a sewing room, a warehouse and new counting houses on the

southern - the corner of Petty Cury. The work, which was carried
out in two stages, was delayed at first because certain legal
matters had to be settled, but finally, on 13 July,

> all hands busy clearing out the cutting room as the workmen are coming
> in on Monday . . . we have moved out machines and stuff to Chater and
> Osbourn's tailors room *pro tem.*

All through July, August and part of September the builders
were at work, interrupted at times because objections to the
proposed new roof - an iron one - were raised by Mr. Cook, the
florist and seedsman at No. 40 Petty Cury, whose shop adjoined
that of Chater & Osbourn. The difficulties were, eventually,
solved and on 15 August the old roof was completely stripped.
'It has been awfully dusty', Josiah wrote. 'I found a brick in the
chimney with a date and initials on it: 1682 I H'.

On 18 August the workmen left at 11 o'clock in the morning
because their employer, 'gave his establishment their annual
holiday - an excursion on the river'. On 7 September Josiah was
able to record,

> Had a good day with the work; they have nearly finished glazing and
> lathing for plaster . . . I promised that if we get finished enough for
> tomorrow night we might perhaps have a leg of mutton for supper; it
> was astonishing what a spirit seemed to be infused in the men.

On 8 September

> Glass all in complete before the rain came to do much damage. At half
> past five the men all set to work in good earnest, cleared the room and
> set up a table and seats, and at 8 o'clock we began supper. Twenty-two
> of us sat down, and the men were all very jolly indeed and not one the
> worse for beer. All left at half past eleven. Annie[16] cooked the supper,
> Ethel and Lizzie helped to take it up and Milly, Ernest and Junia, with
> Alfred, all waited upon them. After supper they all sang and drank the
> health of the firm, Mrs Chater and the waiters.

There was still, however, a great deal of inside work to be
completed. and it was not until 2 October that,

> we had the room cleaned and scoured and got all the machines in,
> though the work people will not commence before Monday morning.

On 6 October the second stage of the alterations were begun,
the brewhouse and stables being pulled down for the building of
a new workshop for Chater and Osbourn's tailors and new
counting houses. Once again Josiah had to be down at the shop
by six o'clock in the morning to supervise the men, as he had
been doing from July to September. The new machine room,
meanwhile, was busy with 11 girls and three men at work in it.

In November a new warehouse for the ready-made clothes was begun, and it was not until January 1872 that Josiah could record, with a sigh of relief, that the last of the workmen had departed.

'Our manufactory', as he called his wholesale garment-making, proved successful, the supplying of police and Rifle Volunteers' uniforms being among several contracts obtained. By 11 April 1872 Josiah and his brother had 17 girls and three men working, while six days later:

> We have 20 women in our workroom and four men; next week we expect 25, as Mrs Randall, whose 2 children died of smallpox, wants to come back; then we shall have half our complement, as I am planning the place laid out for 50 comfortably.

One woman had had to be dismissed in February because she was caught stealing cotton, Josiah hoping that her dismissal would serve as a lesson to her and a warning to the other workers. Thefts by shop assistants were dealt with as severely in the 1870s as they had been when Josiah was an apprentice with Mr. Lilley.

On 28 August 1874 the diary recorded,

> After dinner my clerk told me that his suspicions were true respecting Burling, for he *has* been taking money out of the till. Yesterday, Campbell, one of our assistants, marked some money and left him alone in the shop and on his return he found sixpence taken. He then got Mills to ask Burling for two sixpences in change for a shilling, and one of these was the missing marked one. I had him in and talked a long time with him, but he vowed he had never taken anything. I told him that I would have him before the magistrates tomorrow, but he would not confess. I then dismissed him, but on his asking for his wages I told him to come in tomorrow.

The luckless Burling arrived at the shop next morning, but still refused to admit the theft, 'so we had a policeman in and at 11 o'clock he was tried before the Mayor and sentenced to 6 weeks hard labour'.

But although Josiah could be a stern employer he was also a kindly one, and the diary reveals many acts of charity on his part, and on Agnes's, whenever any employee had domestic troubles. The elder Chater girls, too, were encouraged to follow their parents' example, and Josiah wrote more than once of their 'having a Dorcas[17] - making some clothing for some of our workwomen'.

More alterations and improvements were carried out at No. 1A

Market Hill in December 1872 and from January to March 1873, when the cellar was cleared out and deepened to make a lower warehouse,

> and a splendid place it will be, about 54 feet long by 13 broad, boarded sides and ceiling, windows and cement floor.

The wages bill for the steadily increasing number of employees rose, of course, in proportion: Josiah paid out £14, for example, in the week ending 30 August 1872. In 1873 this sum had become, on average £20 to £22. On 26 March 1872 he paid £5 10s. for a gold watch for his daughter Ethel,

> for her services in the counting house. She has been a very good girl and up to last Christmas has been our clerk.

Following the passing, in 1871, of the Bank Holiday Act[18], many shops in Cambridge began to close on Easter Monday, Whit Monday, first Monday in August and on 26 December. So, on 20 May 1872, Josiah wrote,

> I amused myself at the warehouse all day, it being Whit Monday: most of the shops closed under the new Act.

On Monday, 5 August 1872:

> We closed our Factory and sent all the hands that liked to Yarmouth; all went but two, making 25 tickets at 3s. 6d.

In 1873, although W.G. & J. Chater and Chater & Osbourn, in company with, 'most of the shops except college shops', closed on Whit Monday, Josiah was, 'busy all day at the warehouse as our work people did not close'. They made up for this, however, in August for on Friday, the 8th, Josiah wrote,

> Our work people have all made holiday this week. We gave them tickets for Yarmouth on Monday and many have taken the week, so we had a short pay day, only £8 or £9.

On the Whit Monday of 1876, 'our work people came at 6 o'clock and left at half past eleven'.

Chater & Osbourn on King's Parade

At the end of 1872, the tailoring and robe-making firm of Brown & Sons, No. 13 King's Parade, was in financial difficulties. In February 1873 Mr. Brown was advised to file a petition in the Bankruptcy Court and, on the 21st of that month, Josiah, one of his creditors, was appointed receiver. Meanwhile, James Osbourn and Alfred Chater had looked over the premises and decided that they would do admirably for an extension of their Market Hill business and as living accommodation for James Osbourn.

For several weeks, although very busy with the alterations being made on Market Hill, Josiah was extremely occupied, winding up Brown's affairs and arranging for his brother Alfred and Osbourn to take over on King's Parade. An agreement was, after much discussion, drawn up, but Mr. Brown, shocked and bewildered by his failure, refused for some time to sign it. At last, on 20 April, the day after Jabez Chater died so suddenly, he consented to do so.

The End of the Partnership

In 1875 business relations between Josiah and his brother William became, on occasions, somewhat strained. William, who had re-married[19] in 1873, had come to undertake fewer journeys, employing a traveller, at a salary of £100 a year, to do much of this work for him. The extra expense, coupled with several bad debts, alarmed and worried Josiah.

By the middle of 1876 it had become obvious that the partnership, with the expenses of the business continually rising, could not, probably, continue much longer. William was prepared to stay on by himself, but Josiah, with a large family to think of and with Agnes expecting the birth of her 13th child, had to face the thought of making a new career for himself. With his early training at Mr. William Lilley's, and with all his subsequent experience, accountancy seemed the obvious first choice for such a career.

By October 1876 Josiah had made up his mind, 'not to go on any longer', and there followed many discussions with William, and with business friends, as to the future of the Market Hill premises. It was an anxious and an unhappy time for Josiah. Finally it was arranged that the grocer William Bond would take the premises, allowing William Chater to continue on a 10-year lease at No. 1A, and Chater & Osbourn at No. 1. On 30 December Josiah spent a long time, 'making a rough estimate of expenses for the last year', and then

packed the books away and felt very sad; but I feel sure it is the right step to take. It is almost enough to break my heart after 26 years.

Holidays and Social Life, 1866 to 1876

There were no continental holidays for Josiah in the period 1866 to 1876, although he and Eaden Lilley did have a day's trip to Calais, in 1875, when they were staying in Dover for a few days. He had several short vacations, too, on the East coast, usually with his friends Edwin Barrett and Alex Macintosh, and in 1866 he went to Scotland for a week's grouse shooting. Agnes, also, was able, early in this period, to have a short holiday in Cromer, with a friend, or with the children in Saffron Walden.

In the summer of 1873 the youngest Chater children spent several weeks in the village of Linton, Agnes and the servants going with them and leaving Josiah to be looked after at home by his two eldest daughters. Agnes, however, returned to Fitzwilliam Street, from time to time, to see that all was well and it was on one of these visits that Josiah decided to make up a party of friends and take them and his wife to Linton and there pick up the children for a day's outing. A horse and van were hired on 7 July and ordered to be,

> at our back gate at the *Little Rose* at 12 o'clock. We got off about 1 o'clock and had a jolly ride. I took Charles Richford to play to us on his concertina, so we had music all the way. Reached Linton about half past two. There we found a lot of boys and girls. The biggest we sent on by foot to Bartlow, and after a little rest we took all the others and the servants in the van and a wagonette to Bartlow. After a stroll on the hills we had tea in a little garden at the back of the inn, then we adjourned to a field and had a dance; then supper by moonlight in the garden and returned to Linton and Cambridge, making a very jolly day. Weather beautiful. We got home about 1 o'clock.

In 1874 Josiah leased a house in Chesterford and this was used, each summer, as a holiday home for Agnes and the children, Josiah going there for odd days or for a weekend whenever he could spare the time.

Both Agnes and Josiah went to a number of concerts at the Town Hall in these years 1866 to 1876, as did their three oldest girls, Ethel, Lizzy and Milly. There was much visiting too, between the young Chaters and their friends - sons and daughters of Josiah's married contemporaries. Agnes and Josiah dined at friends' houses and entertained at home, and it was in these years that Josiah seems to have acquired a liking for the game of whist.

Theatrical performances and charades were the main features

of the parties that were given in Fitzwilliam Street. On 20 January, 1868, for example, Josiah,

> went home to dinner early and began at once to make arrangements for our fun this evening. By 4 o'clock I had all things in readiness; our theatre rigged up and the supper room (our nursery) properly decorated. At 5 our company began to arrive and at half past tea commenced. At half past six we adjourned to the nursery and had the Xmas tree, which took an hour; then my company were prepared to play the first act of our charade, *viz* the Trial Scene in the *Merchant of Venice* . . . the word chosen was Judgement, divided into two Acts, the second of which I chose from the last scene in *The Winter's Tale* . . . We then went up to supper and danced and sang until 12.30

On 21 January 1869 three scenes from *Henry VIII* were performed, apparently not as a charade, at a party given by Agnes and Josiah, while in 1873 they entertained 30 of their friends with a performance of scenes from *Twelfth Night,* followed by supper and dancing until half past two in the morning. Their friends, too, provided similar entertainment. In March 1873 the Chaters were invited to a party given by Neville Goodman[20]:

> We had a reading from *As You Like It* and there was also a charade - *Bagdad* - specially written by N. Goodman.

At this period Josiah seems to have mellowed somewhat in his attitude to professional theatrical performances which, in his younger days, he had regarded with some disapproval. On 15 January 1873, when up in London for the day, he even went twice to the theatre:

> Finished what business I had to do by 3 o'clock, then went to Drury Lane to see the Pantomime. The transformation scene was very fine, and the Burlesque after was very amusing. Met Eaden Lilley, Alex Macintosh and E. Turner,[21] we had dinner at the London at 5.30 and then tried to get into Drury Lane but could not get a seat, so went to the Lyceum and had a private box and enjoyed the play - *Charles I* - but did not like the principles of it — too Tory!

On 11 August 1869 Josiah and Agnes were invited to a quadrille party in the village of Comberton:

> We had a jolly evening and did not get home till six o'clock in the morning. Had a tent on the lawn and everything went very nice indeed. I danced in nearly every dance and enjoyed it very much, and so did Agnes. I made her a present of a gold chain necklace and locket, the only piece of jewellery I have ever given her in my life. She looked very nice indeed . . .

Almost a daily event in the Chaters' lives was a visit by Josiah,

Agnes or one of the children, to No. 5 St. Peter's Terrace, where lived Miss Sophia Simpson - Aunt Sophy - a sister of the late Mrs. Adams. She was an old lady who took a great deal of interest in everything that went on in Cambridge in general, and in Fitzwilliam Street and the shop on Market Hill in particular; nor was she slow to voice her disapproval when anything occurred to displease her. Almost as much preoccupied with thoughts of death as Mrs. Adams had been, she constantly arranged and re-arranged her financial affairs in order, chiefly, to make provision for old maidservants who had been in her employment. Josiah was frequently asked to see to such matters, or to carry out small commissions for her in the town; he, and Agnes too, did indeed give a great deal of their time to her. But they knew that the lonely old lady looked forward to their visits, for she seldom left her house and then only in summer, when she went for short drives in her carriage, often with Josiah or Agnes, or, on rare occasions, walked the short distance to Fitzwilliam Street.

Both William and Josiah belonged to a Book Club - referred to once in the diary as the Union Club - whose members, apparently about 20 in all, met monthly in each other's houses, the host for the evening providing supper. Volumes were purchased out of the subscriptions, were circulated amongst the members, and were then, from time to time, sold, at below cost price, at one of the meetings. Two or three such clubs[22] still existed in Cambridge in the 1870s, even though the free Public Library had opened in 1858.

The meeting of the Union Club on 10 January 1870 was a somewhat unusual one:

> At 9 we met at Mr Wetenhall's and had a very pleasant evening and presented Mr Barrett, senior,[23] with his portrait painted as the Father of the Club. He has been a member for upwards of 60 years. We also each had a copy of it as a *carte*, very nicely done. We did not leave until half past twelve.

On 5 December 1870:

> Had the Book Club to supper this evening, it being my turn. There were ten of them and I gave them boiled fowls and ham, roast neck of pork, stuffed beef, sweets, &c.

Sometimes, when the Club met at Josiah's house, he would have a meal sent in, to save Agnes the extra work, as on 3 May 1875:

> Book Club this evening. I did not want to give Agnes much trouble, so I

went to the cook of Peterhouse and made arrangements for him to
supply us with supper. Miss Simpson had had a quarter of lamb sent
her, and she had given Agnes the shoulder, so this made a good dish for
one end. I got 4lb. of salmon for the other, and at the sides a dish of
cutlets and sweetbreads; no sweets, but a good salad with cucumber and
cheese completed the bill of fare. There were 12 of us in all and we had
a jolly evening, the last leaving at one o'clock.

In the school holidays the young Chaters were often taken
for walks round Cambridge, occasionally to London for the day
and, in true Victorian tradition, on a pilgrimage to the cemetery
in Histon Road. This had been opened in 1843, the Cambridge
General Cemetery Company which promoted it, and in which
Josiah, by the 1870s, was a shareholder, having been formed in
1842. The ground was unconsecrated and was much used for
Nonconformist burials. it was principally to see the vault of his
uncle, William Adams, that Josiah took his children to the
cemetery. As early as October 1845, when he was still apprenticed to William Eaden Lilley, he had recorded in his diary
that he had been, 'up to the cemetery before breakfast, and
very nice it looks. There are some very pleasing tablets already
erected'.

On 6 February 1870 Milly, Junia and Ernest were taken to
Newmarket Road,

to see the gas house; the girls were frightened, but Ernest was very
interested. We saw the result of the accident to the great gasometer.

This accident had occurred on 13 January. The large gas holder,
erected in 1867, overturned in a gale, and the 300,000 cubic feet
of gas which it contained escaped and, accidentally became
ignited. There were, fortunately, no casualties.

In 1874 Josiah was asked by Mrs. Lilley, senior, if he would
take her elderly cook, Rachael Adshead, to London and see her
safely embarked for New Zealand, where she was going to live
with a nephew who had emigrated some years previously. Accordingly, on 11 August he called for Mrs. Adshead early in the
morning and, on arrival in London, went with her to the New
Zealand Shipping Office and booked a passage on the *Mataura,*
paying £23 2s. 6d. with £1 3s. 6d. 'for sundries'. They both then
went, in a cab, to the South West India Dock but, finding it was
too late to board the boat, left most of Mrs. Adshead's luggage
in the office, went on to Greenwich and found rooms at the *Star*
Hotel.

On the following morning, Josiah returned to the Dock, by

train and boat via Tilbury.

> to see after luggage and berth for the old lady. By one o'clock I got the
> luggage all on board and arranged with the carpenter how her berth
> should be built. The ship was all in confusion.

He then travelled back to Cambridge and, on the following
evening, Sunday 16 August, caught a train to Stratford and went
from there to the docks:

> Had great difficulty in finding the *Mataura* which had left the quay and
> gone into the basin ready to start at 4 o'clock in the morning. I asked
> the steward if I might stay on board and go down with the ship to
> Greenwich, and he said yes. So I undid the bedding and soon after ten
> I laid it on the luggage and had a good rest until 4 o'clock when the row
> began overhead and I got up . . . At 7 o'clock we reached Greenhithe
> where we had to wait for the compasses to be adjusted. I immediately
> went ashore and caught the 8 o'clock train to Gravesend, went to the
> Mitre and had a jolly good breakfast. Then I found the old lady, and we
> walked about to the pier to get a few requisites for her voyage. I took
> her to be photographed - paid 4s. 6d. for half a dozen to be sent to me.
> Then took her to the Falcon and had a good dinner, and at 2 o'clock we
> were told the ship had arrived, so we immediately embarked. The berth
> was not complete, so we walked about for an hour or two, then set to
> work to get her cabin ship-shape. I screwed all the hooks in and knocked
> a lot of nails around; had a table fixed and made the place very comfort-
> able. At 8 o'clock I bid her goodbye - most likely I will never see her
> again, poor old soul.

He duly reported all these activities - which he enjoyed because
they were, 'so very novel', - to Mrs. Lilley, who was relieved to
hear that all had gone well, and very pleased to be given the
photographs when they arrived a few days later. Five months
later, news of Mrs. Adshead's safe arrival was received.

In 1875 Josiah went for the first, and within the period of
the diary, the only time to watch the Oxford and Cambridge
boat race.

On 20 March he travelled third class to Royston and from
there took a first class excursion train to Moorgate Street, 'with
a nice hot water bottle', for his feet as the weather was very
cold. He attended to some business matters in London before
going on by train to Hammersmith where he found the friend
who had invited him to view the race from his uncle's barge.

> At half past one the cry came 'they're off', and every eye and ear was
> strained to catch a glimpse of the competitors. The huge steamers were
> plainly visible before we could see the two little 8-oars. First the cry
> was 'Cambridge leads', but this soon turned to 'they're neck and neck',

soon it was 'Oxford draws ahead - Oxford leads'. By the time they were opposite us Oxford was ¾ of a length ahead, and at Hammersmith Bridge over a length . . . we could not see them beyond the bridge but we soon heard the result: Oxford ahead by 10 lengths. . . They returned on board the Oxford boat, preceded by the umpire and the other steam boats. The Prince of Wales and Prince Alfred were there, and crowds of people lined the banks and the boats all along the river. It was a grand sight, but had the weather been warm as well as dry, it would have been far pleasanter.

Leisure Activities

The Rifle Volunteers

By 1866 the 8th Cambridgeshire Rifles had become merged in the 1st Volunteer Corps in which, by then, Josiah held a Lieutenant's commission. On 10 July of that year he went by the Great Northern railway to Ludgate Street, his fare costing 4s. 5d., then on to Putney where he spent the night at the *Red Lion* Inn after walking out on to Wimbledon Common where the Rifle Corps was encamped. On the following day:

At 11.30 we shot 200 yards for the Queen's Cup, but I only made 12. I then hastened back to Cambridge, had a walk with Agnes in the garden till 7 o'clock, then down to the shop for an hour. On returning, I met Mr Carter, the doctor, who told me Agnes was confined - another girl.[24]

He returned to Wimbledon on the next day, Thursday, but scored only 10 points, and having spent the night in London, went again on Friday,

down to Wimbledon and finished shooting at 600 yards: only made 8 or 9 alas. Very bad! Then home to Cambridge.

On the Monday he went to London on the first train and 'finished shooting'.

Later in 1866, on 1 October:

I went to our Rifle Butt and shot for our annual prizes but was not one of the successful ones.

2 October:
This morning we had the Battalion Prize shooting at the University Ground. I did better, but not well enough for a prize.

In March 1867 Josiah resigned his commission as, 'I dare not risk any exposure on account of my health'. He was, throughout the period of 1866-1876, often afflicted with headaches, rheumatism, and digestive disturbances. But he continued to take an interest in the Rifle Corps and in 1871, for example, when the Queen's Cup was won at Wimbledon by the son of Dr. G. Humphrey, the Professor of Anatomy at Cambridge, walked with his two eldest daughters on to Hills Road to see the victor return in triumph.

> Major Barber and the Town and University Rifles went to the station to meet him and escorted him round the town . . . Men carried torches and the bands played *See the Conquering Hero Comes, etc.,* and it was very jolly.

On several occasions, alone or with Ernest, he went to the Rifle Butts to watch the Corps at shooting practice, or competing for the annual awards.

The Cambridge Building Society

Josiah added to the number of his activities, in the period, by becoming a director of the Cambridge Building Society[25], in which he was a depositor. On 8 March 1871 he attended the Annual General Meeting and,

> after the Report was moved I offered some remarks and asked a few questions . . . The Chairman asked me to allow myself to be moved as one of the Directors, that I might go into the accounts and satisfy myself of the workings of the Society . . . I consented and was elected unanimously.

Thereafter, in this period, he attended committee meetings and also went, at regular intervals, to assist in the taking of the monthly deposits, as on 15 May 1871 when,

> for the first time we took over £1,000. It was a wonderful help to a great many people who wish to purchase houses or land.

The Penny Bank

Josiah continued to serve on the committee of the Penny Savings Bank and to spend a few hours on one evening, in every week or so, taking deposits. In 1871 he recorded yet another incident illustrative of the harsh measures which, in his day, were taken against petty offenders:

12 February:
> Last night the Managers of the Penny Bank caught a young gentleman in the act of robbery, and put him in gaol. He took 6s. 6d., which was laid ready for him, and young Moore, who was hidden under the desk watching, came out and seized him - a boy about 11 years old, from Occupation Road.

13 February:
> Went up to the Town Hall and heard the lad tried before the magistrates

this morning. He was sentenced to six weeks' imprisonment and twelve
stripes of a birch rod.

The Working Men's College

At the end of 1858 the Principal of the Working Men's
College, the Rev. Harvey Goodwin, had been appointed to the
Deanery of Ely, whilst very soon afterwards another founder of
the College, the Rev. Francis G. Vesey, who had been its
secretary, left Cambridge where, for the past three years, he
had been a curate at Great St. Mary's church. With the departure
of these two men, the College began to languish. Classes were
held until the middle of 1865, and then seem to have ceased,
and Josiah makes but few references to the College in the years
1866 to 1876. However, on 28 August 1867 he, and at least
three of the old Student's Committee,

> met the Working Men's College at 2 o'clock and we went down the
> water to Clayhithe; reached there at 3.30 and spent the afternoon in
> games. Had tea about six and after it a jolly evening, singing and
> speeching till 10 o'clock.

He mentions that the Chairman, on this occasion, was a
Mr. Boning from London, so the outing was probably one for
members of the London College. Certainly there was an excursion to Cambridge made, a few days later, by the Ipswich
College, for on 2 September:

> At 9.30 this morning I went up to the station to meet the Working
> Men's College from Ipswich. They arrived in good time and we all
> marched off at once to the Botanic Garden. Dr Christian was at their
> head, and he went round with them. I was with them all day till 6.30,
> and so were Flack[26] and Boning.[27] They went back by 6.30 train to
> Ipswich; they are a decent sort. Dr Christian would have Flack, Boning
> and me go with them to Newman's[28] where he ordered us each a bottle
> of sherry and port and made a little speech to thank us.

In 1868, on 29 January, Josiah had supper with Walter Flack,
a fellow member of the Students' Committee, and together they
chose, from some pieces of plate sent to them on approval, one
to give as a testimonial to, 'Mr Gray[29], our secretary to the
Working Men's College'. On 20 February the committee met in
Fitzwilliam Street and drew up an address to, 'be presented to
our Secretary with a silver inkstand. We then had supper together
and a very pleasant evening'.

No further reference is made to the College or its affairs

until 20 September 1871:

> At 9 I went to a meeting of the Working Men's College to wind it up. I
> and four others were appointed to a Committee of Execution and we are
> to dispose of the property in a month. Mr Gray, the Secretary, was
> there and acted as Chairman. We decided to give the books to the Free
> Library, the Working Men's Hall, New Town[30] and the Industrial
> School,[31] and any surplus to the Industrial School.

The committee met again on 13 December, 'to divide the
estate', and, for the last time, on 20 June 1872 when Josiah
reported, 'we signed the balance sheet, having distributed all the
effects'.

Charities

By 1867 Josiah Chater was serving on the committee of two
Cambridge almshouse charities: the Knight's and Mortlock's and
the SS. Anthony and Eligius. The former was established by
Elizabeth Knight of Denny Abbey, near Cambridge, who, in her
will dated 18 May 1647 left instructions for the sum of £400 to
be spent in building a house for two poor widows and 'four
poor godly ancient maidens', and for land to be purchased to
provide money for their maintenance. In 1648 the almshouses
were erected on the south side of Jesus Lane, on the site of the
houses now numbered 63 to 69, and an estate of 60 acres was
acquired in the open fields of Swaffham Prior.

In 1818 William Mortlock, the Cambridge banker and, for
many years, treasurer of the charity, gave £500 for the rebuilding
of the almshouses and, in 1826, the first of several sums for
their upkeep; his name was, therefore, added to that of Elizabeth
Knight as a perpetual memorial of his charity. In 1880 the almshouses were rebuilt in King Street.[32]

The hospital dedicated to St. Anthony and St. Eligius was
established in c.1361, by Henry de Tangmer, for the reception
of sufferers from leprosy, but with the decline of the disease
the house became a refuge for the elderly poor. It stood,
originally, on the east side of Trumpington Street, not far from
its junction with Lensfield Road, but was pulled down in 1852
because the buildings projected over the pavement. The inmates
were moved to new buildings in Panton Street.

Josiah's diary records his attendance at meetings of the
Trustees of both charities to elect inmates of the houses from

the long list of applicants, or, as on 28 March 1867, refers to
his going,

> as one of the visitors for the year, to inspect the Knight's and Mortlock's
> almshouses, found them in a decent state, also the property belonging to
> the charity.

The Y.M.C.A.

Of all the societies and institutions with which Josiah was
connected, the Y.M.C.A. occupied the greatest amount of his
spare time, his energy, interest and enthusiasm in the years 1866
to 1876, years which were extremely important and exciting
ones in the Association's history.

In 1866 Josiah seems often to have been unwell, so he does
not refer often, in his diary, to attending Y.M.C.A. functions,
though he was evidently, with his eldest daughter, a member of
the singing class which had recently been formed. Towards the
end of that year, the landlord of the premises in Hobson's
passage gave the Association notice to quit at Christmas. Josiah
and his brother William discussed the possibility of making
rooms at No. 1 Market Hill available, but on 28 November
Mr Attack the builder, who had been asked to submit an
estimate, reported, 'to make two rooms for the Y.M.C.A. will
cost us £170 to £180'.

Accommodation was, however, found in St. Edward's Passage
where, on 12 February 1867, Josiah

> Attended the opening meeting of our new lecture room . . . We had a
> nice dessert, then readings, speeches and singing.

With the move to the new rooms, the life of the Y.M.C.A.
which, since 1859, had been in jeopardy, chiefly through lack
of money and support, was suddenly renewed.

By 1867 a Gymnastics Club had been established, for on 7
March Josiah went to watch a competition which was judged by
three university men and in which '13 competed in 2 squads
divided by height: 5ft 6in. and upwards, and under 5ft 6in'. An
elocution class, formed in 1867, at which members' readings of
prose and verse passages were discussed and criticised, did not,
apparently, survive for long. The Cricket Club, established
in 1866, flourished, one of its regular events being a match
between married and single members. The debates, which had
been so popular in the early days of the Association, had ceased,
and the Annual Report for the year 1867-68, stated that no

attempt had been made to revive them. Later, however,
discussions, if not in the shape of formal debates, were
frequently held on important issues of the day.

Public lectures, which brought in funds for the Association
through the sale of tickets, continued to be arranged. Many
distinguished speakers were engaged, for although a substantial
fee had, often, to be paid to them, their reputation usually
ensured a large audience, and so a satisfactory profit. Occasionally, though, less eminent lecturers were invited. On 10 April
1867, for example, Josiah went to hear a Mr. Bryant[33] speak at
the Town Hall on Electro-Biology.

> There was a good bit of fun, but he is an awful duffer of a lecturer,
> However a university man gave us a slight history of the science and
> did it very well indeed.

A more expensive speaker was Professor Pepper of London
who charged a fee of £40 for lecturing on 28 and 29 October,
1867, on *A Visit to the French Exposition,* illustrating his talk
with dissolving views[34], Josiah went on both nights. On the
first he reported,

> The illusions are very good, but being the first time they have been
> shown out of London they did not go quite so easily as I would have
> wished. Lizzy and Milly liked *The Heads of the Decapitated Speaking*
> better than *The Cherubs.* The views of the Exposition were tolerable.

on the second, 'the show was somewhat better'. In all, the lecture
just covered the expenses.

At a meeting held on 30 August 1867 the Y.M.C.A. committee
decided to give an entertainment to the Association's officers as
a reward for their services during the past 12 months. A circular,
sent out to members, announced that the event would be held
on Trinity College Cricket Ground, that tickets would cost
1s. 6d. each or 2s. 6d. for two, and that in addition to croquet
and other games, a return match between married and single
would be played. The entertainment took place on 11 September
when the diary recorded,

> Down at shop by 7.30 this morning to make sundry arrangements about
> the party and get things ready to send up. After breakfast I went to the
> ground and stayed there until the company arrived. I set the tables and
> dusted nearly all the crockery, and as the guests arrived set them to
> work. At 4 I went home to dress - just back in time to take my innings
> at cricket: got 3 runs in about half a dozen balls. We had 4 sets of
> croquet at work, archery, bowls, quoits, 2 sets of bat and trap besides
> other amusements. At 6.30 we had tea and lighted up the place . . .

Mr Wetenhall was in the chair and Eaden Lilley had quite an ovation. We kept it up till 9.30 then had a committee meeting . . . altogether it was a perfect success.

On 8 April 1868 Josiah,

attended a preliminary meeting of the members and others of a Boat Club in connection with the Y.M.C.A. and was elected Chairman. They determined to form a club and induced several members to join it.

The Club, on 27 June, 'entered an 8-oar' in the Town Races. On 29 and 30 June Josiah took his daughter Ethel to watch them, and could record, on the first occasion, 'our Y.M.C.A. boat keeps its place well', but on the second,

it got bumped by a very unlucky stroke of No. 5 oar who caught a crab and became paralysed, so that they were obliged to stop and the Town II caught them.

Earlier in that summer of 1868, the Y.M.C.A. and the Church of England Young Men's Society had made a joint excursion to Matlock. About 850 members of the two societies and their friends went on the trip, and arrangements were made with the Midland Railway Company so that both societies would make a profit.

On 8 July Josiah and Eaden Lilley, as joint Y.M.C.A. secretaries,

went to the station and after inspecting the saloon carriage we went to the rooms and made the final arrangements for tomorrow. Came home and packed up a long tin box with eatables &c. - cold tea, claret, sherry, potted beef, rolls, cakes, hard eggs, &c. &c.

9 July:

Agnes made a mistake and got up at half past three; I lay till half past five, but could not rest well. We had a cup of coffee and at 6.30 our train started - my party and I in the 2nd class saloon . . . Pryor drove our old Tom up for us and brought with him a jolly good lump of ice which we placed in our 'archives' and during our journey found it very good, placed in a cup of claret or sherry or cold tea. Macintosh and his two daughters, Fred and Harriet Barrett, Annie and Alfred Chater, Agnes, Ethel and I made up our party. We reached Matlock at 11 o'clock and, on emerging from the station, Wetenhall stopped us and wanted us to go with him to Chatsworth. I declined, but Alex Macintosh ultimately joined him. We then determined we would take a trap and go on to Chatsworth, and a very agreeable ride we found it after the heated atmosphere of a railway car. We reached Chatsworth at 1.30 and drove up to Mr Speed's[35] where we might have dined, as he had prepared a dinner for his brother and Jabez by appointment but they had not arrived. We made off at once for the House and were delighted with a stroll through the Chapel . . . as we left we met Jabez and his party going in . . . At Mr Speed's we had biscuits and wine then we all looked over the gardens and left at 5 to drive back to Matlock. Reached the station just in time to start for Cambridge . . . reached home about 11, of course tired, but highly pleased with the enchanting scenery of Chatsworth and glad we did not more weary ourselves by ascending the hills about Matlock, as most of the excursionists did . . . Several stayed behind until Saturday when they may return by ordinary train by paying an extra half-crown.

Five days later, Eaden Lilley entertained seven of the Y.M.C.A. committee and seven of the Church of England Society's at his home. They spent the evening playing bowls, croquet and quoits and, after supper, talked and sang songs till past midnight. It was, wrote Josiah, 'a capital summing up of the excursion'.

At the end of September 1868 Eaden Lilley and Josiah, though both continuing to serve on the committee, resigned as joint secretaries for a year, and were replaced by Edwin Barrett and George Warren[36]. At the Annual General Meeting, held in October 1868, the report of the retiring secretaries showed how successful the past year had been. Membership had risen to 389, over 2,000 volumes had been issued by the library, and the conversation room, which was open every weekday from six o'clock in the evening until ten o'clock, had 'proved a great boon'. Reference books, writing materials and sets of chess, draughts and other games had been placed in the room and had been much used.

This obvious renewal of the Association's vitality led, doubt-less, to the conversation recorded by Josiah on 22 October:

Eaden Lilley, Munsey and I have been talking over the idea I broached some time since, of building rooms for our Society.

The idea must have been discussed more widely, for on 2 November Josiah was 'placed on a Committee for considering a plan to build new rooms'.

23 November:
Have been busy about our new building for the Y.M.C.A. Bond and I went to see Robert Sayle and he approves our plan to buy a piece of the Red Hart estate on lease for 40 years.

This estate, occupied in the 17th century by the *Red Hart* Inn[37], lay in and behind Petty Cury, between Falcon Yard and Alexandra Street. Its sale had, since mid-October, been ad-vertised on behalf of the Master and Fellows of Corpus Christi College, as of three sites fronting on to the Cury and 11 more facing on to, 'a new street to be called Red Hart Place',[38] all on

40-year building leases.

After much discussion, however, the Y.M.C.A. committee decided not to bid for any of this leasehold property, but to try to obtain of Richard Miller, the wine merchant, a freehold site nearby, on the corner of St. Tibbs Row. On this site stood the old *Brazen George* Inn[39], with stables and coach house then leased as livery stables, and an adjoining double tenement. The property was dilapidated, fit only for demolition, but the site, especially in view of the improvements to be made following the sale of the *Red Hart* estate, was a valuable one.

Mr. Robert Sayle undertook to approach Richard Miller who, on 26 November, told him that he was willing to sell for £1,110. By 30 November, five guarantors[40] for this sum had been found, and on 2 December the task of raising funds for the proposed new building began. By the end of that day, Josiah was able to record that £1,100 had been promised, and that Mr. H. Gotobed, the solicitor, had, in addition to making a donation, promised to 'execute the conveyance and make a trust deed for us and do all our legal business *gratis*'.

Throughout the rest of that month of December 1868, Eaden Lilley and Josiah, with, sometimes, other members of the committee, walked or drove about the town asking for subscriptions; by the 10th over £1,400 had been promised them. Even part of Boxing Day was spent in fund raising:

> Eaden called for me in his chaise and, with James Nutter, we went over to Shelford to try and get up some subscription, but did not succeed very well.

On 7 January 1869 a grand tea party was held in the Town Hall; it realised £50 for the Building Fund which, by then, had reached £1,750.

> We must have had nearly 1200 people there . . . it was a great success and one of the finest things that has happened in our town of late years.

Such a large function could not be expected to pass off entirely without a hitch. The committee had to spend some time soothing the ruffled feelings of one member's wife who, inadvertently, was not asked to form one of the group of ladies providing trays of refreshments for the party. Her husband threatened to withhold his promised donation to the Building Fund, but was perusaded to change his mind on being assured that no slight to his wife had been intended.

A public lecture given by C.H. Spurgeon, in April, added £51 to the Fund, while the Duke of Devonshire, in response to an appeal letter from Eaden Lilley and Josiah Chater, sent a cheque for £50. On 16 May 1869 a Rose Show, arranged jointly by the Y.M.C.A. and the Horticultural Society, was held in the grounds of Mr. G.E. Foster's house in Brooklands Avenue. The event, however, only just paid for itself, for the weather was very cold, 'with drizzling rain and the wind blowing great guns', as Josiah recorded.

Because the excursion to Matlock in 1868 had been so successful, the Association and the Church of England Young Men's Society[41] agreed to arrange a second one in 1869. On 19 June, each provided by the Midland Railway Company with a free first class ticket, Edwin Barrett and Josiah travelled to Matlock and on to Chatsworth to make arrangements. They spent two nights away, taking the opportunity to visit Bakewell and Haddon Hall, and returned on the third day, having arranged that the *Edensor* Hotel at Chatsworth should provide 'a good cold dinner for 140 or 150 at once at 2s. 6d. each, and for carriages to meet us at the station'.

By 3 July Josiah could record, 'lots of country people have been enquiring about our excursion', as a result of the fly bills which had been posted about the town.

5 July:
We have been busy all day selling extension tickets for persons to stay at Matlock for 2 or 3 days after Thursday.

7 July:
We have sold more then 1,000 tickets for tomorrow, so that we are sure of its paying.

The excursion was a financial success, the Building Fund profiting by just over £50; several people, however, were disappointed that only 30 persons at a time were allowed in the grounds of Chatsworth House.

The public lectures arranged by the Y.M.C.A. added to the Fund, although some controversy was aroused in October 1869, as Josiah recorded after he and Eaden Lilley had supped with two other members of the committee and discussed the forthcoming programme:

The vexed question is whether, as the Y.M.C.A., we should have Professor Huxley, an Atheist,[42] to lecture for us on Science. He had intimated, through Mr Macmillan, his willingness to come, and some of our 'straight ones' think it a little too much for them.

The choice of such a lecturer certainly displeased several people, not all of them members of the Association, and letters of disapproval were sent privately to the committee and also to the local newspapers. Josiah received one very bitter one from the secretary of the Church of England Young Men's Society, in which he accused the Association of betraying Christian principles in order to add to their Building Fund. The lecture was, however, delivered on 28 March of the following year, and made a profit of £14 18s. 8d.

Meanwhile, Alfred Waterhouse had been selected to design the new buildings and his plans were finally approved in August 1869. He had, in 1866, designed the Union Society building in Bridge Street and was to do, in the 1870s, more work[43] in Cambridge, not all of it very beautiful, than any other architect. On 12 October the old buildings on the site of the new Y.M.C.A. were sold by auction as building material, for £102. They were reported by Josiah, on 25 October, as, 'being pulled down but not very rapidly'.

Four days later, an advertisement for tenders from builders was inserted in the local newspapers; by 10 November 12 had been received, and on Waterhouse's advice that of William Loveday[44] was accepted. On 1 January 1870 Josiah wrote,

> Our clerk of works called on me and took the plans of the Y.M.C.A. building and began the work, *i.e.* he staked out the ground. Mr Loveday came in this afternoon; he tells me he signed the contract this morning. I went with him to the Town Clerk's office to sign the licence to build scaffolds &c. so that we are now right off.

There was still money to be raised, however. The collecting cards which had been issued to members and which were brought in every month had, since the end of November 1869, added £300 to the Building Fund which, on 5 January 1870, was increased by £59, the profits of another large and successful tea party in the Town Hall.

On Monday 7 February:

> Seven of our Y.M.C.A. met on our new ground and I laid the first brick of the new building, just at the corner where the heating apparatus is to be. I wished Eaden Lilley and Edwin Barrett to lay the first bricks, but they would persist in my doing it, and I felt great pleasure, as the Secretary of the Building Committee, in performing the operation. Eaden Lilley laid the second, Edwin Barrett the third, Harry Johnson[45] the fourth, W. Vawser[46] the fifth, Al Chater the sixth and Harry Young[47] the seventh. No more members being present, we adjourned to

Harry Johnson's and had a bottle of sherry and some beer and biscuits, the Clerk of the Works, Mr Tift, and George the foreman, joining in.

Work on the building progressed satisfactorily, apart from a week's stoppage in February, due to bad weather, and in early March plans were being made for the laying of the foundation stone. The Duke of Devonshire and Lord Shaftesbury had each, in turn, been asked to perform the ceremony, but both had declined; however, an invitation sent to Mr. W. Fowler, Member of Parliament for Cambridge, proved more successful, and 30 March was fixed for the event. Mr. Loveday, the builder, offered to pay for a silver trowel which Josiah selected and which cost £5 10s., including the engraving. On 30· March the diary records:

I walked round this morning with Mr Hills[48] to see where best a photograph could be taken, and settled on a loft I had selected which belongs to Mr Basham, and he gave it up at once to the photographers. At 2 o'clock, went to the Old Rooms in St Edward's passage - crammed with friends. At twenty minutes past we set off down the Parade, St Mary's Street, Sidney Street, Post Office Terrace and on to the New Buildings. We had had the ground floor covered with boards, which made a capital platform . . . The service went off very well indeed, and at the conclusion we retired to luncheon at the Red Lion Hotel - 126 sat down to lunch. After it we sat for 3 hours listening to a first rate lot of speeches, and in the evening adjourned to a public meeting in the Town Hall.

On the following day, about 40 of the bricks which each represented a half-guinea donation, were laid. Josiah in his account of the foundation stone-laying, omitted to say that the procession from St. Edward's Passage to the new site was headed by two standard bearers, followed by the chief constables with their halberds, and the mace-bearer who walked in front of the Mayor. He made no reference, either, to the objects which were placed in the cavity of the stone: a bottle containing the history of the Association, two or three newspapers and several coins.

Progress of the building, in the months to come, was halted from time to time, chiefly through late delivery of materials. Thus, on 23 May Josiah reported,

Our new building is quite stopped owing to the builder not being able to get the iron flitches for the 2 great beams.

On 14 June:

Our building work is stopped again for red bricks - through neglect in not ordering in time.

These delays meant that the completion of the work, promised for 29 September, was postponed, and it was not until October that tenders were invited for the furnishing of the rooms.

All through that summer of 1870, various activities were arranged in aid of the Building Fund. On 22 June a Rose Show was held in the grounds of Sidney Sussex College, making a profit of only £2 9s. 2d. because, as Josiah wrote, 'attendance was thin'. There was another excursion to Matlock on 7 July; Josiah did not go on that occasion, although he saw the train go off at 5 o'clock in the morning. About 350 people went on the outing -'a sad falling off from last year'.

On 9 July, travelling with free passes given them by the railway company, Josiah and Ebenezer Brown[49] went to Leamington to make arrangements for yet another excursion. They slept at the *Crown* Hotel and, on the following day, Sunday, walked about the town, attended service at the Baptist Chapel and after it, seeing the Y.M.C.A. sign over a building, enquired the whereabouts of the President. They then called on him and were invited to a public service in the Town Hall in the afternoon, and to take tea with him in his home.

On the Monday, Josiah and Brown hired an open carriage and drove to Warwick, were shown over the Castle by the steward, and then went on to Kenilworth where they arranged with the landlord of the *Queen and Castle* Hotel for the dinner on the day of the excursion.

On Tuesday, 12 July, the President of the Leamington Y.M.C.A. breakfasted with the two Cambridge men at their hotel and then took them,

> to see the new method of pumping and utilizing the sewage of Leamington. It is a first rate system called the A B C method . . . a liquid made of alum, blood and clay which, in small proportion, is mixed with the sewage and immediately precipitates all the organic matter and is then filtered, bringing out the water comparatively sweet and perfectly clear. We intend bringing it prominently before our Cambridge public.[50]

The planned excursion took place on 28 July,

> We took only about 120 from Cambridge and 20 from Bedford. On arrival at Bletchley several of us got out to get refreshment, and before we could regain our seats the train moved on, leaving us behind. So we paid and went on by the next train, reaching Leamington at 1.15. Ethel and the others awaited us at the station, and after a severe scolding we took a carriage and drove to Warwick and Kenilworth, returning to Leamington by 7 o'clock from where we started out and reached Cambridge at 12.

On 4 November, still waiting for the new building to be completed, the committee met,

> to consider how to get up the remainder of the money so as to enter our New Rooms free from debt. G.E. Foster was in the Chair. We passed a resolution that all should write or see 4 people to get money; then Eaden Lilley stated that 4 gentlemen would double any amount that was got between now and next Thursday.

With this incentive, the committee worked hard, and on the Thursday Josiah was able to record that they had collected £100,

> which will secure to us, from the challenge of last week, another £100 and thus relieve the guarantors to that amount. The works are progressing very rapidly and the lift is nearly fitted.

On 14 November the committee gave a supper to the workmen in the lecture room of the new building. Josiah was asked to make the arrangements, and he decided that the meal should be a hot one.

> I asked Mrs Lenton[51] if her man might cook it and she very kindly allowed it, and splendidly it came up, all steaming hot: a round of roast beef, roast ribs, 2 boiled legs of mutton, 2 roast ditto, with all the necessary vegetables. Plum puddings were made at different places and sent in smoking hot. After supper we spent the evening with pipes and speech and song.

Throughout December 1870 the diary recorded the progress of the building - the installation of the heating apparatus, of the gas lighting, the completion of the plastering, and so on, until on Sunday, 1 January 1871, Josiah was able to write,

> After dinner went to our New Rooms in Alexandra Street. We had a splendid meeting - an opening address to young men by Neville Goodman. About 300 were present. Our first meeting in the new building. Twelve months ago we began on the works and now we have them so complete as to be able to use them.

On 10 January:

> The first of our opening meetings began by a Devotional Meeting at 8 o'clock this evening, after which we set to work and cleared the room and placed the tables &c. all ready for the breakfast in the morning.

For on the next day, the building was to be officially opened.

> I was up at half past five this morning and took Ethel and Lizzy to the breakfast at 7 at the new building . . . about 140 present. Mr Foster sent his gardener and some men who hung festoons of evergreens on the walls of the rooms, which gave it a nice appearance. At 1 o'clock the Committee met the Trustees and formally handed over the Building to them. At 2 o'clock 146 set down to a sumptuous luncheon, the food

provided by Mr. Barbier, Cook of Sidney, and the wine by Mr Lincolne
We had some good speaking and this lasted until 6 o'clock. At 8 we met
again: a public meeting, and had the place crammed. Again some
capital speeches.

It must, indeed, have been an exhausting day, but a triumphant
one for all those who had worked so hard for an object which
must, at first, have seemed almost unattainable[52].

The first concert in the new building took place on 18 January
when Sterndale Bennet's sacred cantata *The Woman of Samaria*
was performed, but Josiah was disappointed that only 150
tickets were sold: 'somehow the members did not take to it'.

Although, in the early part of 1871, he was busy with the
ready-made clothing business which he had added to his woollen
drapery trade on Market Hill, Josiah found time, in April, to go
to Birmingham to speak to the Y.M.C.A. there about the new
Cambridge buildings and how the money for them had been
raised. He went too, on the excursion, arranged by the
Association, to Yarmouth and Lowestoft on 6 July. There was
some initial anxiety that the 500 people - the number guaranteed
by the committee to the railway company - would take tickets,
but, in the end, 520 did so. Josiah took Agnes, six of his children,
his sister and a servant and, on arriving in Lowestoft, found
lodgings for them, 'for 6 days at 30 shillings, attendance
included'. He himself returned to Cambridge in the evening.

For the remainder of the period, 1871 to 1876, the references
in the diary to the Y.M.C.A. are mainly those of Josiah's
attendance at the public lectures and discussions, and at
committee meetings. He seems, after 1872, to have ceased to go
to classes, although the number of these, with University men as
tutors, steadily increased; from 1876, several were run in
connection with the Science and Art Department of South
Kensington, whose examinations the students were able to take.

The discussions that were arranged covered many of the
leading topics of the day: the Education Act of 1870, for
example, or the 1871 Ballot Act. In April 1872 Josiah recorded
that a very large meeting was held, 'to meet Mrs Josephine
Butler and hear her opinion on the Contagious Diseases Act'.

The Contagious Diseases Act of 1864 had provided for the
compulsory medical examination of prostitutes, and the
detention in hospital of those found to be diseased, in several
garrison towns. In 1868 the Act was amended and extended to

include Windsor, while, in the following year, it was further extended to cover, in all, 28 garrison towns.

There was much popular agitation in the country, on moral and humanitarian grounds, against the Acts, and Mrs. Josephine Butler, a sister-in-law of Dr. H.M. Butler, Master of Trinity College, Cambridge, was in the forefront of the movement to have them repealed[53]. After hearing her speak - Josiah described her as 'a nice, wholesome-looking little lady, with most marked nose, mouth and chin' - a deputation of Y.M.C.A. members was appointed to see Mr. Fowler, the Member of Parliament for Cambridge, and. 'urge his immediate attention in the matter'.

The new Y.M.C.A. rooms were hired, on many occasions, for meetings of other local societies. On 13 March 1871; very soon after they were opened, Josiah wrote,

This evening a meeting of the Liberation Society[54] was held at our Hall. I got there about 9 o'clock and found a great deal of confusion. Many of the Junior Conservatives were there and they were accused of making a tremendous stench in the place by some chemical compound . . . After I had been at the Physiology class for 10 minutes I heard two explosions, went out and found a policeman at the door ejecting some scavengers from the meeting, and the Juniors in a great state of excitement. I then went into the Hall, and the stench was horrible . . . very like the one I smelt at the Junior Conservative Rooms when I was there on Saturday last with Turner.

On 15 April:

Mr Lilley came to see me yesterday about the blackguard conduct of sundry of the Junior Conservatives the other night . . . H. Matthew[55] came in and talked the matter over with us and he promises to try and find out the perpetrator[56] . . .

With the rooms being so much used both by the Association and by other societies, even without the occasional stink bomb being thrown, it is not surprising that, by 1876, they were in need of redecoration. The last entries in the diary, in this period, record the obtaining of an estimate of £450 to clean and paint the rooms, and a generous offer to defray a third of this sum if the Association would find the rest of the money. The offer came from three people who, all along, had been munificent supporters of the Y.M.C.A.: the brothers George E. Foster and Charles Finch Foster of Foster & Co.'s Banks[57]; and Eaden Lilley.

EVENTS IN CAMBRIDGE 1866-76

Elections

Josiah Chater was naturally delighted when the two Liberal candidates, Sir R. Torrens, and Mr. W.E. Fowler, were returned for Cambridge at the Parliamentary election of 1868. He played no great part in canvassing for his party on this occasion, not feeling well at the time, but on 16 November, on his way home to dinner, he,

> met the Whigs going down the Parade to the Hoop Hotel and accompanied them. Heard Torrens and Fowler speak from a window - Torrens has wonderfully improved.

17 November:
> Polling day, so of course no business doing. Closed shop at 2 o'clock. Market Hill and the whole town all excitement, which culminated in a very furor of joy at 4 o'clock, the Liberals leading the poll by 480 majority. The members addressed the crowd from one of the rooms of the Independent Press Office. So ended a terrific conflict in a glorious victory. William and Alfred dined with the committee; I was not well enough so spent a quiet hour with Aunt Sophy.

He had recovered sufficiently, next day, to go on to Parker's Piece at noon to hear the declaration of the poll by the Mayor, and to see the successful candidates set off on a triumphal march round the town and down to Chesterton and Barnwell.

Josiah continued to take his part in assisting the Liberal cause in municipal elections and recorded, on 1 November 1872, his first experience of such an election after the passing of the Ballot Act which abolished the public declaration of votes:

> I have been up at the Town Hall in the Alderman's Parlour acting as agent for Whibley[58] and Thoday[59] ... Being the first trial of the ballot in Cambridge it was a little exciting as to how it would work, but everything went very well and very satisfactorily, I think - all but the result, which unfortunately leaves Whibley and Thoday over 90 in the minority.

The first Parliamentary election following the Ballot Act was held on 3 February 1874 when Josiah was,

> appointed on to a committee but had not much to do. The Ballot is a most easy and simple method and I like it very much. No one could tell how the election was going, but up to 8.15 all seemed confident that Torrens and Fowler must be returned, and we waited anxiously until 9 o'clock. The Hill was crammed, and at 9 o'clock the Mayor made his appearance at one of the windows and announced a majority for the Tories ... There was a great row on the Hill until very late, but no fighting.

The Great Gas Controversy

On 1 June 1868 Josiah wrote in his diary,

This evening our new Gas Company lighted up the town with paraffin lamps - the Old Company also lighted up, and we looked very brilliant.

This is the first reference to a controversy which had raged in Cambridge for some months, and was yet to be settled.

In November 1867 the Improvement Commissioners had advertised for new tenders for lighting the streets of Cambridge, and for supplying private consumers with gas, because their contract with the Cambridge University and Town Gas Lighting Company[60] was due to expire on 1 June 1868. The Gas Company duly stated its prices. The Commissioners decided that these were too high, and on 17 December 1867 met to consider fresh tenders, one from the University and Town Gas Company and another from a newly-formed company, the Cambridge Consumers' Gas Company Limited, whose shareholders were a number of prominent local men.

The prices quoted by the new company were lower than those of the old, and so were accepted, whereupon the latter threatened to file a bill in Chancery so that, as soon as the newcomers on the scene should begin to take up the streets for the laying of gas pipes, proceedings could be taken against them. The Town Council then tried to mediate between the two companies, but failed to do so, and the bill was filed.

The affair became the talking point of Cambridge and the columns of the local newspapers were filled, week after week, with readers' letters, some in favour of and some against the idea of having two gas companies in what was, then, a small town. There were angry letters, too, from the directors of the old company who resented the accusation, which they said was implied in the prospectus of the new company, that they were over-charging for gas in order to pay dividends owing to shareholders for some years.

A sufficient number of shares, however, were taken in the new company - Josiah bought one - for the building of gas works to be commenced on Coldham's Common, near the railway line, and for several thousand pipes to be ordered from Sheffield. On 15 April 1868 the first Annual General Meeting of the Cambridge Consumers' Gas Company was held[61]. Two days later about 200 people assembled on the Common to witness the laying of the foundation stone under the first gas holder, refreshments being served in a tent after the ceremony.

By early May, it became obvious to the directors of the new company that they would not be able to keep to the contract to begin lighting the streets on 1 June. They applied, therefore, to the Gas Contract Committee for an extension of one month, suggesting that during that period the streets might be illuminated with oil lamps. The Committee, by the casting vote of the chairman, granted the extension and some wooden posts, topped later by glass oil lamps, began to appear on the streets of central Cambridge, causing great amusement to at least one reader of the *Chronicle*, who wrote to the editor to ask, 'what all those clothes posts with whisky bottles on top of them were meant for'.

On 1 June the paraffin lamps were lit for the first and only time, because the Improvement Commissioners immediately reversed the Gas Contract Committee's decision to allow their use for one month, and declared the contract with the new company to be null and void. 'One night's experience of the farce was quite enough', declared the *Chronicle*, 'the lamps gave a most feeble light . . .'. Indeed, without the existing gas lamps of the old company the streets could certainly not have been so 'brilliant' as Josiah Chater described them to be.

Even he, however, was obliged to record on 2 June that,

during the night some very malicious fellows went round in a fly and smashed about 100[62] of the new lamps.

The Consumers' Company was, apparently, undeterred by the cancellation of its contract. On 5 June Josiah went to a private meeting of the shareholders and reported,

They want to dispose of some more shares to give the contractors some confidence in the prosecution of their works. Over £1100 were subscribed at the meeting and great confidence was expressed in the position of the Company, notwithstanding the adverse attitude of the Commissioners. It came out that the men who broke the lamps were known and would be prosecuted in a few days.

The lamp-breakers - William Peed, son of the solicitor and secretary to the University and Town Gas Company, Harold Balls and James Brown, both sons of local magistrates - were duly summonsed and, on 12 June, as Josiah wrote, were, 'dismissed, for want of sufficient management in the evidence, as I think'. The magistrates, it was reported in the *Chronicle*, decided that the evidence was so conflicting that it did not justify any conviction being made.

Meanwhile, the University and Town Gas Lighting Company had applied for an injunction to restrain its rivals from proceeding with its intention of laying gas pipes in the streets. Judgement was given, by Vice-Chancellor Malines, on 1 July when Josiah wrote:

> The law case between the old and new gas companies was decided against the new, so I lose my £10.

But the affair dragged on. The Consumers' Gas Company lodged an appeal against the injunction and seemed determined to continue with its aim to supply gas to Cambridge, although it was experiencing some difficulties with the contractors who had begun to build the gas works. On 7 October Josiah attended a shareholders' meeting when it was decided,

> the affair must be wound up, the contractors not being willing to wait until the Company can get an Act, and we do not mean them to run off with all the plunder.[63] It is a bad job for a good many who have invested in it.

The new company's appeal against the Vice-Chancellor's injunction which prohibited it from digging up the streets to lay down gas pipes, was heard in November by the Lord Chief Justice, who reversed the Vice-Chancellor's decision. But the injunction had by then become unnecessary, through the Consumers' Company's failure to keep to its contract date, and the subsequent declaration by the Improvement Commissioners that this contract was null and void. The Town and University Gas Lighting Company had, in fact, already re-contracted with the Commissioners. But, by the Lord Chief Justice's decision, the company was to have to pay certain costs, and the long-protracted affair was finally settled by compromise, as Josiah Chater recorded on 5 February 1869 after attending a shareholder's meeting of the new company at which,

> a resolution was passed to compromise with the Old Company for a sum of £5,500, they to have our ground and works and to pay all expenses, and to guarantee the shareholders not to lose more than 50% of their shares. I suppose it is the best thing that could be done in the circumstances.

Throughout the controversy, the editorial views expressed in the *Cambridge Chronicle* were almost wholly in favour of the Town and University Company. Those of the *Cambridge Independent Press*, however, were far more in sympathy with the Consumers' Company which had, it considered, been unjustly treated. The threat of legal proceedings, the paper pointed out, had prevented many would-be shareholders from

risking their money, while the seven weeks during which the
Town Council had tried to mediate between the two companies,
had greatly delayed the building of the new gas works and so
prevented the Consumers' Company from keeping to its contract to light the streets on 1 June 1868.

Consecration of St. John's College Chapel[64]
On 12 May 1869 Josiah noted in his diary,

> The town has been all alive today with parsons, this being the day of
> Consecration of St John's Chapel. Bells ringing all day, and not much
> business doing.

The building of the new Chapel, from the design of Gilbert
Scott, had begun in June 1863, the foundation stone being laid
a year later. The consecration was attended by about 900
people, many of whom travelled to Cambridge, on the day
itself, by the special train which had been provided. Large
numbers of non-residents, however, arrived earlier, in order to
attend, on May 11, the concert given in the Guildhall by the
Musical Society of the College.

Public Celebrations
On 2 June 1869 Queen Victoria celebrated her 50th birthday,
Josiah recorded,

> at 12 o'clock the shops all closed and business was generally suspended.
> The Riflemen paraded on the Piece and the Band of the University and
> Town played at intervals. At 4.50 Mr Coxwell's balloon went up. Agnes,
> with Ethel, Ernest, Sophie and Baby[65] had Miss Simpson's carriage and
> rode round the Piece to see the ascent of the balloon . . . in the evening
> I went to the Market Hill to see the fireworks, which were very good.
> The Mayor gave a grand dinner to the Corporation and friends at the
> Lion.

The recovery of the Prince of Wales from a severe attack of
typhoid fever was celebrated throughout the country on 27
February 1872. In Cambridge the shops were closed, but Josiah
spent most of the day at No. 1a Market Hill, attending to
various business matters. In the evening,

> Alfred called for me with Ethel, Lizzy and Ernest and we went on to
> Parker's Piece to see the fireworks and the bonfire, after which we
> hurried round the streets to see the illuminations, which were not very
> grand; but plenty of people about. I then took the children home and
> went for Milly and Junia, who had been to Mrs Banham's in Regent

Street whose back way looks on to the Piece, and where they had a splendid view of the fireworks.

Two Gala Days are mentioned in the diary in this period, one on 21 August 1873, the other on 30 July 1874. Both were arranged by W.H. Poole, a teacher of singing who lived in Green Street, and both took place in the grounds of Downing College. On each occasion the band of the Coldstream Guards played, a juvenile ballet company performed, there was a grand firework display and the usual balloon ascent, always a popular feature of such events, was made.

In both years Mr. Arthur Deck, the chemist of No.9 King's Parade, was one of the passengers in the balloon which, in 1873, came down about 15 miles away, near Isleham. It ascended just as the down express was leaving Cambridge station, and it managed to race the train to Ely. In 1874 the balloon descended in Westly Waterless, 13 miles from Cambridge.

Readings by Charles Dickens

Charles Dickens visited Cambridge twice in the period 1866-76, to give readings from his works in the Guildhall. On the first occasion, 28 March 1867, Josiah referred to the visit but wrote in his diary, 'we did not go'. On 18 March 1869, however, he accompanied his father, who had come over from Saffron Walden for the day,

to hear Charles Dickens, who gave us some readings at the Hall from *Martin Chuzzlewit* and *Holly Tree Inn*. I liked it very much.

Shop Assistants' Ball

From the 1840s leading Cambridge business men, notably William Eaden Lilley and Robert Sayle, had tried, by closing their own shops at seven o'clock in winter instead of at the usual hour of nine o'clock or later, to encourage others to do the same. The question of shop closing hours was frequently discussed by members of the Working Men's College and of the Y.M.C.A., but not until the period 1892-9[66] were the first very limited steps taken towards regulating the employment of shop assistants. Owners of shops, especially of small ones, were naturally reluctant to reduce the number of hours in which they were open for business.

Josiah's diary records instances of the long hours worked by two of his daughters. In May 1876 Milly Chater, then 15 years old, began to help, on Saturdays, in the linen drapery shop of her father's friend Frederick Smart, Josiah thinking, 'It would be getting her into business habits'. She began work at 10 o'clock in the morning and finished at half past 10 in the evening; for this she was paid two shillings, but had her meals with the Smarts.

In August 1876 Josiah's eldest daughter, Ethel, went as clerk to Whichello's grocery shop in Trumpington Street:

> She goes at 7.30 a.m. and leaves at 8 or 9 in the evening, according to season - has all her meals and £26 a year.

In 1871 the practice of closing shops at four o'clock on one afternoon in the week, in the summer months only, was introduced in Cambridge. The Mayor of that year, Mr. Samuel Peed, was largely responsible for the innovation.[67] On Saturday, 24 June 1871, Josiah noted,

> Most of the shops close at 4 p.m. on Thursday afternoons during the summer months. Last Thursday was the second time; it seemed very strange.

21 September:

> This is the last day of closing shops at 4 o'clock, to commemorate which the Mayor gave a ball at the Town Hall to young people thus engaged.

Between four and five hundred people attended the ball and danced to a Quadrille Band from eight o'clock until midnight. Josiah's brother, Jabez, made a gift of the flowers which decorated the room. In the April of the following year the shop assistants presented to the Mayor a silver salver, as a token of their gratitude for his help in obtaining the Thursday half-holiday, and for inviting them to the ball.

Opening of the Reform Club

On 20 December 1871 Josiah wrote,

> The Reform Club was opened today. The members came down and dined at the *Hoop* and had a public meeting in their new rooms[68] in Green Street . . .

The establishment of such a Club, preparatory to the passing of the Ballot Act was essential, as the *Cambridge Independent Press* pointed out on 23 December, 'if for no other purpose except for procuring a place for the holding of political meetings when the system of holding them in public houses shall be abolished'.

The 'new Club in Cambridge', the newspaper continued, 'will no doubt prove a puzzle to our Conservative friends, but it is an organization which they will have good cause to fear. Its promoters do not look to popular favour by the hackneyed aid of amateur theatricals, or by the introduction of carefully selected lectures, but they appeal to the members of their party to uphold the club as an institution for political organization and political discussion'.

Josiah referred, occasionally, to attending Liberal party discussions and 'political conversaziones' at the Club which, in December 1873, was congratulated by the satirical periodical *The Lantern of the Cam,*[69] for being in a 'flourishing condition'. The anonymous writer of the article, however, while praising the Reform Club for substituting political discussions for the theatrical performances arranged by the Junior Conservative Club, questioned 'the advisability of keeping the political strife-pot constantly at seething point by means of somewhat inflated sermons - we beg pardon, "papers" - read by gentlemen who may be destined to be saviours of the land . . . but whose more immediate concern seems to be the appearance of their names . . . in the weekly press'.

The New Congregational Church and the Universities Tests Act

On 19 November 1872 Josiah attended the laying of the foundation stone of the 'new Independent Church' in Trumpington Street. This church - the Emmanuel Congregational Church - was built on the site of the old *Half Moon* Inn[70] and replaced the Independent Chapel in Downing Place,[71] which Josiah had so often attended in his early years in Cambridge, especially between 1848 and 1854 when the Rev. George Bubier was its minister.

The stone-laying ceremony was performed by Mr. J. Morley, Member of Parliament for Cambridge. After it Josiah,

> went to dinner at the Y.M.C.A. rooms - a very nice dinner it was, and several good speeches, Mr Morley was Chairman; he has given £500 and promised £250 more if they can go in free of debt.

The new church was opened for worship in 1874, the first minister being the Reverend Dr. Matthew Robertson who had come to Downing Place in 1872. Josiah recorded, on 24 September of that year, 'Agnes, Ethel and Lizzy went to the tea at the Y.M.C.A. for Dr Robertson's ordination, and they attended, on the following day, at Downing Place Chapel, 'when Dr Robertson was ordained'.[72]

The need for a larger Congregational Church than the small one which had for so long existed in Downing Place, became apparent following the Universities Tests Act of 1871, which led to an increasing number of Nonconformist undergraduates coming up to Cambridge.

Although, since the Cambridge University Act of 1856, Nonconformists were allowed to take degrees, except in Divinity, without subscribing, as hitherto, to the Thirty-Nine Articles of the established church, they remained debarred from membership of the Senate and from holding any office in the University, while colleges could still exclude them from fellowships. So, for example, when W.S. Aldis of Trinity became Senior Wrangler in 1861 - a fact which Josiah noted with pride in his diary - he could not, because he was a Baptist, be elected to a fellowship even though so distinguished a scholar might well have been an asset to his college.

The question of religious tests remained under discussion for many years, and from 1862 there was a growing demand for their abolition. A Bill, introduced in 1870, sought to abolish all religious tests in the Universities of Oxford, Cambridge and Durham, imposed either by Parliament or by the statutes of the Universities and colleges. But it made no provision for a layman to hold a college or University office which was restricted to men in Holy Orders, and in many Cambridge colleges a certain proportion of the fellows had to be clergymen of the Church of England.

A society, founded in Cambridge in 1870, and known as, 'The Association at Cambridge for the Removal of Religious Disabilities from the Universities', strove particularly, for the abolition of all clerical fellowships. Its leading figure was William Aldis,[73] who was then living in Cambridge and working as a private coach, and it had, as one of its secretaries, Neville Goodman of Peterhouse, the friend of Josiah Chater. Josiah, himself, seems to have played no part in the society, although he makes several references to it and to attendances made by his friends at its meetings.

The Bill of 1870 never became law, but in 1871 a new Tests Act did come on to the Statute Book. In future, no declaration of faith was to be required to enable any person to take a degree, other than in divinity, to hold office, other than divinity professorship, or to hold a fellowship.[74] Although the Act did not go so far as such men as Neville Goodman, W.S. Aldis and others would have liked, for it did not do away with all clerical fellowships, yet it went a long way to meeting the demands of the opponents of religious tests.

In 1875 the Senior Wrangler was John William Lord, a Baptist and son of a Baptist minister, who had come up to Trinity[75] in 1871. The sixth Wrangler, that year, was also a Nonconformist - T. Crompton-Lewis, a Wesleyan. John Lord, by virtue of the 1871 Act was able, in 1876, to be elected to a fellowship at Trinity, which he held until his early death, at the age of 33, in 1881.

The Nonconformists' examination successes of 1875 were celebrated, on 19 February, by a party given in the Y.M.C.A. rooms by Mr. G. Foster, the banker and Y.M.C.A. president, and others. Josiah Chater was invited, and he and his daughter Ethel[76]

> at 7 o'clock had a fly and drove to the Alexander Rooms. Our names being announced at the door, we were received by Mr Foster and ushered into the Room. Many were already assembled, and many more came after. The Room was very nicely arranged, carpeted, and the windows hung with curtains. Orchestra and gallery fitted out with shrubs; couches &c. all about the Rooms. In a few minutes, tea and coffee were served, with biscuits, then we sat chatting and quietly enjoying ourselves with glees and songs &c. Ices and wine were served in the interval. Mr Goodman made a neat little speech suited to the occasion and was responded to by Mr Lord, the Senior Wrangler of this year, and by Mr Harris,[77] a high Wrangler of last year. Then came a most elegant light supper, after which carriages were ordered. We got home about 12 0'clock, after a very pleasant evening.

The Cambridge Hoax

In 1873 the Shah of Persia came to this country for a visit lasting almost three weeks. Arriving at Dover on 16 June he was met by the Prince of Wales with whom he travelled to Buckingham Palace, where he was to stay and where a special telegraph line was placed at his disposal so that he could have direct communication with his wives in Teheran.

The Shah carried out a number of official engagements in

London and then, from 24 June, spent three days with the Duke
of Sutherland at Trentham, during which time he visited Crewe,
Liverpool and Manchester. It was not beyond the bounds of
possibility that he might, at some time during his stay, visit
Cambridge, so no suspicions were aroused when news was
received that he would be doing so on his way back from
Trentham to London.

On 28 June Josiah Chater wrote,

> About 11.30 the bells began ringing and the Bugler of the Rifles sounded
> the Assembly about the streets, and the Town Clerk went tearing about
> like mad. On enquiry I was told a telegraphic message had been received
> saying that the Shah of Persia was coming to visit the Town. The Vice-
> Chancellor, Mayor and Corporation all hurried up to the station to meet
> him. They waited an hour and then found out a cruel hoax had been
> practiced upon them; the telegram had been laid on the Hall Keeper's
> table and had not come through the wires, and although the Mayor was
> told by Mr Turner, the Postmaster, that it was not right, he would
> persist in going and was thus made a fool of . . . The Town Council are
> awfully wild.[78]

The Town Clerk might well, as Josiah expressed it, 'have been
tearing about like mad', for in the short period between the
reception of the bogus telegram and the departure for the station
of the official welcoming party, there was a great deal to do.
Members of the Town Council had to be summoned, the police
had to be alerted, and decorations had hastily to be put up in the
streets. Horses and vehicles, including an open carriage drawn by
four greys, with two postillion riders, were ordered, and the
landlord of the *Bull* Hotel was told to be ready to supply the
Shah with any refreshment he might need after his train journey.

On the realisation that the telegram was a hoax, efforts were
made to discover who had sent it. On 12 July Josiah's diary
recorded,

> The telegram has been traced to Mr Neville. He is the man who was
> engaged in the stench business at the Y.M.C.A. rooms two years ago.

Cambridge was, naturally, a little sensitive after this incident,
and exception was taken to the fact that the actor playing the
part of the 'Shah' in the production of *Kissi Kissi* at the
Barnwell Theatre Royal, was too realistic in his make-up. The
theatre manager, therefore, announced that, in future performances, the player would whiten his face.

United Religious Meetings
On Monday 5 April 1875, Josiah's diary recorded,

> A Prayer Meeting was held in the Town Hall last evening in anticipation of Moody and Sankey's coming to Cambridge in May. It is to be continued every Sunday in April and on the first Sunday in May, Churchmen and Dissenters uniting.

The American evangelist, Dwight L. Moody, had, since 1860, devoted himself to city missionary work in Chicago where, in 1870, he had been joined by the singer, Ira D. Sankey. Between 1873 and 1875 the two men had come to England, on a series of revival missions, and, from March to July 1875, they held a particularly successful campaign in London.

The proposal that the evangelists should come to Cambridge in the summer of that year was made by a number of undergraduates, supported by many of the local Anglican and Nonconformist clergy. The united prayer meetings in the Town Hall, at which Sankey's hymns[79] were sung and addresses were given by various local preachers, were intended to prepare people for the hoped-for visit. In Barnwell, still a somewhat disreputable neighbourhood of Cambridge, the Theatre Royal was hired for a month[80] for united prayer meetings similar to those held in the Town Hall. Although Moody and Sankey did not come in 1875, the meetings were attended by large numbers of people, and the hymns made popular by Sankey were, probably, as much whistled by Cambridge errand boys that year as they were by their London counterparts. Townspeople, especially, were, because of the meetings, all the more enthusiastic in their welcome when the evangelists did eventually visit Cambridge in 1882.

Although Josiah Chater's wife and daughters went to all the Town Hall meetings in 1875, he himself apparently, attended only the last one on 2 May, when there was,

> a tremendous meeting for United Prayer at the Town Hall - it quite crammed 4 rooms. They then filled all the rooms of the Y.M.C.A.

Proposed New Bridge
From about 1872 onwards Cambridge people were beginning to agitate for a bridge, capable of carrying traffic, to be built over the Cam at Chesterton, to connect the growing neighbourhoods on either side of the river.

On 10 June 1875 Josiah Chater

attended a Town Council meeting and heard a good debate about a
bridge over the Cam, which was lost on division.

The Council's decision came after a public meeting in the
Guildhall arranged as a result of one held in the Castle End
district of the town by traders in that area. Shopkeepers in
Bridge Street and Magdalene Street were opposed to a bridge at
Chesterton, declaring that it would deprive them of trade. Those
in favour, on the other hand, argued that one of the many
advantages of the bridge was that it *would* relieve, 'nasty,
narrow, overcrowded Bridge Street'.

Years passed, and the bridge remained unbuilt although, as
the town grew, the need for it became more obvious. The matter
was raised frequently in Town Council meetings and in townspeople's letters to the local press. In the late 1880s, though
still opposed by the Bridge Street traders, the public demand
became even more pressing, on the grounds that trade generally,
including that of Bridge Street, would be increased, that the
bridge would shorten the distance between Chesterton and
Barnwell by about a mile, and that a pleasant drive would be
provided to the northern end of the town.

A public meeting in the Guildhall, followed by a town poll,
revealed almost unanimous support for the scheme, and work
on the bridge and on the construction of the new access road to
it - Victoria Avenue - across Midsummer Common, was at last
begun. On 4 November 1889 the foundation stone was laid by
the Mayor, who placed under it a bottle containing, among
other things, silver coins, local newspapers, and a copy of the Act
of Parliament which had allowed the long-desired bridge to be
built.[81]

Fires and the Fire Brigade

As had always been his custom, Josiah Chater recorded, in
the period 1866-76, any outbreak of fire in Cambridge of which
he had knowledge. On 23 May 1875, for example, he wrote,

whilst at the Building Society last night, about 8 o'clock, we heard a
fire had broken out in Market Street, next door to Mr Lilley. I went off
at once and found Smith's shop[82] on fire, but it was nearly out; a lot
of goods burnt through. The gas had set fire to one of the windows.
Fortunately all were at work and it was soon put out, but it was a
narrow escape.

26 May:
> Smith has settled the amount of his claim with the Insurance Company -
> £278, and he buys the salvage for £32. 10s. He has opened again and
> begun selling off.

It would seem that this fire was dealt with by Smith's own
employees, and not by the brigade of the Insurance Company. It
would, in any case, have been among the last of Cambridge fires
to which an Insurance Company engine would have been
summoned, for about this time the Volunteer Fire Brigade was
formed, composed of a captain, lieutenant, two buglers, two
turncocks and 24 firemen.

The first call on the Brigade's services was recorded by Josiah
on 26 August 1875,

> The fire brigade was called out this evening for the first time, to a fire at
> Coulson's[83] in East Road, and rendered very effective service.

The New Corn Exchange

A new Corn Exchange was opened in Cambridge on 6 November 1875. At two o'clock, the Mayor and Corporation and
several prominent residents of the town and county walked in
procession, led by the Cambridge Rifle Band, the High Constable
and the mace bearers, from the Guildhall to the new building in
Wheeler Street, for the opening ceremony. Josiah Chater,
strangely enough for one so interested in local happenings, made
no reference to the occasion. Indeed, the entry in his diary under
the date 6 November is unusually brief: 'Business not at all
brisk'. Customers, doubtless, were assembled in Wheeler Street
to watch the proceedings.

He had previously, however, referred many times to the new
building, the erection of which had, from 1868 to 1872, been a
matter of some controversy. On 23 March 1870, for example, he
went to

> a public meeting at the Town Hall called by the Mayor to consider the
> question of the new Corn Exchange. The meeting was about equally
> divided. Clement Francis proposed that the Council be asked to stop its
> proceedings as regards the site in Wheeler Street, and Peas Hill was
> recommended.

On the following day:
> I went to the Council meeting and heard the debate on the Corn
> Exchange. The Wheeler Street site is to be built upon at once.

But on 9 June:
> Attended Council meeting. The accepting of tenders to built the Corn
> Exchange is again postponed on the motion of Mr Samuel Peed.

The first Corn Exchange in Cambridge was erected in 1842 on
St. Andrew's Hill; prior to that date the weekly corn market had
been held in the open, on Market Hill, opposite Rose Crescent.
As early as 1859 it had been suggested that a new and larger
Corn Exchange be incorporated in a group of municipal buildings - Assembly Room, Free Library and School of Art - which
were eventually opened in 1862. A large number of rate payers,
however, objected to the plan on the grounds of its cost, and for
the next 12 years the scheme remained a matter of violent
debate in Town Council meetings and in letters to the press, and
a subject of much legal inquiry.

Argument hinged on whether a new Corn Exchange be built
on Peas Hill - although, by 1869, the site there was considered
by many to be too small - in Wheeler Street, or, indeed whether
one should be built at all. A proposal to rebuild on the same
site on St. Andrew's Hill was rejected. The Town Council, as
Josiah Chater recorded, was fairly evenly divided on the question
of the Wheeler Street and the Peas Hill sites, but those in favour
of Peas Hill obtained an injunction to restrain the Corporation
from building in Wheeler Street and from using borough funds
for any new Corn Exchange.

In 1873 an appeal against this injunction was lodged, and on
10 June, Josiah Chater, who had spent that day in London on
business met a friend, by chance, on King's Cross station and
learned from him that

> the Lords have decided the Corn Exchange question against the
> Relators[84] and in favour of the Corporation.

The Lords Justices had decided that Wheeler Street could
properly be thought of as part of the market place, for the
enlarging of which an Act of Parliament had been obtained in
1850, following the fire of 1849. The Corporation, they declared,
had power to borrow money for the new building in Wheeler
Street as it had had power to borrow for the improvement of
Market Hill.

The Wheeler Street site was, therefore, cleared by the
demolition of the premises which stood on it, and work on the
new Corn Exchange, designed by R.R. Rowe of Cambridge, was
begun. The Mayor, Mr. John Death, laid the foundation stone
in 1874 and, as one of his last public acts of his year of office,
opened the building on 6 November 1875. He was criticised,

on that occasion, in the *Cambridge Independent Press,* for extravagance, the sum of £100 having been voted him by the Town Council for the expenses of the ceremony. A few days later he was to suffer more than criticism from a section of the student population of Cambridge.

Undergraduates' Riot

On the whole, relations between Town and Gown seem, in the period 1866-76, to have been fairly peaceful. Once or twice Josiah Chater recorded 'a row at the Town Hall', usually on the occasion of a concert or lecture, but each 5 November passed, apparently, without incident, thanks, as he wrote, to the banning of fireworks by the University authorities.

In 1875, however, there were a number of outbreaks, culminating in a noisy interruption, on 8 November, of a concert in the new Corn Exchange. Undergraduates stamped, yelled and whistled throughout the performance, to the great annoyance of the audience which included the Mayor, Mr. Death, and most of the Town Council.

Throughout his year of office, Mr. Death had shown a firm determination to curb rowdyism, which had not made him popular with undergraduates. When, therefore, seven men were arrested as a result of the Corn Exchange disturbance, some of their supporters decided to avenge them. So, on 10 November, as Josiah recorded,

> This evening the University men burnt Death in effigy on the Market Place.

On the following day the seven men appeared in court:

> The Market Place has been pretty lively all day, the University men being up before the magistrates for the row on Monday night. The Courts have been crammed from 11 o'clock till half past seven. Three of them were fined £10 each; one £5; one £1. After it was over, a lot of them went to J. Death's house[85] and broke his fence and windows and committed other breaches of the peace, and I think 2 or 3 got locked up.

The mob which attacked the Mayor's house were restrained by the police, but not before a great deal of damage was done to surrounding property.

On 16 November Josiah wrote,

> Yesterday, Herrison of Christ's was fined £15 for rioting at Death's last week and sent down from the College.

The Perse School Affair

On 2 May 1876 Josiah, whose eldest son, Ernest, had been a pupil in the junior section of the Perse School in Cambridge since September 1874, recorded in his diary,

> At the Post Office this evening, Mr Maxwell, one of the Perse School masters, told me he had had a letter of dismissal from Mr Allen, the Headmaster, because he is a Nonconformist.

Francis Charles Maxwell, M.A., of St. John's College and a Wesleyan, had been appointed at the school, on leaving college in 1871, by the then headmaster, Frederic Heppenstall. Since 1873 Maxwell had been head of the junior department, receiving a salary of £150 a year and being allowed to take boarders in his house in Bateman Street.

The letter that he received, at the end of April, from Mr. Heppenstall's successor, J.B. Allen, stated clearly the writer's reasons for dismissing his assistant: Maxwell's religious beliefs differed from those that Allen wished to see held by his staff, and there was 'a certain difference of social position' between him and the rest of the masters.

On 9 June Josiah Chater noted,

> Maxwell's dismissal is making a great stir in the country'.

This was no overstatement. On the previous day, at a meeting of the Town Council,[86] a Nonconformist councillor had raised the matter which had already been given publicity, in the *Cambridge Independent Press,* by the publication of Allen's initial letter and the ensuing correspondence between the headmaster and Maxwell.

A day or so later, indignant letters on the affair, under such headings as *Religious Intolerance in Cambridge,* were appearing in the *Times,* the *Telegraph* and in many local newspapers up and down the country. By 5 June a question had been asked in the Commons of Lord Sandon, Vice-President of the Committee of the Council of Education, who replied that he had no knowledge of the case and no jurisdiction over grammar schools.

The *Cambridge Chronicle,* which all along had urged, ' the exercise of calm thought upon the different aspects of this unfortunate dispute', printed in its issue of 17 June a letter from Dr. W.H. Bateson, Master of St. John's College, on behalf of the School governors, which sought to calm the mounting hysteria.

Dr. Bateson, while regretting that religious beliefs had become involved in the affair, explained that Maxwell would never have been dismissed solely on the grounds of being a Nonconformist. The real reason for his dismissal was the bad report made on the lower school by the independent examiners appointed by the governors at Midsummer 1875. When Mr. Allen came to the school in place of Frederic Heppenstall, he was asked to enquire into this report and, having done so, had sent his letter to Mr. Maxwell in an attempt to induce him to retire voluntarily from the school. The governors, however, had informed him of their regret that he should have named Maxwell's religion as an excuse for dismissing him.

Maxwell, in a letter to the *Times* and to the *Cambridge Chronicle,* at once defended himself against this attack on his teaching ability. The unfavourable report, he declared, referred to Latin only, out of the 10 subjects in which the junior school classes were examined, to one class only and to one examination paper only. His defence was supported by, among others, a letter from Mr. Heppenstall, now headmaster of Sedburgh School, which stated that Maxwell was, 'the right man' in the 'right place' and that he could 'teach well more of the subjects required in such a school than most men'.

The unfortunate controversy continued and on 7 July the school governors met to consider two petitions, one signed by a number of Cambridge residents, the other by Nonconformist ministers, both asking for the dismissal of Mr. Allen. It was decided that, as the whole affair had been thoroughly examined and Allen had been rebuked for expressing his unwillingness to have a Dissenter on his staff, the matter was now closed. No further action would be taken save to allow Mr. Maxwell, if he so wished, to remain until Christmas.

It was not surprising that, only five years after the Act which had freed Nonconformists from many of the disadvantages they had hitherto suffered in the Universities, feelings should run high over what appeared to be religious intolerance in a school. Maxwell left Cambridge in September 1875, and became head-master of the Manor House School, Clapham Common, where he remained until his death in 1898. His son, born in Cambridge in 1874, succeeded him at the school.

An Execution in Cambridge

On 25 November 1876, Josiah Chater recorded,

Browning was tried and sentenced for the murder of a girl on the Common last August.

Robert Browning, a 25-year-old tailor of Bradmore Street, Cambridge, had visited the *Garrick* public house[87] on the night of 24 August and had got into conversation with Emma Rolfe, 16 years old, who had left her home, two weeks before, and was then lodging in Crispin Street.

After leaving the *Garrick*, Browning and Emma walked on to Butt Green and there, seemingly without provocation, Browning attacked his companion with a razor, almost severing her head from her body. A policeman, called by horrified passers-by, found him standing by the body; on being questioned he admitted 'I know I've done it, I couldn't help it'.

Browning was convicted at the Norwich Assizes and brought back to Cambridge where he was lodged in the Town Gaol in Gonville Place, overlooking Parker's Piece. Despite an appeal for his sentence to be reprieved, he was hanged at the gaol on 14 December 1878, at 8 o'clock in the morning, when many people assembled on the Piece to see the black flag hoisted. When the gaol was pulled down in 1878, his remains were taken for re-burial at the County Gaol on Castle Hill. Browning's execution was the only one to take place at the Town Gaol, which was built in 1839, and the first, in Cambridge, to be carried out in private since the last public hanging, on Castle Hill, of John Green in 1864.

NOTES TO PART IV

1. He had been engaged to drive Josiah and his brother William on business journeys.

2. Nos. 19-22 Fitzwilliam Street are now a hostel of Peterhouse. Extensions have been built on the gardens at the rear and there is no longer an access to the *Little Rose*.

3. *Pea jacket:* A short, stout overcoat of coarse, wollen cloth, commonly worn by sailors. *O.E.D.*

4. George Peck, chemist, of 30 Trumpington Street. The shop continues under the name of G. Peck & Sons Ltd., but is no longer a family business.

5.   There has been a chemist's shop at this address since 1815 when
      Isaiah Deck transferred to it the pharmacy business founded by his
      father on Market Hill in 1804. The last of the Deck family to trade
      on King's Parade was Isaiah's grandson Arthur A. Deck (1860-1948)
      who succeeded his father in 1903. In 1914 the business became Deck
      & Pain until A.A. Deck retired in 1929; it was then continued by his
      partner, G.N. Pain, until 1932 when it was acquired by G. Peck
      & Sons Ltd. under whose name it continues.

6.   Rowena 1867, Hubert 1869, Augustine 1870, Vernon 1871, Olivia
      1873, Llewellyn 1876.

7.   She had been resting having been up for most of the previous night
      because three of the children were ill.

8.   A well-known wine merchant in Cambridge.

9.   In 1871 he had also bought a nursery garden business in Mill Road
      which was sold, shortly before his death, to George Tredgett and his
      son. The Tredgetts for many years had a florist's shop on Market Hill;
      after 1879 when much of Mill Road, including the site of the nursery
      was sold for building purposes, they moved to the Ainger Nurseries
      in Histon Road.

10.   The Gonville Nursery was bought by the firm of Lyles & Speed who
      had a shop at 15 Petty Cury. A few years later, re-named the Newnham
      Nursery, it was acquired, with the Petty Cury shop, by James Sanders
      under whose name the seedsman's business now at 42 Regent Street
      continues.

11.   Josiah had suggested a number of improvements to the house and
      had spent much time in writing to builders to obtain estimates.

12.   Jabez's eldest son.

13.   This information was supplied by his son, the late Mr. Leonard Chater.

14.   Plumber and decorator of 4 King's Parade.

15.   Entries in the diary show that Josiah and his brother Alfred had on
      several occasions brewed beer in the brewhouse.

16.   Josiah's sister who kept house for Alfred Chater.

17.   *Dorcas*: Name of a woman mentioned in *Acts*, ix, 36; hence *Dorcas
      Society*, a ladies' association in a church for making and providing
      clothes for the poor. *O.E.D.*

18.   By this Act Easter Monday, the first Monday in Whitsun week, the
      first Monday in August and 26 December, if a weekday, were declared
      Bank Holidays.

19.   His first wife died in January 1866.

20.   He lived in Shaftesbury Road, Cambridge. Born 1831 in Wyton,
      Hunts. Entered Peterhouse in 1862 to read Natural Sciences; took
      his M.A. degree in 1869 but because he was a Nonconformist was

ineligible for a fellowship. He made entomological collections in South America and contributed frequently to scientific journals. A keen skater and co-author of a *Handbook to Fen Skating,* he was a founder member of the National Skating Association established in Cambridge in 1879. He was Hon. Secretary of the Association for the Removal of Religious Disabilities, formed in Cambridge in 1868, and wrote pamphlets urging the abolition of the University Tests Act. He died in April 1890.

21. Edward Turner, son of J.H. Turner, Postmaster of Cambridge. Usually referred to in the diary as Ted Turner. He later qualified as a barrister.

22. The earliest was, probably, the Bull Book Club founded in 1748. It met weekly at the *Bull* Hotel until it was dissolved in c.1841. It had a library of over 2,000 volumes.

23. Agnes Chater's uncle, grandfather of Josiah's friend Edwin Barrett.

24. Sophia.

25. Established 1850.

26. W. Flack, a boot and shoe maker, 9 Bridge Street.

27. R. Boning, tailor, 19 Pembroke Street.

28. Either E. Newman, beer retailer of 14 Silver Street or F. Newman, landlord of the *Bell and Crown* Inn, 67 Bridge Street.

29. Charles Gray, M.A., Trinity College.

30. This was the Working Men's Institute in Russell Street, in the area developed in the early 19th century, west of Hills Road, and named New Town.

31. This owed its foundation, chiefly, to Rev. Harvey Goodwin and was designed to educate and, if necessary, reform boys over 13 years old and to provide a home and training for unemployed youths. It opened in 1850 in Victoria Road, instruction being given in reading, arithmetic, tailoring, shoemaking and gardening. In 1894 the school was transferred to the C. of E. Waifs and Stray's Society (now the Children's Society) and re-named the Harvey Goodwin Home in 1901. In 1894 premises were erected for the Home (now called the Harvey Goodwin Nursery) in the newly-made Harvey Goodwin Avenue.

32. Josiah Chater's name appears, with those of his fellow Trustees, on the stone tablet, on the front of the almshouses, which records the building of the houses on their King Street site. New premises are due to be erected in Chesterton.

33. Thomas Bryant, 19 Market Street, is listed in Mathieson's *Cambridge Directory* for 1867 as a homeopathic chemist, medical galvanist and mesmerist. He had public galvanic baths on his premises.

34. These were produced with two magic lanterns placed side by side or one on top of the other. The fronts of the lanterns were slightly inclined to each other so as to make the illuminated discs, projected by each lantern on to the screen, coincide. By means of a pair of thin

metal shutters terminating in comb-like teeth and operated by a lever, the light from either lantern could be gradually cut off at the same time as the light from the other was allowed to fall on the screen. In this way one picture appeared to melt or dissolve into another.

35. Head gardener at Chatsworth and brother of the man who bought Jabez Chater's nursery garden in 1873.

36. Partner in Warren & Nicholls (later Warren & Sons), grocers of 4 Market Hill and 51 Bridge Street.

37. This inn is mentioned in *The Diary of Samuel Newton, Alderman of Cambridge 1662-1717*, ed. J.E. Foster (1890). (Cambridge Antiquarian Society Publications No. XXIII). Newton records the suicide in 1688 of Richard Herring, son of Alderman Herring of Cambridge, after losing £100 when playing dice, 'at John Dods at the Red Heart in Petticury'. John Dod, with many other 17th-century tradesmen, faced with a shortage a small coinage, issued his own trade token. It bears the figure of a hart and an antelope, the date 1667 and the words, JOHN DOD AT THE RED HART AND ANTELOP IN CAMBRIDGE HIS ½.

38. It was, for a short time, called Red Hart Lane but was soon re-named Alexandra Street.

39. The original *Brazen George* was on the west side of St. Andrew's Street. In the early 16th century it was given to Christ's College and served, for many years, as a hostel for undergraduates. In 1850 the Post Office moved from Green Street to the old *Brazen George* site and remained there for 35 years. The public house which carried on the licence and the name of the older inn lay in St. Tibbs Row; it could also be approached by a narrow passage, called the Black Ditch, leading from Petty Cury.

40. William Eaden Lilley; G.E. Foster; Robert Sayle; James Nutter; John Lincolne.

41. This society merged with the Y.M.C.A. in 1918.

42. Thomas Huxley (1825-95), biologist and champion of Charles Darwin.

43. At Jesus, Pembroke and Girton Colleges.

44. A Northamptonshire builder then working on the new All Saints Church in Jesus Lane, Cambridge.

45. Stationer and bookseller then of 28 Petty Cury, later of 3 St. Andrew's Street.

46. Hosier and draper of 32-33 Petty Cury.

47. Jeweller of 8 Bridge Street.

48. Partner in the firm of Hills & Saunders, photographers, 15 King's Parade.

49. Draper of 1 King's Parade.

50. Sewage disposal was then a matter of some concern in Cambridge.

Many letters were written to the local newspapers complaining of the pollution of the river by sewage.

51. A neighbour of Josiah who lived at 14 Fitzwilliam Street.

52. The Y.M.C.A. building was demolished in July 1972 because of a redevelopment scheme which embraced much of the surrounding area, including the south side of Petty Cury. A new building, with hostel accommodation, has been erected in Gonville Place, overlooking Parker's Piece.

53. The Contagious Diseases Acts were not repealed until 1886. An earlier public meeting held in Cambridge in March 1871 had also condemned them.

54. The Society for the Liberation of Religion from State Patronage and Control.

55. Henry John Matthew, a leading member of the Y.M.C.A. He was in partnership with his father, George Matthew, in the grocery business at 20 Trinity Street which was continued by the Matthew family until it closed in 1964.

56. He was discovered to be John Wright Neville, a member of the Junior Conservative Club and later a partner in the firm of Barlow, Palmer & Neville, solicitors. See Part V for Josiah's account of Neville's trial and conviction for embezzling money belonging to the Cambridge Improvement Commissioners.

57. Foster's Bank opened 11 November 1813 at 55 Bridge Street; in 1836 it moved to 14 Trinity Street and in 1898 to 3, 4 and 5 Sidney Street where, in 1903, it amalgamated with The Capital & Counties Bank to be absorbed, in 1919, by Lloyds Bank Ltd. Foster's name is carved on the stonework of Lloyds Bank, which now occupies Nos. 1-5 Sidney Street and extends round the corner in Hobson Street.

58. Mark Ives Whibley, a well-known Cambridge Liberal. He came to Cambridge from Brighton to join the grocery firm of Brimley & Bond, 32 Market Hill, which eventually became Brimley, Whibley & Co., until it closed in 1934. Mark Whibley's son, Herbert George, was Mayor of Cambridge 1907-8; his grandson, Stuart Whibley, is the only surviving founder of the Cambridge Rotary Club, which was established in 1922. The Whibley family had a long association with the Y.M.C.A.

59. Francis Thoday of the firm of Thoday & Clayton, builders.

60. Petty Cury and a small area of central Cambridge had been lit by 'oil gas' since 1832 by John Grafton who, a few years later, entered into a contract with the Improvement Commissioners to light the streets with 'inflammable air or gas obtained from coal'. He set up the first gas retorts in the former Gas Lane, off Staffordshire Street, but by 1830 had moved his plant to River Lane off Newmarket Road. On 22 May 1834 the Cambridge Gas Light Company was formed to take over Grafton's plant and contracts. This company became the Cambridge University & Town Gas Light Co., in the summer of 1867 and

continued to operate until the gas industry passed into public owner-
ship in May 1949, when the Cambridge works were operated by the
Eastern Gas Board. Much of the plant has been demolished since
1971, following the bringing of natural gas to Cambridge.

61. The report of this meeting which appeared in the *Cambridge Chronicle*
on 18 April 1868 included Josiah's name in the list of those present.
The diary does not record that he attended this meeting.

62. This figure was exaggerated; the culprits were charged with breaking
six lamps. The *Cambridge Chronicle*, 6 June 1869, reported that
others were broken by passing traffic and 'the untrustworthy nature
of paraffin oil placed in a lamp in the highest degree liable to fall
over'. The temporary lighting with paraffin oil and the smashing of
the lamps inspired two of the questions in the Trinity College May
Examination of 1869. See *Cambridge Memories* by Edward Conybeare
in *The Cambridge Review*, 6 May 1909.

63. This included a quantity of gas pipes which had been ordered from
Sheffield.

64. It was built to the north of the old chapel, part of its site occupying
St. John's Lane which had run from St. John's Street to the river.
St. John's Street was widened by the demolition of a row of houses
on the west side.

65. Hubert, born 1 May 1869.

66. Four Acts of Parliament were passed in these years to regulate the
employment of shop assistants, e.g. that of 1892 declared that the
maximum hours worked by an assistant under the age of 18 were not
to exceed 74 a week, inclusive of mealtimes. Not until the Shop Act
of 1904 were certain additional optional powers given to any local
authority to make an order fixing the hours (not earlier than 7. 0 p.m.
or, on one day a week, 1.0 p.m.) at which shops could close. Even
then, as the Secretary of State reported to the Commons, great
difficulty had been experienced in obtaining the required two-thirds
majority among shop keepers in favour of the order.

67. The practice was maintained. On 3 June 1868 Josiah recorded that
Cambridge solicitors had agreed to close their offices at 2.0 p.m. on
Thursdays.

68. These were at No. 29, above the premises of J. Ryder, tailor and
robemaker. They eventually became, until 1881, the headquarters of
the Liberal Association.

69. Three numbers only of this were published 1871-3.

70. This was demolished for the building of the church, the licence being
transferred to 5 Little St. Mary's Lane which remained the *Half Moon*
until 1915 when it became a private house.

71. Two wall-tablets and various silver vessels of the 17th, 18th and 19th
centuries were removed from the old chapel to the new Congregational
church.

72. The meeting on 24 September was, probably, the occasion of Matthew Robertson's ordination, either for life or for the period in which he was at Downing Place. The meeting on the following day would have been his induction.

73. At the end of 1870 he became Professor of Mathematics at Durham College of Science, Newcastle-on-Tyne, and later Professor of Mathematics at Auckland College, New Zealand.

74. The former ineligibility of Nonconformists to be elected to fellowships had led, as Neville Goodman emphasised in the pamphlets which he wrote at the time, to the loss to the University of many eminent scholars.

75. He had already graduated at London University in 1870.

76. She went in place of her mother, who was unable to attend the party because five of the young Chaters were ill.

77. James Rendel Harris who, as a member of Clare College, joined Emanuel Congregational Church in June 1875 but left two years later. He remained in Cambridge for some time as a Fellow of Clare, later becoming Director of Studies at Woodbrooke, Birmingham. He was a noted New Testament scholar.

78. They probably were, although the *Cambridge Chronicle* on 5 July 1873 reported that, when the welcoming party at the station realised the whole affair was a hoax, 'even the members of the Corporation joined in the general laughter at the clever ruse which had drawn together so many people - there must have been 1,500 - by a well-planned practical lark'.

79. Ira Sankey compiled over 700 hymns which were published under the title *Sacred Songs and Solos*. He himself wrote the music of some of the hymns.

80. It was available for hire because theatrical performances in term time were banned by the University.

81. The building of bridges in Cambridge can be slow. It was in 1890 that proposals were made for a bridge to be constructed over the river from the end of Abbey Road. Not until 13 July 1971 was the Elizabeth Bridge opened. It crosses the river from the end of the now-demolished Walnut Tree Avenue, a few yards east of Abbey Road.

82. W.H.C. Smith who had bought the drapery business of John Barrett, Agnes Chater's father, at 13 Market Street.

83. P.T. Coulson, pork butcher of 190 East Road and 9 Sussex Street.

84. *Relator*: An informer, *spec.* one who supplies material for an information by the Attorney General. *O.E.D.*

85. This stood on part of the site of the present Wesleyan Chapel in King Street.

86. The Council declined to take any action on the grounds that, although it had representation on the Perse School Board of Governors, the Board was an independent body.

87. This stood at the Four Lamps Corner near the end of King Street.

V

1877 to 1883

A NEW CAREER

Affairs at Home

By January 1877 the number of Josiah Chater's children had increased to 12, Rowena having been born in 1867, Hubert in 1869, Augustine in 1870, Vernon in 1871, Olivia in 1873 and Llewellyn in 1876. In August 1876, Ethel, then aged 22, had left home to live for three months in St. Leonard's, Sussex, with the owners of a glassware and china shop, prior to her father's purchasing the business for her and for his third daughter, Milly.

On 26 March 1877 Josiah travelled to St. Leonard's, found lodgings for Ethel and her sister at 10s. a week, 'for all except washing', and on the following day, when Milly arrived with her mother who was to stay for a few days with her daughters, completed the formalities of the purchase of the china shop. The day was, as he noted in his diary, 'an ever-to-be-remembered one in our annals'.

Throughout most of the period in which Josiah continued to keep his diary, he wrote many times of his daughters' progress. He visited them often, with Agnes and the younger children, and gave them much helpful advice in the keeping of their accounts. He was extremely proud of the way in which Ethel showed how much she had profited by her training with the previous owners of the business and, as he watched the two girls, he must often have been reminded of his own early venture, with his brother William, into the world of commerce.

Hardly, however, had he seen his daughters settled in Sussex than he and Agnes passed through a period of great distress and sorrow. On 15 April 1877 he wrote,

> Had Peck in to see Ernest and he says he has the measles. Rowena is very queer too and I fear some of the others are sickening for it. Poor Agnes is in a terrible way.

Two days later Ernest had 'come out with the measles all over his body', and 12-year-old Junia and her sister Sophy, two years younger, had been sent to stay with their uncle Alfred in the hopes that, since they appeared, so far, to be well, they might escape the infection. On 19 April,

> Agnes sent for Dr Carter to Rowena and Ernest; he says Ernest has the measles very severely and Rowey must be taken great care of.

Three days later Hubert was taken ill with bronchitis and his two younger brothers, Augustine and Vernon, were obviously sickening for measles.

23 April:
> Hubert and Rowey were so bad when I got home to dinner that I sent for Carter, who was out. I then went to Dr Latham;[1] he came at 4 o'clock. Then Hubert got so much worse that I went again for him; He came at 10.30.

24 April:
> Poor Hubert was fearfully bad all night; he nearly suffocated. Agnes and I sat up all night - we both thought he must have choked. Dr Carter and Dr Latham both came this afternoon.

By the next day Hubert not only had bronchitis but measles as well; four-year-old Olivia was in bed, her brother Vernon 'scarcely knows how to hold his head up, poor little fellow'. News had come, moreover, from Josiah's brother Alfred, that the two children staying with him were also in bed with measles.

By 27 April Agnes had eight children in bed, including the baby Llewellyn; only Lizzy, the eldest daughter now at home, remained well and able, therefore, to be of great help to her mother in nursing the invalids. It must have been some relief that Junia and Sophy were being cared for by Alfred Chater and his sister, especially when, on 28 April, Josiah returned from visiting them with the news that they were now suffering from whooping cough as well as measles. The children in Fitzwilliam Street had also, by then, contracted the second complaint.

On 9 May, however, Josiah was able to record that they were 'slightly mending, but very slowly', adding, on the following day, that the baby was very ill. Agnes, by this time, was able to rest more at night thanks to Mrs. Whibley, wife of Josiah's friend Mark Whibley, coming in from time to time to sit up with the sick children. 'It is', Josiah wrote, 'very good and kind of her to lend a hand in our time of need'.

On 14 May,

> Our poor little dears are not doing very well this morning. Poor Baby was very restless all night and had no sleep. I noticed his eyes had become quite crossed and he was a good deal convulsed. I gave him

some milk in his bottle at one o'clock, but he could not swallow without a struggle . . . Today, after dinner, we thought him a little better and I left to go to Macintosh's.[2] Had just taken off my hat and coat and set to work when Alfred came in and said Agnes wanted me directly; she thought the baby was dying. I called at Carter's but he was out; then went on home with Al and found Peck and Dr Latham there. The poor little dear had died at half past three in Agnes' arms; she had taken him up in a fit of coughing and he suddenly seemed to be suffocated. It must have been a fit. The poor little dear - just 16 months old last week, and a fine little fellow . . . Poor Agnes and the children are all distracted. I took them all up to see him in the evening and he looked so naturally asleep they did not mind it in the least, but cannot understand it.

Llewellyn was buried on 17 May in the cemetery in Histon Road, beside his little sister Polly, who had died in 1865. Agnes had little opportunity to give way to her grief, for she was kept fully occupied in looking after the other whooping cough sufferers. Mrs. Whibley called often and occasionally took a turn in sitting up at night, while Miss Simpson - Aunt Sophy - too feeble, now, to call in person, sent a servant daily to make enquiries and to bring dishes of blancmange and savoury jelly to tempt the childrens' appetites.

With brief periods of remission the illness lasted until June, although Ernest, the first to be affected, had by then recovered. Then, on 14 June, Josiah wrote,

The children are very bad; Gussy had some sort of fit so Agnes sent for Carter and Peck as she thought he was dying. They all seem worse; what to do we don't know.

With some difficulty he persuaded Dr. Carter to call in Dr. Latham, which he finally agreed to do, although,

he was very angry and put himself out, saying 'Damn it, if you haven't confidence in me then it's no good at all'. I told him that was not fair . . . the children were very ill and did not seem to mend, and another person might suggest something to their advantage.

Not until 27 June were the young Chaters declared, by Dr. Latham, to be well enough to travel to St. Leonard's to recuperate. On 3 July the large family party set off:

We had 3 flys and got to the station in good time with all our luggage, which we packed into one compartment of a first class carriage. Ernest, Hubert, Gus, Vernon and I took the other end, and Mother, with Aunt Annie, Sophie, Rowena, Junia and Olivia in the middle compartment. . . We got away very comfortably and were soon landed at Kentish Town where we took the Metropolitan to Victoria. It was rather tedious and

the Underground was a little too much for Rowey - dark and stuffy - it
made her a little faint. At Victoria we were soon on our way again and,
with half an hour's stop at Sevenoaks, arrived very nicely at St Leonards
at 9 o'clock. Ethel and Milly[3] met us and in two cabs we arrived at our
journey's end . . . Poor Ethel was quite knocked over to see Rowey and
the others looking so bad; she had not seen them for six months. We
soon got them all to bed and, with a little coughing and sickness, they
went off to sleep. The boys enjoyed the journey amazingly and stood it
famously. I think it has cost me in all £8. Everyone has been very kind
to us.

In view of their experience in 1877 it was fortunate for Agnes
and Josiah that, when their daughter Junia contracted diphtheria
in May 1878, she was away at school in Huntingdon and so did
not spread the infection to her brothers and sisters. Josiah
received the news by letter and at once set off to visit the child,
Agnes not daring to risk catching the disease as she was expecting
the birth of the child who was to be named Leonard.

Josiah found Junia isolated in a cottage used as the school
infirmary, and although he was assured by the doctor that she
was progressing satisfactorily, he naturally regretted that he was
not able to take her home with him. Returning to Huntingdon
the next day, however, he was encouraged to find that his
daughter had been joined by one of her class mates and that both
were in the charge of a pleasant nurse:

Poor child, I could not bear to leave her, but she is very good and
patient. I thought to stay the night and tomorrow with her, but after
seeing she was in such good hands I thought it best to come home.

His last visit was made on 30 May when he found Junia, though
still in bed, 'quite cheerful and bright'. The owners of the school,
however, were 'in a dreadful way, having sent two more girls
home - one had just been taken to Peterborough'.

It must have seemed to Agnes and Josiah that their children
were never going to be free from illness for, in that same year,
on 20 December 1878, nine-year-old Hubert went down with
scarlet fever. The other children were at once sent off to stay
with their uncle Alfred, although Agnes kept the baby Leonard,
born on 26 May, at home with her in Fitzwilliam Street.
Fortunately neither he nor any of the others caught the fever.
Throughout these two difficult years, Agnes had domestic help
in the house and seems to have had none of the servant problems
which had earlier beset her; at any rate, none are recorded.

Earlier, on 15 November 1878 Aunt Sophy Simpson had died
at her home in St. Peter's Terrace, Trumpington Street. All but

two of the young Chaters seemingly escaped, on this occasion, the ordeal of being taken to see the body before it was placed in the coffin:

> I went to No 5 this evening and wrote some letters; everything seems very strange and I cannot realise it. I have made all the arrangements for the funeral; the shell was taken up today and the corpse placed in it. Ernest and Hubert went with me to take their last look at the old lady.

Recreation and Leisure

Holidays, in this period of the diary, were usually spent by Agnes, Josiah and their children in St. Leonard's; in 1880, however, Josiah accompanied his daughter Ethel on a five-day visit to Paris.

On Sunday, 1 October 1882, he bought two tickets, at 5s. each, for himself and Ernest and the pair travelled on the special excursion train to Manchester which left Cambridge at half past three on the following morning. The journey took seven and a half hours. After a short walk in the city, father and son went, after dinner, to the Belle Vue Gardens:

> We amused ourselves by examining the Zoological Collections and the flowers and other sights, especially the Dancing which was quite new and amusing to Ernest - some hundreds of dancers on an immense platform in the open to a very good Band ... There were any quantity of steam roundabouts, while boating on the lakes kept us going until 8 o'clock when a magnificent display of fireworks closed the performance. Before it had quite subsided we bolted off to the railway station at Ashbury and secured our comfortable second class compartment and settled ourselves for the night. We were nearly an hour late in starting and lost a little time on the way, but ultimately reached Cambridge and were just turning into Fitzwilliam Street as the clock struck six on Tuesday morning.

Small dinner and supper parties were regularly given, and attended, by Agnes and Josiah while amateur theatricals continued to be popular with the Chaters and their friends. On Christmas Day 1882, for example, the back parlour of No. 19 Fitzwilliam Street was converted to a theatre and the young Chaters, with the help of some friends, acted *Aladin's Lamp* before an invited audience, although Josiah had to confess,

> It certainly was rather rough, it being more of a rehearsal as it was the first time they had all been together. After it we went upstairs and had a capital dance. We had 18 to dinner at 9 o'clock.

Neither on this occasion, nor on the many others on which, throughout the diary, Josiah records attending or giving dances at home, does he tell us who provided the music. There were, however, many musicians - chiefly violinists - listed in 19th-century Cambridge directories, and these were frequently engaged for private parties.

In summer Josiah often went to bathe at Newnham with his sons Ernest and Hubert, or took them on long walks to Coton, Madingley, Grantchester and other nearby villages. He never, if possible, missed an opportunity to skate whenever the winters were severe. Thus, in December 1878, he went several times on the ice at Grantchester, with three or four of the younger children, and on the 18th of that month he wrote,

> Went, after 4 o'clock, with Brimley Johnson and had half an hour's skating on Stirbitch Common. Some of the Corporation men have been pumping water on it for the good of the town.[4]

There was another prolonged frost in 1881 and, although Josiah himself was too occupied with business affairs to be able to take advantage of it, Ernest and some of his brothers and sisters skated several times on Lingay Fen at Grantchester, and watched the Amateur Skating Championships held under the auspices of the National Skating Association.[5] They saw, too, the race between 'Fish' Smart,[6] the famous fen skater and then Open Champion, and a specially selected team of the best speed skaters in the district.

In his spare time Josiah continued to take a regular turn at helping to receive deposits at the Penny Bank; he remained on the committee of the Borough Charities and also on the committee of the Y.M.C.A., although his busy life in these years did not allow him to attend many of the Association's functions. He went, however, to the Conversazione on 14 January 1878 when he,

> saw the Electric Light, the Phonograph, some conjuring and many other things. A good lot of people there and I think it must prove a success.

At the end of 1881 the local newspapers advertised a lecture, to be given at the Alexandra Hall of the Y.M.C.A. on three evenings in early November, by 'The Escaped Nun'. She was Miss Edith O'Gorman who, for six years, had been in St. Joseph's Convent in New Jersey. On 1 November Josiah wrote,

> Mr Porcher, the secretary of the Y.M.C.A., came to tell me that the Vice-Chancellor had sent for him and told him he expected there would be a row at our Rooms at the lecture by the Escaped Nun.

2 November:
> Mr Porcher tells me this morning that the Proctor had seen him and

told him he ought to have had permission of the Vice-Chancellor, as
the advertisement bills are too dramatic. I went up to the Room at
8 o'clock and looked in several times, but it was very orderly and no
row whatever.

Miss O'Gorman's lecture, described in the *Cambridge Chronicle*[7] as, 'a graphic account of the evils and iniquities connected
with the conventual system . . . and of the austere and unnatural
penances enjoined by the rules of such places', does not seem to
have attracted the expected noisy attention of the undergraduate members of the University. Indeed, attendance was
reported to be only 'fair'.

Business Affairs: A New Career

The beginning of the year 1877 saw Josiah busy with the final
stages of the winding-up of his partnership with his brother,
William, in the Market Hill business and with the final disposal
of the lease of the property. By 9 January the agreement was
signed with William Bond the grocer, who was taking over the
premises and allowing William Chater a seven-year lease.

Meanwhile, on 8 January, Josiah had begun his new career as
an accountant:[8]

This morning at 11 o'clock, I entered on my new duties as Chief
Accountant at Alex Macintosh's establishment, and I began by going
through the Petty Cash Ledger and sorting the Bills out. I stay till half
past one; home to dinner and back at 3 till 5 or half past. I like it very
well.

On the following day the Actuary of the Cambridge and
Cambridgeshire Savings Bank[9] died, and it was suggested to
Josiah that he might apply for the vacant post. He was not, in
the end, elected, but there was no lack of work for him in other
fields.

The years 1877 to 83 seem to have been lean ones in Cambridge
and a number of local businesses[10] failed; in many cases Josiah
was appointed as trustee or receiver. The burden of the correspondence involved was eased, initially, by his using a device,
owned by Mr. Vawser, the Petty Cury draper and hosier, which
enabled a number of circulars, notices and other written
material to be duplicated. Thus, in May 1877, he recorded.

I knocked off about 100 circulars in about half an hour by the patent
Papyrographic System.

This was, probably, the device, patented by E. de Zuccatto in 1874, whereby a stencil was made by using a thin sheet of paper, called by the inventor 'papyrographic paper', which was lacquered on one side. The writing or drawing to be duplicated was inscribed on the paper by means of a steel pen and ink; copies were produced by pressing in a writing copying press.

In the August of that same year Josiah wrote,

> I have today been at Vawser's practising a new method of writing from which to multiply copies, called the Electric Pen. It seems to require a good deal of practice.

However, he seems to have mastered the art of using it because, three months later, he wrote of sending out a number of notices which had been written 'with my electric pen'.

On 12 February 1878 he:

> took my Electric Pen and Battery to Vawser's and we cleaned it and I got a new inner for the Battery and made it go first rate.

In May, however, he had to take the pen to London to be cleaned. It was returned to him by post, he 'made a new battery' for it and on 8 May was able to record,

> The pen goes very well and I have been striking off about 500 double circulars about the trams.[11]

The electric pen was, doubtless, that invented by T.A. Edison and covered by the British Patent No. 3762 in the year 1875. There is an example to be seen in the Science Museum in South Kensington. By means of Edison's invention, a paper stencil plate was rapidly prepared for producing a large number of copies of the original writing by running an inked roller over the back of the stencil.

The instrument used consisted of a stylus, from the end of which protruded a needle point which was connected to a small fly-wheel and electric motor at the end of the instrument. By the rotation of the motor the point of the stylus was rapidly protruded and drawn back again so that, in passing over a sheet of paper, it left a finely perforated track. Power was supplied to the motor by a portable galvanic battery.

The Cambridge Reform Club Building Company

On 15 June 1877 Josiah was asked by his friend, Mark Whibley whether he would act as secretary to the Cambridge Reform Club Building Company which it was proposed to establish. That same evening Josiah went to see Robert Sayle, one of the promoters, and reported,

> He was very good and congratulated me about the Y.M.C.A. which, he said, would never have been built if I had not played the part I did. I returned the compliment, and he declared this new company must be a success and I was the man for its secretary.

Three days later he wrote to Mark Whibley, accepting the post of secretary at a basic salary of £25 a year with 'extra for promoting the Company'.

On 25 June the Promoters of the Company met to discuss the drawing-up of a prospectus and Articles of Association. These were finally drafted a month later and, on 28 August, Josiah 'spent the day in getting signatures to the Memorandum of Association'. Two days later he wrote,

> I opened an account at the Bank yesterday and placed £125 of the Reform Club Building Company; placed today £130 more. I called on Ginn[12] and enquired about an office he has to let. I think I must have one in the town somewhere.

He occupied this office, at No. 2 Alexandra Street,[13] for the first time on 16 October. Meanwhile, on 14 September:

> Knowles sent for me to say he had received the Certificate of the Registration of the Cambridge Reform Club Building Company, Ltd. I then wrote a circular with my electric pen calling the Directors to a meeting at my office at 7.30 tomorrow evening. Called on Sayle and he is agreeable to having the office of the Company at my office.

The Company was incorporated on 10 November 1877. Its objects were to purchase or rent lands in Cambridge and, in particular, to carry out a contract entered into by the solicitor, Philip Knowles, with the trustees of the late William Newby of Cambridge, for the purchase of freehold property in Green Street.[14] A Club House for political and social meetings was to be provided, either by altering the Green Street property or by pulling it down and erecting a new building on the site. This Club House was to be let to the Trustees of any political or social club whose rules were approved by the Company in which the shareholders were, for the most part, prominent Liberal business men of Cambridge.

Some of the property in Green Street was acquired by purchase - £1,000 was paid for No. 29, for example - but the Company's affairs seem never to have been very prosperous. On 24 January 1880 Josiah recorded, 'we are just paying our way, but no dividend'. On 13 February of the same year:

> At 12 a meeting of the Reform Club Building Company. They have had to cut my salary down from £25 to £10; not a pleasant performance, but as they cannot pay a dividend they must reduce expenditure.

The Company managed to survive until 1891 when it went into liquidation, the winding-up meeting being held on 26 January of that year.[15]

The Cambridge Steam Laundry Company

In 1881, although extremely busy with the affairs of several companies and with many bankruptcy cases, Josiah took on yet more work in connection with the new steam laundry[16] then being established. On 11 February the diary records,

> Had a pipe with Ginn the solicitor; he told me about a new project of a Laundry Company he had in view to which I am to be secretary if it comes off. He has the offer of an estate of 4 acres, with buildings on it, at Cherryhinton, opposite the Waterworks, and he has a capital man in view as a manager.

Josiah was duly appointed secretary and on 5 March he attended the first meeting of the Directors of the Steam Laundry Company:

> I am ordered to get a Prospectus printed and a set of books for the Company:

17 March:
> Last evening we had a meeting of the Steam Laundry Company and allotted about £1,300 worth of shares. Sealed the Contract; the public seem satisfied it is going to pay.

At the end of April the Directors selected a plan for the laundry building and agreed to the demolition of the brewery which stood on the site. The brewing utensils were sold for £90. By 7 August Josiah could report that the walls of the laundry were ready to receive the roof, but he thought the workmen were making slow progress. On 14 September he

> went to the laundry. It is nearly all covered in and the shaft of the chimney is going up well.

29 September:

> Borrowed Alex Macintosh's tricycle and rode over to the Laundry. They have most of the machinery there now and are getting on rapidly.

On 8 October Josiah found the machines almost ready for use and the boiler, the engine and the shafting installed. He then called on the Warden of Cavendish College[17] and arranged with him that the Laundry should begin to do the College washing at 7s. per 1,000 articles of household linen and 1s. a dozen for personal items.

His salary as secretary was fixed on 13 October 1881, by a meeting of the Directors, at £25 a year. It was agreed, at the same time, to pay the Manager £1 a week, with a commission on dividends to be decided later, and the Manageress £1 10s. a week.

Work at the laundry began on 18 October, the first customers being Cavendish College and Mrs. Todhunter, wife of Isaac Todhunter M.A., Honorary Fellow of St. John's College. Josiah, going to Cherry Hinton two days later, to advise on how the books should be kept, found the women 'all busy ironing'. However,

> the men tell me that the engine will not do its work, and I expect we shall be obliged to have a new and more powerful one.

The new 8-horse-power engine, needed surprisingly soon after the laundry had opened, was ordered five days later. It had arrived by 8 November when Josiah was able to report that the work was increasing and 'being done very satisfactorily'.

On 20 January 1882 there was

> A Grand Tea Meeting for the employees at the Laundry. Lizzy and Junia and I went at six o'clock. Mr. Tillyard[18] was Chairman. Macintosh and his wife were there and their three daughters. Had a little speech, two readings, some songs and duets, then a jolly dance. It was a capital evening. Home about 11 o'clock.

Affairs were less satisfactory in the February of that year. Josiah found the books in a bad state and recorded that he did not think the manager and his wife were competent. The same opinion was voiced in February at a general meeting of the shareholders. No fault was found with the quality of the work being done in the laundry, but there seem to have been many mistakes made in sending customers' linen home. Meanwhile, eight cottages for the work hands had been built near the laundry, and the Directors had consulted Dr. Cunningham, a graduate of Harvard University who was then living in Cambridge, on the problem of disposing of the soap suds without interfering with the sewage system.

Proposed Telephone System
One of Josiah's activities, in the last years of his diary-keeping,

was an attempt to get a telephone exchange established in Cambridge, because he realised what an advantage this would be to local business men. On 1 August 1882 he recorded,

> I have been busy this week calling on bankers and lawyers and others about the Telephone Exchange and getting a memorial signed. Have succeeded very well.

Three weeks later he travelled to London, visited the offices of the National Telephone Company and there learned, 'a company is being started for an Eastern Counties District Company Ltd'.

The last-named company never came to Cambridge; it was not, indeed, until 1892 that the National Telephone Company[19] established an exchange in the town. Within four years it had 128 subscribers. The company's offices were at No. 12 Market Hull until, in 1908, they moved to No. 2 Alexandra Street.

The Cambridge Improved Industrial Dwellings Company

On 25 April 1883, eight days before Josiah ceased so abruptly to keep his diary, he wrote,

> Professor Liveing,[20] Mr Clay.[21] Mr S.L. Young[22] and Whibley called in this afternoon to ask me if I would take the secretary-ship of the Cambridge Improved Industrial Dwellings Company Limited. After a little consultation I agreed.

This Company had been formed in 1878 when what was known as the Mendicity Property, consisting of Mendicity House in Newmarket Road, a number of adjoining small cottages and some land lying to the back of them, came on to the market.

Mendicity House, previously known as the Old Manor House, had been leased in 1847 from its owner, Thomas Parker, by the Anti-Mendicity Society[23] which had been formed in that year to assist the large number of labourers who passed through Cambridge in search of work. The Society opened the house for wayfarers - 16 men and eight women - who could obtain a night's lodging under the care of a resident master and matron. Those in urgent need were, on approval, given bread and cheese when they arrived and breakfast before they left on the following morning.

The Mendicity Property passed eventually to Thomas Parker's grandson, Octavius Parker, who died in 1876. When it became known that, for the benefit of his creditors, it had to be sold, the Anti-Mendicity Society gave up its tenancy of Mendicity

House. A number of townspeople and members of the University, however, appalled by the bad housing conditions in Barnwell, decided to form the Cambridge Improved Industrial Dwellings Company, with the initial view of purchasing the property, improving the cottages adjoining Mendicity House and building decent tenements on the back-land. Their intention was, also, to buy any other similar property which might come on to the market, and either improve or rebuild it.

By the time the sale took place, in August 1878, the proposed Company had not yet been fully established and less than half the necessary money had been raised. However, with the aid of an overdraft of £1,035 from the Bank and an advance of £1,064 from three members of the proposed Company, the whole of the Mendicity Property was purchased for £3,472.

Once the Company was established its work proceeded with vigour. At the end of nine months the Directors were able to report that 15 dilapidated cottages had been demolished, 25 had been repaired and 25 more cottages were in course of erection. In 1879 new houses were built on the corner of East Road and Crispin Street, two of them being taken over by Mr. C.J. Clay, the University Printer, and the Rev. H. Trotter, Vicar of Christ Church, Newmarket Road, for use as a coffee tavern and lodging house.[24] Behind Mendicity House 11 cottages were built facing on to a new Road, Leeke Street,[25] named after the Rev. E.T. Leeke, a former Vicar of Christ Church.

In 1884 18 cottages were built in Gloucester Street,[26] at the top of Castle Hill, and were let at 2s. 6d. a week, while more property was erected, six years later, in the same district of Cambridge, where housing was almost as bad as it was in Barnwell.

Professor Liveing, one of the deputation which approached Josiah Chater to ask him to act as secretary, remained Chairman of the Company until he retired, in 1923, at the great age of ninety-six. By that date housing conditions in Cambridge had greatly improved and the Directors reported, 'they deemed it desirable that the holdings should be realised at the best prices obtainable'. By 1927 the Company was no more. To its last days it had a number of the Chater family as its secretary, because Josiah's third son, Augustine, partner in the chartered accountancy firm of J. Chater & Sons, succeeded his father in the office, as he did in that of secretary to the Steam Laundry Company.

Nonconformist Affairs

After his aunt, Miss Sophy Simpson, died in 1878, Josiah was able to resume attendance at St. Andrew's Street Chapel on Sunday evenings, a practice he had foregone, over the preceding 12 months, in order that he might spend an hour or two reading to the old lady. He had, however, regularly attended the morning services, and it was on 6 January 1878 that he recorded in his diary an incident which provides an interesting reference to the history of Nonconformity in Cambridge.

On his way to Chapel that morning Josiah met his friend, Mark Whibley, who persuaded him to,

> Accompany him to the Alexandra Room of the Y.M.C.A. Here Mr Harris[27] conducted a service for the benefit of those who have split off from Dr Robertson's congregation. There were about 50 there, and it was very sincere and very good.

Dr. Matthew Robertson had been appointed the first minister of the new Emmanuel Congregational Church in Trumpington Street which had opened in 1874. Josiah had already referred, in his diary, to the somewhat strained relations which had grown up between the minister and his congregation and which were not improved by the former's failure to inform his flock that he was about to marry. In December 1877 following a disagreement over what, today, would be considered an extremely trifling matter, Dr. Robertson resigned his ministry and a number of his followers withdrew, also, from the church. It was for these that the service was held in the Y.M.C.A. rooms on 6 January 1878, the first Sunday following Dr. Robertson's exodus.

Dr. Robertson continued to live in Cambridge and became editor and part proprietor of the Radical newspaper, the *Cambridge Independent Press*. He died on 22 April 1891 and, despite his secession from the Congregationalists, the Dead March was played at Emmanuel Church, on the Sunday evening after his death, in tribute to his memory.

It is possible that the service which Josiah attended with Mark Whibley on 6 January 1878, the first of several to be held in the Y.M.C.A. rooms, had some connection with the establishment of St. Columba's Presbyterian Church in Cambridge. In 1879 Mr. James Rae, a Borough Councillor and a former deacon of Emmanuel Church in Dr. Robertson's time, together with a number of leading University men, mainly Scotsmen, petitioned the London Presbytery that Presbyterian services might be held in Cambridge.[28] Their request was granted, and by the October of that year a room in the Guildhall was being used for worship. The large number of undergraduates and townspeople who attended the services soon made it apparent that a permanent church would be desirable, and on 1 November 1879 Josiah recorded in his diary,

> Dr Robertson[29] has commissioned me to look out for a site to build a new Presbyterian church.

It so happened that, just at that time, a large property known as the Lensfield Estate, at the corner of Hills Road and Lensfield Road, had come on to the market. It had not long been in the possession of Henry John Matthew, of the Trinity Street grocery firm of Matthew & Son, whose sudden death on 12 September 1879, at the early age of 39, had been sorrowfully recorded by Josiah in his diary. The estate, previously owned by Joseph Wentworth, a well-known Cambridge auctioneer, consisted of a large residence - Lensfield House[30] - with orchard, stables, and extensive grounds; it was offered for sale as one lot or as four separate building lots.

Josiah thought that part of the estate would provide a suitable site for a Presbyterian Church so, having obtained particulars of the sale and shown them to Dr. Robertson, he wrote on 25 November:

> I attended the sale of the Lensfield Estate; had a commission to buy Lot 3[31] for £1,010, but it was sold in one Lot for £6,100, so I lost my chance.

Although no Presbyterian Church came to be erected on any part of the estate, this important site was destined to be that of the Roman Catholic Church of Our Lady and the English Martyrs, which replaced the smaller Church of St. Andrew built,[32] in 1841-3, in Union Road close by the Lensfield Estate.

In March 1880 Josiah Chater was again approached on the matter of finding a site for a Presbyterian Church. He took a Mr. Bullman

> to the Reform Club Building Society and showed him over it and he seemed to like it well. I also took him to the Old Chapel[33] in Downing Place and gave him particulars of each.

Not, however, until nearly ten years later was a site purchased by the Presbyterians in Downing Street.[34] Their new St. Columba's Church was formally opened in May 1891, by which date Josiah had ceased to keep his diary.

EVENTS IN CAMBRIDGE 1877-83

An Election

There was a General Election in 1880. Josiah reported, on 10 March, that electioneering was 'going full steam' in the town, and that Hugh Shield, Q.C., one of the Liberal candidates, was already in Cambridge. His fellow Liberal candidate, William Fowler, was in Egypt but on Sunday, 14 March, Josiah received a telegram from him announcing his imminent return. Josiah took the telegram with him to St. Andrew's Street Chapel that evening, and there, 'distributed the news'.

On the following day he,

> went to a political meeting at the Town Hall - one of the best I have ever attended. Shield, the Liberal candidate, spoke well; Neville Goodman was superb; Courtney Kenny[35] and Lawrence[36] of Downing were excellent, and Oscar Browning[37] of King's was very good, although, as he came late, full justice was not done to him . . . The talk went on till 11 o'clock and the Hall was crammed.

16 March:

> Electioneering is going on at a terrific pace. Every vacant wall space is covered with bills of all sorts, and canvassers are out all over the town. This evening I rode over to Chesterton in a fly and heard a speech delivered at the School . . . We then drove to Castle End to another meeting where Shield spoke a few words.

Josiah attended several more Liberal meetings that week and then, on 2 March, wrote,

> All anxiety about Fowler's coming home. We expect him on Wednesday and intend giving him a good reception. The Tories, fearing they may be outdone, have issued bills calling all good Conservatives to go down to the station to meet Mr Marten, their candidate, who is coming down tomorrow.

The Tories duly obeyed the order but, Josiah reported, 'a fine set-out they made of it - a regular rabble'.

The Liberals were, apparently, determined to do better when their candidate arrived, for on 24 March,

> We hear Fowler has arrived in Paris and will be in London tomorrow morning and has ordered a special train which will arrive at Cambridge station at 8 o'clock. The Junior Liberals, about 200 strong, are to act as bodyguard. They have a lot of songs and music and have been practising them up for the occasion.

25 March:

> The train arrived with Fowler, his two sons and Whibley. A tremendous procession met him and escorted him through Barnwell, down Fitzroy

Street, Jesus Lane and to the *Bull*[38] where he spoke a few words. Every-where he was received most enthusiastically - it certainly was a glorious reception.

The election took place on 31 March when Josiah,

> Went to the *Lamb* inn, Guildhall Street, at 8 o'clock and there I kept till 4, except for about 15 minutes for my dinner. Alfred was at the Free Library as Personation Agent. At five I went home, had a warm bath[39] and tea, and then on to the Hill to await the verdict. No. 1 was well attended, all the ten windows filled with occupants, and the Market Place was literally crammed. About 9.15 the Mayor made his appearance but we could not make out the result. Then Ted Turner came and announced the Liberals were in by a 300 or 400 majority. At the nick of time Arthur Chater[40] had a blue light ready on the top of the house, which he lit up, and that announced to the multitude the Liberal victory. Then went up a mighty shout which continued for nearly half an hour.

Student Protest

It is not unknown for present-day undergraduates to voice, on occasion, their disapproval of college food by refusing to eat in Hall. That their predecessors sometimes behaved in similar manner is shown by an entry in Josiah's diary which he made on 26 February 1877,

> Corpus College undergraduates struck dining in Hall tonight and 90 of them went to Peeling's[41].

Today such an action would, probably, merit at least a paragraph in the local newspaper, but in 1877 reporters either were unaware of what had occurred or chose to ignore it.

The Neville Case

On 4 August 1877 Josiah Chater wrote,

> Ted Turner came in and told us all about J. Neville who has been found out at last, having embezzled about £700 of the Improvement Commissioner's money. A sub-committee was formed yesterday to find out the defalcations, and J.H. Turner[42] is appointed accountant. Neville has been forging receipts and they expect to find out much more yet.

The affair caused a great stir in Cambridge and was reported at length in the local newspapers. John Wright Neville, a member of the firm of solicitors, Messrs. Barlow, Palmer & Neville, was initially charged with stealing the relatively small sum of £50 which he had received, by cheque, on behalf of the Cambridge Improvement Commissioners to whom he was acting as Assistant

Clerk. This position he had held since 1875, when the senior member of his firm, Frederick Barlow, the permanent Clerk to the Improvement Board, had, on being elected Mayor, chosen Neville to replace him.

The cheque had been received on 21 July. Neville signed it, stamped it, 'for scavengers' work', then told a clerk to cash it for him. When the man returned with the money, Neville put it in his pocket and then left Cambridge for a two weeks' holiday in Halesowen, Worcestershire. It was while he was in Halesowen that he was arrested.

Josiah reported his arrival in Cambridge, under police escort, on 11 August when he was lodged in the gaol in Gonville Place. Two days later the accused man made his first appearance before the magistrates.

Further thefts and forgeries were then disclosed and Neville was ordered to be remanded in custody, application for bail being refused. By 1 September 1877 he faced six charges: the original larceny of £50, the forgery of a receipt for £100 in August 1876, another for £150 in 1875, larceny by cheque of £100 in 1877, larceny of a cheque for £147 10s. and forgery of a receipt for the same amount. He was committed for trial at the Winter Assizes to be held in Ipswich in November. On 2 October 1877 it was reported to a meeting of the Improvement Board that, since 1867, Neville had been concerned in 13 frauds involving a sum of £3,092, and that it was not unlikely that further offences would be discovered.

At the Assizes Neville pleaded guilty and was sentenced to six years' penal servitude and brought back to the gaol in Cambridge. His was a typical case, the Judge pronounced, of a young man who, because he did not receive a very high salary and yet had certain standards of living to keep up, was tempted to take, for his own use, sums of money which passed through his hands in the course of his work.

On 10 November, soon after the verdict was passed, Josiah recorded,

> J. Neville tried to hang himself this morning and nearly succeeded; he has been removed from the Gaol to London.

Visit of the Prince of Wales
In 1878 the Prince of Wales visited Cambridge to unveil a statue[43] of his late father, who had been Chancellor of the

University.
On 21 January Josiah wrote,

> The town is all agog preparing for the Prince of Wales who came here this evening at 6 o'clock to unveil the statue of the late Prince Consort in the Fitzwilliam Museum. There was a great deal of rowdyism and a bonfire on the Market Hill. Some illuminations about the town. Chater & Osbourn had a star but, with others, it could not be lighted as the wind was so high.

22 January:

> The Prince performed the operation at the Fitzwilliam Museum this morning at 12, and returned to Sandringham at 4 o'clock. There has been a lot of bell ringing &c. all day and, in the evening, a repetition of the fireworks and bonfire on the Hill. Last night it was put out by the Fire Brigade, for which some rogues went and broke some of the windows of Henry Hall, the captain, in his house in Maids Causeway.

Gales and Floods

On the night of Saturday, 2 August 1879, severe storms, accompanied by torrential rain, swept over East Anglia and the Home Counties. Josiah was in St. Leonard's that weekend but, on his return on Tuesday, recorded that many shops and houses in Cambridge had been flooded and that Robert Sayle and William Eaden Lilley were to hold a sale of damaged goods in the old and new Corn Exchanges.[44] Both firms had suffered damage to the amount of several thousand pounds, while W.T. Palmer, a wholesale boot manufacturer of No. 54 Sidney Street, had over 1,000 pairs of boots and shoes ruined by flood water.

The local newspapers carried full reports of the storm, during which over three inches of rain fell in the town in six hours, and of the havoc wrought to property and crops in the surrounding countryside. Trees were uprooted, houses were struck by lightning and set on fire, and numbers of sheep and cattle were killed.

In 1881 a gale caused a great deal of damage in Cambridge. On 14 October Josiah wrote in his diary;

> There was a regular hurricane last night and all day. It blew down the wall at Petersfield along the side of Basham's garden,[45] also part of Downing College wall and the old Botanic Garden wall in Pembroke Scores of trees in St. John's and all along the Backs were blown down, as well as several on Jesus Green, and a woman was killed.

15 October:

> Walked round St. John's to look at the havoc made by the hurricane; it

is frightful. The finest trees, and many of them, are all prostrate. Two
splendid elms, known as 'The Sisters', are lying flat, side by side.

On the following day, with Alex Macintosh, Josiah walked to
the Steam Laundry and,

found two large poplar trees blown on to the roof. The wonder is that
so little damage is done; only a few tiles broken.

The Baking Powder Case
On 8 January 1880 Josiah recorded,

The great baking powder case came on today and the Corporation lost it.

This case, heard at the Cambridge Borough Sessions, aroused
some interest in Cambridge, especially among housewives and
grocers. George and Edward Warren, proprietors of grocery shops
on Market Hill and in Bridge Street, were accused by the
Improvement Commissioners - the Urban Sanitary Authority - of
selling baking powder, manufactured by a Norwich firm, which
on analysis by the Medical Officer of Health, had been found to
consist of 41.5 per cent ground rice, 15.76 per cent alum and
42.74 per cent soda bicarbonate. The alum, it was claimed, was
a harmful ingredient, but this was denied by the Warrens and by
a representative of the Norwich makers who said that the baking
powder had been on the market for nearly 40 years.

The case rested, Josiah reported, on whether the ground rice
and the soda in the baking powder could be considered as foods,
since the powder itself was not a food.[46] A doctor from
Addenbrooke's Hospital, however, told the court that, in his
opinion, the alum would cause bread made with the baking
powder to be deprived of a certain amount of the soluble
phosphate which was necessary to health. Anyone eating such
bread over a long period would, he declared, inevitably suffer
from indigestion. This was denied by other medical experts and
the conviction was finally quashed by the Recorder, who said he
was not satisfied that the baking powder was injurious to
anyone who used it.

The Market Ward Election Petition
Great interest was taken by Cambridge people, about two
weeks later, in the proceedings which began at the Guildhall on
20 January 1880. Under the Corrupt Practices Act of 1872, Mark
Whibley had entered a Petition in the Common Court of the

High Court of Justice against the return of W.B. Redfarn[47] and
Charles Turner as representatives of the Market Ward at the
Borough Election held in November 1879. Mark Whibley had
been a Liberal candidate at this election but, as Josiah had
recorded on 1 November 1879, a day he had spent almost
entirely in Whibley's Committee Room, 'the poor old chap was
defeated by 78 voters'. This defeat, Mark Whibley was convinced,
was due to bribes by his Conservative opponents in the form of
money, beer and entertainment.

Josiah was too busy with his own affairs to attend all the court
proceedings, but he took pains to discover, every day, how
matters were progressing. Thus, on 20 January, he wrote,

> The great conflict began this morning. Cockerell[48] made a grand opening
> speech; even his opponents say it was cleverly done.

On the following day he spent half an hour in court and
reported,

> Whibley's witnesses are being examined; Cockerell seems very well
> satisfied at present.

On 22 January he had 'a good spell in court this morning and
afternoon', but on the following day he was

> very busy, so could not get up, but I hear they are getting on very well.
> Saw Whibley this evening and had a rubber of whist with him. The judge
> has pronounced the case not to be frivolous or vexatious, so Whibley, I
> think, will not have to pay the respondents' costs even if he loses. All
> the witnesses for the Petitioner have been examined and the Counsel has
> made a four-hour speech for the defence and begins examination of the
> witnesses.

Josiah spent most of 24 January at the Guildhall, listening to
the evidence of the witnesses called by Redfarn and Turner, one
of whom, in Josiah's opinion, 'convicted himself in two deliberate
lies'.

> From what I can learn it has been a good day for Whibley; at all events
> his opponents are not quite so elated as they have been.

Amid growing excitement in the town, where memories of
the old days of election bribery and corruption still lingered,
the case continued until 29 January when,

> Judgment was delivered by Mr Prideaux at 4 o'clock. It took him two
> hours and he dismissed the Petition, charging Whibley with costs - a very
> sad end for him and a great disappointment, as well as a surprise to the
> Respondents who are, of course, very jubilant. After tea a grand

torchlight procession came round King's Parade, Benet Street and on to the Market Hill, with Whibley hanging on a gallows, and there they burnt him and had a great bonfire.

The Commissioner, Mr. G.G. Prideaux, in delivering judgment declared, as the *Cambridge Chronicle* reported on 31 January, that Mark Whibley[49] had acted in good faith when he brought the Petition. 'I should be sorry', Prideaux continued, 'for it to be supposed that I had to pass censure upon him except to express regret that, in his party zeal, he should have allowed himself, and those who assisted him, to impute charge against the respondents'.

A large crowd waited outside the Guildhall to learn the result of the case, and when this was known the bells of Great St. Mary's rang out while Mr. Redfarn and Mr. Turner were carried, shoulder-high, to the Junior Conservative Club on Peas Hill. From the balcony of the Club, later in the evening, the two members for Market Ward addressed the mob who had carried the effigy of Whibley - not, as the diary somewhat alarmingly suggests, the unfortunate man himself - through the streets and placed it on the bonfire on Market Hill.

Mark Whibley's costs, as he ruefully told Josiah, amounted to £600. In February a meeting of the Reform Club was held to discuss the raising of a fund to help him to meet this sum which, the meeting felt, had been incurred in the defence of the Liberal cause.

Sankey and Moody in Cambridge

Early in 1882 J.E.K. Studd, an undergraduate of Trinity College, Captain of University Cricket and President of the Cambridge Inter-Collegiate Christian Union,[50] proposed that the American evangelists, Dwight Moody and Ira Sankey, be invited to Cambridge in the following Michaelmas term.

As we have seen (page 157), in the spring of 1875, United Prayer Meetings had been held, not only in the Guildhall and the Y.M.C.A., but also in the Theatre Royal, Barnwell, to prepare for the expected visit of the two evangelists, who were then conducting their successful London mission. These Barnwell meetings proved so popular that it was decided, even though Sankey and Moody did not, in fact, come to Cambridge in 1875, to continue them once a week in the New Street Ragged School.

The Theatre Royal, at that time, was faring badly but it

managed to survive until July 1878, when it was put up for auction. W.T. Mowll of Corpus Christi College, and the friends who had been assisting him in holding the services in New Street, decided to buy the theatre and convert it to a non-sectarian Mission Hall. At the auction sale they limited their bid, at first, to £1,200 but Ion Keith-Faulkner, son of the Earl of Kintore, persuaded them to raise their offer to £1,650. The young men, however, were unsuccessful and the theatre was sold, for a larger sum, to Robert Sayle who intended to turn it into a more respectable, and certainly more profitable, place of entertainment than it had been in its last days. Learning, though, for what purpose Mowll and his friends wanted it he let them have it for £1,200. Keith-Falconer paid him at once, with his own money, then opened a subscription fund to which he, his father and his future father-in-law made substantial donations.

On 18 November 1878 the former theatre was opened as the Barnwell Theatre Mission Hall.[51] Free teas were provided for 600 people, W.R. Mowll presided, three addresses were delivered and 'Miss Chater sang very sweetly', the *Cambridge Chronicle* reported.

Josiah went to the Mission Hall in the evening of the opening day; he was unable to attend in the afternoon because he was busy making arrangement for the funeral of Miss Simpson, which was to take place two days later.

> After tea I went up to the Theatre; they have had a grand opening tea meeting. Fanny[52] came over to sing a solo but I could not stay to hear her. But Agnes heard her; they say she sang very well. The place was crammed.

Sankey and Moody finally arrived in Cambridge in 1881. Their first service, for townspeople, was held on Sunday, 5 November in the Corn Exchange which had been adapted to hold 2,500 people and was nearly full. Josiah tried to get into the hall but was unable to do so because of the crowd, while Agnes and their daughter Olivia, who had gone earlier, came out before the service began, so frightened were they by the crush of people.

The evening meeting, that Sunday, was for members of the University and was, at the outset, an extremely noisy one. Undergraduates rushed into the Corn Exchange and laughed and talked as the hall filled, and sang rowdy songs when an under-graduate choir began to sing hymns. A fire cracker was thrown from outside against a window, but the Proctors and some senior members of the University quickly and quietly ejected some of the most troublesome in the audience before stationing themselves at the back of the hall to keep a watchful eye on things.

Throughout Moody's address he was interrupted by shouts that he could not be heard, by the shuffling and stamping of feet and by loud mimicry of his American accent. But he continued to speak and when, at the end of the meeting, the Vicar of Holy Trinity Church suggested that some of those present might like to remain for prayer over 400 undergraduates stayed and peace was restored. Ernest Chater[53] attended that meeting and reported to his father that it had, on the whole, been a good one.

Subsequent University meetings were held in the Gymnasium in Market Passage and were increasingly well attended. Any rowdyism that occurred was instantly quelled by the singing of Ira Sankey. The town meetings continued twice daily in the Corn Exchange, with additional ones in Holy Trinity Church; they drew immense crowds, not only from Cambridge but from as far afield as Huntingdon, St. Ives and Newmarket.

The campaign ended on 12 November with two meetings for the townspeople and a third for the University.[54] Sankey and Moody then went on to Oxford, where they met the same initial opposition from a section of the undergraduates and the same ultimate triumph.

Josiah Chater seems to have been unimpressed by the evangelists. He went to the afternoon meeting on 6 November and,

> heard one tune, very nicely sung, but when Moody began his address I was too far away to hear.

He does not seem to have tried again to hear him, though he recorded the excitement that the services aroused in the town and the large numbers of people who attended them.

Trams in Cambridge

The entries in Josiah's diary for the years 1879-83, are mainly concerned with his work as secretary of the Cambridge Street Tramways Company.

In the 1870s trams were becoming a popular means of public transport in many English towns,[55] and it was in November 1879 that Cambridge residents learned, from notices in their local newspapers, that two companies[56] were each applying for an Act of Parliament for authority to lay down tramways in the streets of the town.

The first company envisaged a line along Station Road, Hills Road, Regent Street, St. Andrew's Street, Bridge Street, Magdalene Street and Castle Street, to the junction of Huntingdon Road and Mount Pleasant. A second line was proposed from Hills Road, via Hyde Park Corner, to East Road and Newmarket Road, while a third was suggested from Bridge Street to Newmarket Road by way of Jesus Lane. The gauge of these tracks was to be 3 feet 6 inches.

The proposals of the second company were less ambitious. A track was proposed from the station, along Station Road, Hills Road and Regent Street to a terminus in St. Andrew's Street opposite Christ's Lane.[57] Another tramway was suggested which would run from a junction with the first, at Hyde Park Corner, and thence by way of Lensfield Road, Trumpington Street and King's Parade, to Senate House Hill. The gauge of these tracks would be 4 feet 8½ inches.

In January 1879 the first company applied to Parliament for additional provisions to enable Trumpington Street, Trinity Street and St. John's Street to be included in *their* proposed system of tramways. Their rivals took exception to this and stated their objection in a letter to the Cambridge Improvement Board which was read at the Board's meeting in January. 'We are concerned', the letter stated, 'with a tramway embracing Lensfield Road and Trumpington Street, and we have never heard of a case in which opposing promoters were allowed to adopt important parts of a rival scheme to the detriment of their opponents . . .

'We confidentially assert that the introduction of tramways, of whatever gauge, in such narrow streets as Sidney Street, Bridge Street and St. John's Street would be highly detrimental to the trade and comfort of Cambridge as it would almost stop the traffic in these streets where two carriages can hardly pass[58] . . .'

Judging by their letters to the local newspapers, Cambridge people seem generally to have welcomed the proposal to introduce a tramway system which, as an editorial in the *Cambridge Chronicle*[59] pointed out, would be of great benefit to the town especially as it would link the railway station with the town centre. Opinions, however, were divided on the merits of the two companies' proposals. Traders and residents in Bridge Street and Magdalene Street were certainly not in favour of a tramway being laid along such narrow thoroughfares, while the general view was, that wherever the tramways were eventually laid, the narrow gauge proposed by the first company was preferable to the wider one suggested by the second.

The Town Council, meeting on 31 December 1878, decided to offer no objection to either company in principle, although the Improvement Commissioners, on the preceding day, had declared their intention of withholding consent to the construction of any tramway whatsoever.

At a subsequent meeting, however, on 7 January 1897, they voted, by a majority of two, in favour of the second company's scheme, that is for a tramway from the railway station to St. Andrew's Street, opposite Christ's College, and for a branch line from Hyde Park Corner to Senate House Hill. They recommended that the narrow gauge should be used.

Josiah Chater attended this meeting and recorded in his diary the results of the voting. Three weeks later, on 24 January, he wrote,

> Whibley tells me he has proposed me as Secretary to the new Tramway Company. I gave him my name as a guarantee for £25.

11 February:
> Attended Commissioner's Meeting and heard the discussion on the Tramways Bill and reported to Whibley before he started for Penzance.

At this meeting a preference was expressed for a terminus on Market Hill rather than one on Senate House Hill, and some time was spent in discussing the possible danger that might be involved in turning a tram car from Senate House Hill into St. Mary's Street and so on to the Hill. It was also proposed that a provision be made on the Bill to enable the Town Council to purchase the tramways after a period of 21 years.

On the following day Josiah went to London to discover what he could about the company whose scheme had been selected:[60]

> I was anxious to see about this tramway business and make the acquaintance of some of the leading men in it. I called on Mr Pelton, a large grocer in Croydon, and introduced myself to him, and he gave me the address of Mr Hebb, their secretary. Him I found at home, and had a chat with him. He was very pleased I had come and also pleased to hear the news I brought about the meeting of the Commissioners yesterday.

He gave me more information and promised to be down at Cambridge on the 22nd . . . Pelton and Hebb both told me I was to be Secretary if I liked, and that it would be a good thing.

Mr. Hebb came to Cambridge on 22 February, as he had promised, in company with Mr. Floyd, the Croydon Tramways Company's engineer. Josiah met them both at the office of Mark Whibley's grocery shop on Market Hill, then drove with them to Robert Sayle's house on Trumpington Road to get his signature to a petition, already signed by a number of townspeople, that the rival company should not be allowed to operate in Cambridge. He was able to record,

> Mr Hebb said he had to offer me the office of Secretary in Cambridge; he would retain the London business. I agreed to accept it, and he said I might consider my office as the office of the company and put the name up.

In the March and April of 1879 Josiah, either alone or with Mark Whibley, travelled several times to London to attend meetings of the company's directors held in the office of the Liberator Building Society in Bridge Row, whose Chairman, Mr. J.S. Balfour,[61] was also Chairman of the Croydon Tramways Company and of the proposed Cambridge Street Tramways Company. On 11 March he was able to write in his diary that he had

> had a telegram from Hebb to say our opponents' bill has been withdrawn and we are now safe in Parliament.

Objections, however, raised by the Great Eastern Railway Company to the use of the station approach and of Station Road had to be overcome. The matter was discussed at a meeting in London which was finally adjourned so that Josiah could make further enquiries. On 1 April he learned from the Town Clerk of Cambridge that Station Road was a public highway over which the railway company had no control. This information he at once sent to the Tramways Company's solicitors and was able to record, on 5 April, 'the Great Eastern have withdrawn their opposition to trams in Station Road'.

22 April:
> Busy collecting Tramways Guarantee Fund. Expected to go to London to House of Commons but Whibley went instead. The Bill passed the Commons Committee all right, unopposed.

On 27 May Josiah met Mr. Pelton and Mr. Hebb in London and went with them,

> to the House of Lords to a Committee. Lord Redesdale was Chairman. I had to explain to him about the Station Road and where the authority of the Great Eastern began and ended. He said he was satisfied they could claim no jurisdiction.

The Tramways Bill received the royal assent on 21 July, 1897. Four days later Josiah went to a directors' meeting in London:

> I was appointed Local Manager. The salary to be fixed when the Capital is raised, until then to be £25. I was allowed £25 for my past services, exclusive of the cost of journeys &c.

After a week in St. Leonard's where Agnes and the children were on holiday, Josiah returned to Cambridge on 29 July, stopping in London, on the way, to look at another type of tramway system:

> I found the office of the Patent Steam Car Company and, with an order, I went to Stratford Bridge and saw the car in work and rode round the yard upon it several times. It must supersede horse power, I feel sure; it is vastly superior.

The following weekend, again returning from spending two days in St. Leonard's, he went off to Croydon, 'to see how the new tramway there is progressing', before writing in his diary on 8 August,

> Busy all day preparing for the Banquet tomorrow. Have sent out about 120 invitations, but only about 30 accepted.

The banquet was held to celebrate the passing of the Cambridge Street Tramways Act, and was attended by the promoters of the company and by a number of people interested in the undertaking. The dinner was presided over by the Chairman, J.S. Balfour. On 7 August Josiah wrote,

> Went to Whibley's about 8 o'clock and had some breakfast; all the morning spent in preparation for the feast. At one o'clock I went to the Station to meet the Croydon contingency. A dozen came and we took three flys and drove to the Red Lion where we had a jolly lunch, after which held a meeting of Directors in my office. Then, at 6 o'clock, a meeting of the Guarantors at the Lion, and at 7 the dinner, a tip-top affair; 35 there. A first class glee choir and some good speeches.

Among the 'good speeches', reported fully by the local newspapers, was one by the Vice-Chairman of the company, Mark Whibley. In proposing the toast to the University he said that this body could, in a way, take credit for the trams coming to Cambridge. The first suggestion for forming a Tramways Company had come from a prominent member of the Oxford Street Tramways Company when he was visiting an undergraduate friend who was up at Cambridge. The trams, Mark Whibley hoped, would lead to a closer relationship between Town and Gown, for they would be of benefit to both, and he welcomed the fact that the University was greeting the tramways scheme with none of the opposition with which it had faced the coming of the railway to the town in 1845. Mr. Balfour, replying to the toast to the new company which had been proposed by Henry Matthew, said that it had been recommended that the Board of Directors should consist of three London and three Cambridge men; he saw no reason why the company should not be worked, 'on local ground as a local scheme'.

Throughout November 1879 Josiah was much occupied with trammy business. On the 6th of the month he went to London to discuss the offer made by the engineer, J.F. Meston, to construct the tracks in Cambridge for the sum of £20,000. On the 18th he

> had a very heavy day. At one o'clock I met Pelton and Floyd at Cambridge station and went with them over the ground on which we propose to extend our trams.[62] Three times I have been over it today, the 2nd time with Floyd, after lunch at the Lion, the 3rd time to post notices, with bill stickers, after 9 o'clock. Had a capital meeting of directors at my office; Professor Hughes[63] and Thoday,[64] the two new directors, attended. Mr Balfour came and showed us the Prospectus in draft.

This Prospectus was duly printed, and Josiah was able to distribute copies of it at the end of the month. An advertisement which appeared in the *Cambridge Chronicle* on 6 December 1879, gave particulars of the new Cambridge Street Tramways Company, with its capital of £20,000 in 2,000 shares of £10, and set out the advantages which Cambridge would enjoy by having the centre of the town linked with the railway station which more than 2,000 travellers used daily. On 12 December Josiah could record that he had 'had several applications for shares, but no great rush'. On the following day, however, he 'had an application for 25 shares this evening, which makes 38 today'.

In the first two months of 1880 he devoted a considerable amount of time to endeavouring to persuade Cambridge people to take shares in the company. On 16 February for example, he

> spent the greater part of the day canvassing for Shares in the trams.
> After tea I had a fly and drove round East Road, canvassing; did a lot of
> talking and succeeded in getting 2 or 3 applications, but it is very hard
> work.

Two days later he attended a directors' meeting in London:

> We had an important offer from Mr Meston to construct all the works
> of the tramways and pay all past and present expenses for £24,300, and
> a resolution was passed to accept it. We then adjourned to Croydon,
> inspected the trams there and, after a walk, assembled at Mr Balfour's
> for dinner - a very grand affair it was. Eighteen sat down, and it lasted
> 2 hours.

Josiah's next task was to find suitable premises in which the
horses, which were to draw the trams, could be stabled. On 11
March he looked at sites in Bradmore Street and at the yard of
the *Globe* Inn in Hills Road; none of these, however, proved
suitable. Much discussion followed at meetings in London
between Josiah, Mr. Floyd, contractor to the Croydon Tramways Company, and Mr. Meston who had contracted to lay the
track in Cambridge. The son of the last-named came to Cambridge
on 19 April to take measurements of some possible sites in East
Road and elsewhere; again all of these were unsatisfactory.
Meanwhile, earlier in the month, Josiah had gone with William
Eaden Lilley to look at some property which the latter owned
in East Road 'with a view to make the tram stables[65] there'.
On 7 June Mr. Meston saw this property, accompanied Josiah to
Mr. Lilley's house and 'agreed to buy his estate on East Road'.
On Thursday, 8 July 1880, on his return from a few days' stay
in Sussex, Josiah could proudly record in his diary,

> Found the trams construction had begun - lots of men busy picking up
> Hills Road and laying the rails. They began on Thursday afternoon.

He went to London on the following day, returning with the
contract which had been drawn up between the company and
Mr. Meston; this was duly sealed at a directors' meeting in
Cambridge on 10 July. Work on laying the track then proceeded
apace.

Steel girder rails, 5½ inches deep and 5 inches wide, weighing
71 lb. per yard, were attached by double-ended dog spikes to
transverse sleepers, thus maintaining the gauge of four feet
which had finally been selected. Granite setts were laid between

the rails and over a width of six inches on the outer sides, the remainder of the space between the setts and the pavement being covered with tarred macadam.

The tramway system, when completed, ran from the railway station along Station Road and Hills Road to Hyde Park Corner, thence down Regent Street and St. Andrew's Street to the terminus opposite Christ's College. From Hyde Park Corner a track passed along Lensfield Road, Trumpington Street, King's Parade and St. Mary's Street to the terminus on Market Hill. Another run, from the Hyde Park Corner junction, to the junction of East Road and Fitzroy Street by way of Gonville Place.

From the Roman Catholic Church at Hyde Park Corner to the *cul-de-sac* known as Claremont, between No. 53 and No. 55 Hills Road, the track was a double one; elsewhere it was single except at the terminals and at passing places in Station Road, in Gonville Place, at the junction of South Street with East Road, in Regent Street - opposite the *University Arms* Hotel, and in Trumpington Street - opposite Addenbrooke's Hospital.

The thought of a horse-drawn tram negotiating the steep curve from Senate House Hill into St. Mary's Street, by Great St. Mary's Church, alarmed not a few Cambridge residents. Their fears were expressed in letters sent to the Tramways Company and to the local newspapers. Among those sent to the *Cambridge Chronicle* was one from Mr. Gilbert Ainslie, J.P., of Brook House, Trumpington Street. Josiah Chater went to see him and tried to reassure him: 'I told him we would do all we could, but feared it was too late to alter things now'.

Mr. Ainslie's letter was discussed, on 8 September, at a meeting of the Improvement Commissioners which was attended by Josiah, Mr. Floyd and Mr. Meston:

> They are quite satisfied the course is all right and they consider it quite safe and legal. I wrote to Mr Ainslie and told him I would lay any communication he sent me before the Board of Trade.

But Mr. Ainslie was not satisfied and on the following day he went to Josiah's office with, 'a memorial signed by himself and 25 others objecting to the line'. The objectors, however, failed to prevent the line being laid by Great St. Mary's Church.

On Saturday 9 October 1880 the first two tram cars[66] arrived in Cambridge. Josiah, on the Monday, walked to the Great Northern Yard at the station to inspect them, and he pronounced them to be, 'very nice looking vehicles'. On the following day:

> Meston came in this evening to tell me they intend to try the car over
> the line tomorrow at half past five, and they thought I should like to be
> one of the party, which I promised to do.

So, on 13 October,

> I got up at half past five this morning, had a cup of coffee and, at six,
> caught the first car[67] passing the end of Fitzwilliam Street and rode
> down to the Senate House where we unhorsed and tried to push the car
> round the curve into St Mary's Street, but the rails were not permanently
> laid and the gauge was not quite right - the consequence was that it got
> off the rails and we could not manage it and were obliged to put back.
> We then put the horse[68] to and drove round to Hyde Park Corner and
> down to the Post Office, then up to the Station . . . I like the go of the
> car well, it seems to be thoroughly satisfactory, also the rails.

15 October:

> Mr Meston, senior, and Floyd came down today. I met them at Station
> Road coming down in a car, so I joined them and we drove over the
> line. The course at St Mary's is made right and we went round well.
> They are come to arrange for horses and inspection. I had a letter from
> the Board of Trade saying Major James Hutchinson was appointed to
> inspect the line.

On the next day Josiah was busy 'selling advertising spaces in
the tramways' and was able to report, six days later, that he had
sold '57 out of 60'.

The official inspection of the track was carried out on 25
October 1880:

> At 12 o'clock I went to the station with Whibley, and soon after half
> past 12 Major General Hutchinson and Mr Floyd made their appearances
> via the Great Northern. The General, with the Town Clerk, the Clerk to
> the Improvement Commissioners, the Town Surveyor, Mr Whibley and
> Mr Thoday, Directors of the Tramway Company, Josiah Chater,
> Secretary, J.F. Meston, contractor, and several others walked over the
> course to the Post Office, then jumped in a car and rode to Hyde Park
> Corner and walked down Trumpington Street to St Mary's Church. The
> General very carefully inspected the line. We then all rode in the car to
> the Great Northern Hotel and had luncheon. The General left at 2 o'clock
> and we spent the afternoon in the Hotel . . . All passed off very
> satisfactorily and the line is declared open for traffic. Our traffic manager
> Mr Tucker, arrived this morning.

The commencement of the tramway service was fixed for 28
October.[69] Horses arrived in Cambridge on 26 October while
the horsekeeper, Harry Lunn, came on the following day. Josiah
had to spend most of that day printing 500 passenger tickets,[70]

probably with his electric pen, because those which had been
ordered had not been delivered.

On the great day of 28 October he wrote,

> Up at 7 o'clock and went to the Station and rode down in the first car.
> Hubert, Gussy and Vernon got up and they took tickets Nos. 3, 4 and 5
> and had a ride to the station. We have been running all day at 30 minute
> intervals and have carried 636 passengers - very good. Ernest is my Clerk
> and takes to the work well. Mr P. Wallis is appointed our veterinary
> surgeon to examine our horses. Had a delivery of 11 horses this evening.
> I went to the stables and inspected them.

29 October:
> Another good day - took 801 passengers. Had another car on for 2 or 3
> hours and tried 2 or 3 new horses. P. Wallis examined them all; he
> rejected one. We get rare crowds up and down after tea; have secured
> some decent drivers.

On the following day two cars were run every quarter of an
hour from Christ's College and from the Station, until 10 o'clock
at night; 1,750 passengers travelled in them and between £14 and
£15 were taken in fares.

In the first week of November many of the 14 horses were
taken ill, as Josiah recorded, 'with sore throats, influenza, bad
colds and fever feet', but the trams managed to keep running.
Two large double-deck cars were delivered on 4 November, each
capable of carrying 16 outside and 16 inside passengers.[71]   On
5 November Josiah recorded his fears that fireworks might be
thrown in the streets and so cause the tram horses to bolt; he
was able to write at the end of the day, however, 'all went off
quietly and well'.

One of the large cars was put on the track on the evening of
6 November

> causing much excitement to the public who filled it every time. Horses
> bad, though - obliged to hire four.

On 12 November a public meeting was held in the *Lion* Hotel
to promote the sale of shares in the Tramways Company, and at
the end of the month Josiah was able to report,

> Tramways shares are selling wonderfully well. The list for London is
> closed on Saturday, and tomorrow for the county.

On 3 December:
> Have had over 1,100 tram shares sold in 3 weeks - have got rid of a lot in
> Cambridge and am to have 2s. 6d. a share on all I dispose of.

Troubles in the Company

Josiah was finding, however, that the office of local secretary of the Tramways Company was not without its share of worry and anxiety. At more than one meeting in London J.S. Balfour - the *Great Mogul* as Josiah often called him - and J.F. Meston the contractor, had complained of the running of the company's affairs in Cambridge. Balfour, especially, considered that the opening of the tramway to the public should have been delayed for a while, although Meston himself had insisted that it was imperative the service should start on 28 October.

On 7 December 1880 Meston proposed, at a director's meeting in London, that he should take over the running of the Cambridge trams for a period of 12 months, guaranteeing five per cent to the shareholders. At a further meeting on 20 December Josiah reported,

> Balfour presented a letter from Professor Hughes objecting to any offer of Meston's to take the management of the Company for 12 months. He also read an offer of Meston's to work the line for 12 months: he would pay all and keep on the staff except the secretary. All the four directors then withdrew leaving them to discuss the matter . . . I met Whibley for the 9.30 train and on our way down he told me they had a very stormy meeting and got pretty well to high words. The upshot was that Whibley was empowered to request me to write a letter tending my resignation to the company and asking for a sum of money as compensation, because Balfour was determined he must have an office in London.

This was a bitter pill for Josiah to swallow, and it was made no sweeter by the knowledge that his old friend, Mark Whibley, agreed with Balfour in thinking the secretaryship should be transferred to a London man. Josiah continued, nevertheless, to work extremely hard over the company's affairs, assisted by his son Ernest. The Christmas of 1880 was especially busy; 2,150 passengers travelled on the trams on Christmas Eve and 2,113 on 27 December. On Christmas Day the trams ran until midday and Josiah, although he and Agnes entertained 21 of their family and friends to dinner at half past four, put in seven hours of work in his office, on tramway business.

On 11 January 1881, after a directors' meeting in London, Josiah handed in his letter of resignation as local secretary. He travelled home with Mark Whibley and Francis Thoday who told him that Balfour was considering offering him £100 in compensation, but, 'if I would not accept it he would propose my salary should be £20 a year'. The proposal of so low a salary,

Balfour doubtless thought, would force Josiah to accept compensation and retire.

Josiah was not alone in finding the London directors difficult men to deal with. At a meeting in Cambridge on 5 February 1881, at which Mark Whibley, who by then had had a change of opinion, proposed that Josiah be retained as local secretary at a salary of £80, the Cambridge traffic manager, Mr. Tucker, was, Josiah reported, 'regularly set upon', while 'the engineer got it about the points'. These had, apparently, been giving trouble for on 6 February the diary recorded:

> Floyd the engineer, and his man Hunt, have been down and brought a driver from London to try the points, and when I left them they had been successfully round St. Mary's, but on their return, Tucker tells me, this man missed one set of points and ran off the track to another, so the London man went home without his feathers.

In the spring of 1881 a letter written by Josiah's barrister friend, Edward Turner, and printed in the *Cambridge Chronicle,* caused no little stir in the town, because it criticised the Tramways Company's financial affairs. The letter expressed the writer's misgivings of the way in which the company had, so far, been conducted, and referred to the 'shroud of mystery encircling everything that has hitherto been done'. Edward Turner then asked for replies to three questions[72] relating to money paid to the company's directors.

Josiah first knew of this letter on 14 March when a copy of the *Cambridge Chronicle* was sent to him in Hastings, where he was staying for a few days. Returning to Cambridge on the following day he wrote,

> The town seems quite in a fever about Ted Turner's letter and all manner of questions are being asked, which I studiously avoid answering as I do not mean to be mixed up in the affair.

On 21 March Mark Whibley told him that he had written 'a strong letter to Balfour, telling him that we must have a meeting and the matter must be met'. Three days later Josiah went to London and met 'the Great Mogul', whom he found in conference with his solicitor. It was decided,

> to have a meeting; they fixed it for 8 April. They acknowledged that a mistake had been made in not bringing the remuneration of the Directors and the Secretary before the shareholders.

Edward Turner attended the meeting in Cambridge on 8 April and repeated the questions he had asked in his letter. After a discussion which lasted for two hours,

> The Directors gave up their 100 guineas and their £500. Then Mr Ginn
> proposed that the remuneration of the Directors should be £500 up to
> 31 December, which was carried. Then came the Secretary's remuner-
> ation. Ted Turner proposed that I should have £150 a year, which I
> declined and left myself in the Directors' hands. The Chairman proposed
> that I be paid £100 a year, which I accepted and, on a vote of thanks
> to the Chairman, the meeting ended . . . It is a very nasty affair which
> must have come out some time or other, and so it is now cleared up, and
> they all agreed that we must go on more amicably in future.

After this, relations between Balfour and Josiah seem to have
improved. At a meeting in Cambridge on 23 April Balfour
complimented Josiah on his keeping of the Company's books; he
then expressed his hope that J.F. Meston would,

> see his way to taking the management of the line for 12 months,
> guaranteeing the Company 5% and promising to keep the Secretary, his
> staff and office. He appealed to me if I thought the shareholders would
> agree to such an arrangement and I said I believed the Cambridge share-
> holders would be quite willing . . . Balfour stated his wish and intention
> to resign unless such an arrangement could be made.

On 10 May 1881, after attending yet another meeting in
London, Josiah wrote,

> An offer was received by the Chairman from Mr Meston to take over and
> work the line of trams for 3 years, paying 5% per annum to shareholders,
> which was accepted. He undertakes none of the staff but the secretary
> and he agrees to pay him £100 a year - a very different arrangement to
> the last offer. he made in December - that he would take all the staff
> except the secretary. I was instructed to ask Mr Ginn to draw up the
> contract at once. The Chairman was most complimentary to me.

So the day was one of triumph for Josiah and his feeling of
elation was increased, on the following day, by the birth of his
last child, Bertram, whose name, the diary records, came to be
selected because of Josiah's overwhelming preoccupation at that
time.

> After tea we all discussed, of course, what his name should be. I said I
> had fixed on one and, after a little pause, told them 'Trams!' 'Oh, the
> children exclaimed, that *is* funny'. 'Well, I said, to effect a compromise
> I don't mind adding to it and making it Bertram!' And that seemed
> to suit.

An Extraordinary General Meeting of the Tramways Company
was held in the Y.M.C.A. rooms in Cambridge on 18 June 1881
to adopt a resolution to confirm the contract between the

company and J.F. Meston. Some objections were raised, but after Mr. Balfour pointed out that, under existing arrangements, it would not be possible to pay the shareholders five per cent for the current half-year, the resolution was carried. Under the terms of the contract Josiah had to give notice to the traffic manager, who was replaced by a man from London, while,

> three of the conductors[73] were given notice to quit on Staurday night. Of course, it has caused quite a stir among the staff.

The company's books were moved, for the period during which Meston's contract lasted, to the tram depot on East Road, leaving Josiah's office in Alexandra Street 'very quiet and peaceful'.

Trouble with the Trams

During all this time the day-to-day running of the trams had not proceeded without incident. The number of passengers had increased - 3,087 were carried on 4 June 1881, for example - but the driver and conductor of car No. 1 had been charged, by the local officer of the Royal Society for the Prevention of Cruelty to Animals, with ill-treating one of the horses on 4 May 1881, the day of the Two Thousand Guineas race at Newmarket.

The case was first heard on 13 May. Evidence was given that the tram car, drawn by a seven-year-old mare, had gone along Station Road to the railway station with a load of 42 passengers and had returned, drawn by the same mare, carrying over 30 people. The weight hauled, it was said, amounted to four tons. Josiah attended the hearing:

> I saw the horse at 8 o'clock when she came off her spell of duty, and gave evidence of her not being in any way distressed by her work. After 20 minutes' consideration the magistrates adjourned the case for a fortnight to get more scientific evidence.

At the adjourned hearing the case was withdrawn.

The year 1882, so far as the trams were concerned, was a less anxious one for Josiah than the preceding one had been. Meetings in London and Cambridge passed off pleasantly and it was not until 26 December that he had the unwelcome experience of being served, as secretary of the Tramways Company, with a summons arising from the bad condition of the roads along which the trams ran. On 29 December he wrote,

> At eleven o'clock I attended at the Town Hall before the magistrates to answer a summons for not keeping the roads in repair where the trams

ran. Mr Ginn appeared for the company and got the case adjourned for a fortnight.

The case, brought by the Improvement Commissioners, was heard on 23 January 1883. Josiah and J.F. Meston attended the court and heard witnesses' reports of the bad state of the roads and were reminded, by the prosecution, of the request made by the Tramways Company's solicitor, on 29 December 1882, for an adjournment of the hearing. This request had been granted in view of the company's plan that they had been unable to get the necessary materials for the repair of the roads. They had been granted until 12 January to complete the work, but the same excuse had then been made - that bad weather was holding up delivery of granite. Now they were asking whether sand and gravel might not be used, temporarily, until the granite arrived. However, as Josiah recorded,

> The magistrates pronounced judgement against the Company and fined them £1 a day for 30 days.

Two days later he attended the County Court,

> to hear the case Bolton v. the Tramways Company for causing the death of his horse. He claims £40 damages. The case lasted 3 hours and the Judge condemned the Company in damages - £20 - and all expenses.

The accident to the horse had occurred on 18 October 1882. A witness at the hearing said that he had noticed Thomas Bolton's[74] cart in Station Road, near the junction with Hills Road, where it was being loaded with rubble by a young boy. The cart was drawn up askew between the gutter and the tram line, the horse's head being turned towards Hills Road. A tram had come, 'rather fast', from the station, and although the boy had shouted to the driver and had tried to move the horse and cart, he was unable to prevent the tram, to which no brake was applied, from striking the animal, causing it to be thrown against the fence of a timber yard.

For the Tramways Company it was argued that the horse and cart were stationed in a dangerous position, and that they were in the charge of only one person, a mere lad. But negligence on the part of the tram driver was proved and Thomas Bolton was awarded damages and costs, although the sum of £40, which he claimed was the value of the horse, was reduced by half.

The Last Years of the Trams
    Until the last day of the Cambridge Street Tramways
Company's existence the secretaryship remained in the Chater
family. In 1895 Josiah's sons, Augustine and Vernon, qualified
as chartered accountants and joined their father in the firm
which, from then on, was known as J. Chater & Sons. Vernon
subsequently left Cambridge,[75] but Augustine remained, to be
joined later by his brothers Leonard[76] and Bertram,[77] and
became the company's secretary from 1898.
    Six years before, in 1892, the Corporation, subject to an
annual payment by the company of £325, had taken over the
Tramways Company's liability to repair the roads where the
tramlines were laid. At the end of 1913, three years after
Josiah's death, because the company had fallen into arrears
with this payment, the Mayor and Corporation presented a
petition for the company to be wound up. This was granted
by Mr. Justice Astbury, in the Chancery Division of the High
Court, on 6 January 1914 when a compulsory winding-up order
was made.
    In his lifetime Josiah saw the Tramways Company flourish
and decline. In its early years, with the hotel buses its only
rivals, it had operated successfully, but in 1896 the newly-formed
Cambridge Omnibus Company announced that, from 29 April,
it would operate a horse-drawn omnibus[78] service in the town.
The Tramways Company retaliated by purchasing four omnibuses[79] of its own, two of which they put on to the roads[80] on
1 February, some three months before the appearance of those
of its rivals. The competition, however, had an adverse effect on
both companies. Towards the end of 1900 the Tramways Company agreed to withdraw their vehicles from the routes covered
by the Omnibus Company, while the latter promised to cease
their service to the railway station. The Tramways Company
sold their omnibuses at a loss of nearly £900; the rival company
managed to survive until September 1902.
    Proposals in 1899 and in 1904 to electrify the tramway
system[81] came to nothing, to the relief of many Cambridge
people and, especially, to that of Professor George Darwin of
Newnham Grange.[82] In 1904, learning that it had been proposed
that electric trams should run along Silver Street and the Backs
of the colleges in Queen's Road, he presented to the Mayor and

Corporation a protest memorial which had been signed by many leading Cambridge residents.

On Saturday 15 April 1905 a rival to the trams appeared in the form of a light blue motor omnibus, owned by the Cambridge University and Town Motor Omnibus Company. This was quickly followed, on the same day, by a dark blue vehicle owned by the Cambridge Motor Omnibus Company. Both plied between Market Hill and the railway station. The dark blue omnibus had arrived on the Thursday night and made a trial run; its somewhat shabby appearance showed, as the *Cambridge Express*[83] pointed out, that Cambridge streets were by no means the first that it had travelled along. The light blue vehicle was 'a little more modern'.

On their first day of public service the vehicles were filled on each journey; on 17 April the light blue one, which had knocked down a lamp post on its first day, carried 1,800 passengers, but its rival was off the road for two hours for repair. More vehicles, of both colours, eventually arrived to alarm the tram horses, but the light blue company did not survive for more than six months. In 1906 the licences of the other company were withdrawn owing to the number of accidents in which the double-decked vehicles had been involved.

So the trams remained supreme until, on 19 August 1907, a fleet of four motor omnibuses, owned by J.B. Walford's Ortona Company,[84] appeared on the streets, having ferried passengers to and from the Mammoth Show on 1 August. These vehicles were so safely and efficiently run that more and more passengers ventured on them and by 1912 the trams were only just managing to pay their way. In 1914 they ceased to run.

Their last journeys were made on 18 February; two days later the Tramways Company's eight cars[85] were sold by auction, at prices ranging from £7 15s. to £15 each. At the same sale Blossom, Corporal, Punch, Daisy and 20 more horses and mares, all of them named in the sale catalogue, were auctioned along with sets of harness and various items of equipment. Josiah Chater, had he been alive, would doubtless have been sad to see the end of the company even though, in its first years, it had caused him much anxiety and had led to a temporary coolness in his friendship with Mark Whibley.

For cheap transport to and from the railway station, and for intermediate journeys along their limited routes near the town centre, the trams had their uses; but they were very slow. It was not unknown for small boys to place pistol caps on the rails, then watch with glee as the startled horse covered the next yard or so at more than its usual leisurely pace. So slow were they, in fact, that they were responsible for the Cambridge saying, 'If you are in a hurry, walk; if not, take a tram'.

It would have been fitting if the final entry in Josiah Chater's diary on 3 May 1883 had referred to the tramways. It consists, however, of three words: 'Professor Liveing called' - a visit made in connection with Josiah's latest business activity, the secretary-ship of the Cambridge Improved Industrial Dwellings Company. The last reference to the trams had been made in mid-April 1883 and was almost prophetic in its gloom; indeed, after reading the entry, it is difficult to see how the Tramways Company managed to survive for another 30 years.

Many of the horses were ill that April, and although the traffic manager had bought two new ones in order to give the others a rest, Josiah feared, 'they have come too late'. Visiting the stables on 15 April he found the sick animals 'looking very bad'. Two days later he went to London to meet J.F. Meston who

> wanted to know about selling his shares and debentures. I told him it was a bad time - the Company was under a cloud; the horses were in a most deplorable state; the roads were out of repair and everything looked black. I did not think the shares would fetch £10, but I would do my best.

These last five words are characteristic of their writer. In his long and varied business career, in his religious observances and in his family life Josiah Chater, as his diary shows, was a man who strove at all times to do his best in whatever he undertook.

NOTES TO PART V

1. Peter Wallwork Latham, M.D., Downing Professor of Medicine.

2. He was then auditing the accounts of Alexander Macintosh's iron-mongery and ironfounding business.

3. By then the sisters had a house in St. Leonard's.

4. It was customary for low-lying land in Cambridge to be flooded artificially, in severe frosts, so that skating could take place. The unemployed were able to earn a few pence by sweeping the ice clear of snow or by hiring out chairs to support inexperienced skaters.

5.   Founded by James Drake Digby, Neville Goodman and others. The first meeting was held in the Cambridge Guildhall on 1 February 1879.

6.   George Smart of Welney, Hunts., said to have acquired his nickname because he was a good swimmer. He was professional champion (distance 1½ miles) in 1879, 1881 and 1887.

7.   29 October 1881.

8.   Josiah recorded in his diary on 15 September 1880 that he had visited the Institute of Chartered Accountants in Throgmorton Street, London, to leave his application for admission to the Institute. He was admitted 1 December 1880. The Institute of Accountants, formed in London in 1870, did not receive a royal charter until 11 May 1880, when all existing accountants' societies and institutes were incorporated into the Institute of Chartered Accountants of England and Wales. No qualifying examination was required at the time of its foundation.

9.   Founded in 1816.

10.   Among them were old-established drapers, brewers, builders, tobacconists and ironmongers.

11.   See later for Josiah's connection with the trams in Cambridge.

12.   Samuel Reuben Ginn, solicitor of 64 St. Andrew's Street.

13.   Josiah gave up the office soon afterwards, because it was too small, and moved to 5 Alexandra Street which was occupied by J. Chater & Sons until the mid-1960s. Mr. R. Chater Blows, Josiah's grandson, now carries on the work of the firm at 24 Bateman Street. Nos. 2 and 5 Alexandra Street, with the adjoining property, were demolished in 1972.

14.   Part of this was occupied by the Reform Club.

15.   The documents of the company are now in the Public Record Office: Ref. B.T. 31/3282/11823. Three MS. sheets of accounts, 1879-91, with a list of the directors, are in the Reference Library at the Cambridge Guildhall.

16.   Until this laundry opened, and for some years afterwards, undergraduates' linen and that of many Cambridge residents was washed by private laundresses who worked in their own homes. Laundry work had also been done, since 1842, at the Cambridge Female Refuge, founded in 1838, 'to afford to females who have been leading a sinful course of life, and express a desire of returning to the path of virtue, a temporary refuge where they may be provided with proper instruction . . . until an opportunity offer of restoring them to their friends, transferring them to a penitentiary or placing them in some situation where they may procure for themselves an honest livelihood'. 1st *Annual Report* of the Refuge (1839).

        The Cambridge Steam Laundry, now a member of a group, continues under the name of the Cambridge Laundry and Cleaners Ltd. The works are still in Cherryhinton Road.

17. Now Homerton College for the training of women teachers. Cavendish College was founded in Hills Road, in 1876, by the County College Association to provide facilities for passing through the University course and obtaining degrees at a moderate cost and at the earliest practicable age. It also provided training for intending schoolmasters. The College closed in 1891 and was purchased in 1894 by the Congregational Board of Education for occupation as a teachers' training college by Homerton College London, which had been bought by the Board in 1850. This college dates to the foundation in 1659 of the King's Head Society, formed to aid Congregational churches. In 1723 the Society amalgamated with the Congregational Fund Board and a college for training ministers and schoolmasters was established at the Plasterers' Hall, London in 1730. This moved to Mile End in 1753 and to Homerton in 1769.

18. A.J. Tillyard, M.A., Mayor of Cambridge 1899-1900.

19. In 1892 Cambridge was the only exchange of the company in the country. It was taken over by the Post Office in 1912.

20. George Downing Liveing, Professor of Chemistry.

21. C.J. Clay, University Printer.

22. A draper of 121-4 Fitzroy Street.

23. A society of the same name had been founded in Cambridge, in 1819, to deal with the vagrancy problem arising from the unemployment and high prices which followed the Napoleonic Wars. The object of this society, which lapsed by 1838, was to drive from the town or to arrest, with the help of the parish constables and a special officer of the society, the beggars who loitered about the streets and who often stole from houses and college rooms. The new society was more humane in that it sought to provide food and shelter for those seeking work, and so spare them the need to apply for assistance at the workhouse. In 1879 the society was re-constituted as the Cambridge Charity Organization Society, though it retained the name Anti-Mendicity Society as a sub-title until 1894. In 1915 the Charity Organization Society became the Central Aid Society.

24. A third house was added later and the property was managed by the Barnwell Coffee House Committee as the *Barnwell Coffee Palace*. In 1905 it was re-named the *White Ribbon Temperance* Hotel, and run by the British Women's Temperance Association. Since 1932 it has been a men's hostel run by the Salvation Army.

25. Now demolished.

26. None of these now exist.

27. See Pt. IV, n. 77.

28. After the secession of member from Hussey's Great Meeting in 1696 (see Pt.I, p.10), Presbyterians worshipped in Green Street until 1769 when their chapel closed. It re-opened in 1722 only to be closed again in 1778 because of the unorthodox teaching of the

minister, John Robotham. The small congregation that remained
went to other Nonconformist churches. The Presbyterian chapel was
then used by the Congregationalists, 1781-1819, when they moved
to a building on the opposite side of Green Street. Their vacated
premises were leased for a few years to a group of Strict Baptists
who moved in 1826 to their new Eden Chapel in Fitzroy Street. The
old chapel was demolished soon afterwards and the narrow end of
Green Street on which it fronted was widened. The Congregationalists'
chapel on the other side of the road, now part of W. Eaden Lilley
& Co's premises, was taken over in 1829 by the Wesleyan Methodists,
who moved to Hobson Street in 1850.

29.   Dr. William Robertson, minister of a church in Irvine, Scotland. He
       came often to preach in Cambridge where his sermons, at the services
       in the Guildhall, were extremely popular.

30.   Originally built and occupied by Julius Skrine, banker, this was the
       first house erected in the New Town area of Cambridge. According
       to Josiah's diary Dr. Robertson wanted to live in the house.

31.   This had a frontage of 85 ft. on to Hills Road.

32.   To the design of A.W. Pugin. On the erection of the present Roman
       Catholic church it was moved to St. Ives, Hunts. Until St. Andrew's
       Church was built the only permanent post-Reformation Mass centre
       in Cambridgeshire was at Sawston Hall, home of the Huddleston
       family. From 1828 attempts were made to establish a permanent
       chapel in Cambridge and in 1841 Rev. E. Shanley was sent to
       minister to the Irish colony settled in Barnwell. He raised a sum of
       money and, with help from Major Huddleston of Sawston, the site in
       Union Road was secured. In 1865 Josiah went with a friend to
       St. Andrew's Church; despite his Baptist principles he recorded that
       he, 'found the service very beautiful indeed'.
            To St. Andrew's had come as Rector, in 1843, the Rev. (later
       Canon) Thomas Quinlivan, who eventually built a school and school-
       house in Union Road. The school was held at first in a cottage near
       the church; then the new building, now the oldest part of St. Alban's
       (formerly St. Andrew's) R.C. School in Union Road, was opened in
       1868.
            As time passed the need for a larger church became apparent, but
       the Wentworth family, when approached, refused to sell any part of
       the Lensfield Estate for Roman Catholic use. In 1879, however,
       Henry Matthew's widow gave the Rev. T. Quinlivan a lien on the
       estate, and in May 1880 it was conveyed to him for the sum of
       £6,100. The property was mortgaged in the December of that year
       to secure £6,600 11s. 4d., the sum of £3,000 being guaranteed by the
       Duke of Norfolk.
            The new Catholic Church was begun in 1885 and consecrated on
       8 October 1890. Its architects were Messrs. Dunn & Hansom of
       Newcastle; its builders Messrs. Ratte & Kett of Cambridge. The cost
       was defrayed by Mrs. Yoland Lyne-Stephens. Canon (later Monsignor)
       Christopher Scott, who succeeded the Rev. T. Quinlivan at

St. Andrew's in 1883, occupied Lensfield House until it was demolished to make way for the new church, of which he remained Rector until his death in 1922.

33. Then being used by the Good Templars Temperance Society and others. In 1884 it was bought by Mrs. Sidgwick, then Bursar and later Principal of Newnham College, and her sister in memory of their brother, Francis Maitland Balfour, Professor of Animal Morphology, who had been killed in a climbing accident in Switzerland in 1882. The sisters gave the old chapel to Newnham College for use as the Balfour Laboratory by women students. Later re-sold to the University, it is now occupied by the University Music School.

34. A cottage to the rear of the Downing Street site was also purchased and used, after renovation, for the Church officer. This cottage stood on the site on which the Rev. Joseph Hussey had held the first Presbyterian services in the 17th century.

35. Courtney Stanhope Kenny, Fellow of Downing College, later Reader in English Law.

36. Thomas Joseph Lawrence, born 1849 in Chesterton, Cambridge, educated at the Perse School. Entered Downing College 1868; later elected as Honorary Fellow of the College. Ordained 1874; Warden of Cavendish College, Cambridge 1876-7. Professor of International Law at Chicago 1892-3. Subsequently assistant chaplain at the Chapel Royal, London and Canon of Salisbury Cathedral. Died 1919.

37. Author and historian. Born 1839; died in Rome 1923. Fellow of King's College, Cambridge. Taught at Eton 1860-75. Subsequently lecturer in History at King's College and University Reader in History. Helped to establish the Teachers' Training College in Cambridge of which he was Principal 1891-1901. 'In Cambridge he was a notable figure with his short corpulent frame, the great head, indrawn mouth, the rolling gait . . . the irresistible urge to confide in any listener'. *Cambridge Daily News* (8 Oct. 1923).

38. Now part of St. Catherine's College. The facade remains unaltered but the main part of the building has been rebuilt.

39. He may have taken this in his 'new Patent shower bath' which, he recorded in his diary, he used for the first time on 6 July 1878.

40. Josiah's nephew, son of the late Jabez Chater.

41. John Peeling was landlord of the *Bath* Hotel in Benet Street.

42. Ted Turner's father, Postmaster of Cambridge.

43. The statue, by Foley, was placed in the entrance hall of the Fitzwilliam Museum in 1877. Its cost - £1,200 with an additional £400 for the plinth - was met by a subscription fund started soon after the Prince Consort's death.

44. The old Corn Exchange on St. Andrew's Hill became an arcade of shops until c.1895 when, for a brief period, it was in use as the Arcadia Entertainment Hall. It later became a garage until its demolition in 1951.

45. Mr. Basham's house, then called The Maples and later Petersfield Lodge, stood near the corner of Mill Road and East Road. The house was later used as the Post Office Sorting Office until replaced by the present Sorting Office on the same site.

46. The Sale of Foods and Drugs Act 1875 had defined food as 'every article used for food and drink by man, other than drugs or water'. Many bakers, at that time, added alum to flour in order to make whiter bread, a practice condemned by physicians and chemists. Soon after the passing of the Food Act numerous prosecutions led to the abandonment of the practice. Many baking powders, however, still contained alum and it was thought that, as the powder was used in the preparation of food, the makers and sellers of it could be proceeded against under the Food Act. The high court, however, held that baking powder was not in itself a food and its sale, even if it contained alum, was not an offence. This anomaly was removed by a later Food Act in 1899.

47. Artist and founder, 1875, of the Bijou Amateur Dramatic Club in Cambridge. In 1882 he bought St. Andrew's Hall, St. Andrew's Street, which was then being used as a skating rink, and some time later adapted it for use as a theatre which he named the Theatre Royal. In 1894 the University relinquished its right to licence theatres and plays; Redfarn then pulled down St. Andrew's Hall and built on its site the New Theatre which opened in January 1896. The theatre closed in 1956 and was demolished in 1961.

48. William Cockerell, barrister and Liberal. He was several times councillor for East Barnwell Ward of Cambridge and was later elected as alderman of the Borough.

49. Mark Whibley had made it clear from the outset that, if he won his case, he did not intend to seek re-election. He did, however, represent East Barnwell Ward from 1884 to 1892. The number of Wards was then increased from five to ten and East Barnwell, under that name, ceased to exist.

50. Founded 1876.

51. This closed in 1920 and was then used, 1921-5, by the King's College Club for Boys. It was re-opened in 1926 by Terence Gray as the Festival Theatre but, for financial reasons, had to close in 1934, after which it was occasionally used by various local dramatic societies. The building, which dates from 1816, is now used by the Cambridge Arts Theatre as a wardrobe and workshop.

52. Fanny Chater, Josiah's half-sister.

53. He had qualified for entrance to the University by passing the previous Examination in June 1882.

54. Sankey and Moody's mission had a profound effect on the growth of Ridley Hall which had been opened, in the previous year, by Evangelical members of the Church of England to provide a residential course in theology for graduates who preferred to remain

in Cambridge rather than to go to Theological Colleges elsewhere. In October 1882 the Hall had only 14 members; as a result of the American evangelists visit applications from intending students greatly increased.

55. The first tramways in Great Britain (e.g. at Birkenhead, 1860 and London 1861) were promoted by private enterprise under powers conferred by private Acts of Parliament. In 1870 a general Tramways Act enabled promoters, after obtaining the sanction of the local authority concerned, to apply to the Board of Trade for a provisional order, which then went to Parliament for confirmation.

56. Both called themselves the Cambridge Street Tramways Company.

57. Until the major alterations were made to the east side of St. Andrew's Street in the 1950s this lane, now closed, ran beside Christ's College and gave access to Drummer Street and Christ's Pieces.

58. *Cambridge Chronicle* 11 January 1879.

59. 3 November 1879. The same article prophesied the approaching end of 'those locomotive street cells called omnibuses, with their cramped area, suffocating atmosphere and peculiar odour' - an allusion to the small box-like omnibuses owned by the chief hotels in Cambridge. They carried hotel visitors to and from the railway station.

60. The company chosen to lay the tramways in Cambridge was also responsible for those being laid in Croydon.

61. Jabez Spencer Balfour, principal promoter of the Liberator group of companies which claimed to be building societies but which, contrary to the rule of such societies, engaged in speculative business. Their affairs were so interwoven that when one failed the rest were bound to collapse, as happened in 1892 when their liabilities were over £8,000,000. Balfour fled to Buenos Aires to avoid arrest but was sent back to England in 1895 and sentenced to 14 years' penal servitude for conspiracy and fraud. He was released in 1906. He had been Liberal M.P. for Tamworth 1880-8 and of Burnley 1889-93. In 1883 he was elected the first Mayor of Croydon.

62. The Company had advertised its intention of applying for a provisional order to construct additional tramways: From Hyde Park Corner to the junction of East Road and Newmarket Road with a branch from Newmarket Road to pass along Maids Causeway, Fair Street, Emmanuel Road and thence by way of Emmanuel Street to the line in St. Andrew's Street. 2. From Senate House Hill into St. Mary's Street to terminate in line with the east end of Great St. Mary's Church. The second proposal was approved in 1880 but the Master of Emmanuel College strongly opposed the laying of a track in Emmanuel Street. Authorisation was given for the extension of the line from Hyde Park Corner to the junction of East Road and Newmarket Road but, in the end, the line never went beyond the corner of East Road and Fitzroy Street.

63. Woodwardian Professor of Geology.

64. Francis Thoday, builder.

65. The tram depot, to hold eight cars, with stables at the rear for 30 horses, was begun in October 1880 between Nos. 182 and 183 East Road. A house for the traffic manager adjoined. At the second half-yearly meeting of the company held on 3 March 1881 the buildings were reported to be almost completed. The trams and horses, meanwhile, may have been kept in the Great Northern yard at the railway station.

66. Car No. 1 was a double-deck car seating 18 passengers inside and 23 outside. Car No. 2 was originally a single-deck but was converted later to a double-deck. The number of tram cars owned by the Street Tramways Co. never exceeded eight; all were built by the Starbeck Car & Wagon Co. of Birkenhead.

67. The car used in this trial run was probably No. 2, then a single-deck vehicle.

68. An attempt to use two horses to draw a car proved unsuccessful.

69. The service between the station and Christ's College began on this day; that from Hyde Park Corner to Market Hill did not start until December. The track in East Road was completed on 22 December 1880, but faults in its construction caused the opening of the line to the public to be delayed until February 1881. It was reported at a meeting of directors on 3 March 1881 that traffic on the Market Hill to East Road route had been heavier, in the preceding week, than that between Christ's College and the station. The tram service gradually improved until, by 1908, the service from Christ's College to the station operated every 15 minutes from 8.0 a.m. to 9.0 a.m. and every 5 minutes from 9.5 a.m. to 9.30 p.m. On the Market Hill to East Road route there was a 20-minute service throughout the life of the Street Tramways Company.

70. The fare on both routes was 2d. until 1896 when that to the station was reduced to 1d. Books of tickets could be obtained at a small discount. Season tickets were issued at 6s. for 1 month, 15s. for 3 months, £1 18s. for 6 months and £2 10s. for 1 year. When the trams began to operate, the cab fare, for one passenger, from the station to any part of the town on the south and east sides of the river and up to the Church of St. Andrew the Less in Newmarket Road, was 1s. and each additional passenger was charged 6d.

71. These are the figures given by Josiah in his diary. Double-deck cars seated 18 passengers inside and 22 to 24 outside.

72. These were:- 1. Had the contract for laying the track and supplying the plant contained a stipulation that the contractor was to pay to the directors 100 guineas or any other sum? 2. Had the contract been drawn up privately by solicitors in London or had the solicitors named in the company's prospectus been consulted? 3. Had any money or shares been allotted to certain directors as 'promotion

money' or for guaranteeing the preliminary expenses of forming the company? If such money or share had been given why were they not mentioned in the prospectus or in the report of the company presented at the directors' meeting on 3 March 1881? This meeting had been fully reported in the *Cambridge Chronicle* on 5 March 1881. The paper claimed that the occasion had made possible, 'the first public statement with reference to the past proceedings and future prospects of the Tramways Company'.

73. The diary does not record the wages paid to drivers and conductors. A leaflet of *Rules for Conductors*, in the Cambridge Folk Museum, shows that each man had to deposit £2 with the Tramways Company, 'as a guarantee of his honesty and good conduct'. Conductors had to be on duty 15 minutes before their cars were due to start, had to see that the cars were clean and were expected to help the drivers to reverse the horses at the termini. They were forbidden to allow any drunken persons to enter a car or 'any unclean or improperly dressed person inside the car'.

74. A haulage contractor working for the Improvement Commissioners.

75. For Eastbourne where he became secretary of the Eastbourne Building Society.

76. After the First World War he set up his own accountancy business specialising, initially, in accountancy work for farmers. His sons Leonard and Norman followed him; the latter is senior partner in the firm, now Chater & Myhill, at 10 Jesus Lane.

77. He remained with Augustine in the firm of J. Chater & Sons.

78. The double-deck vehicles ran from Market Hill to the station, Mill Road, Chesterton Road and Huntingdon Road. The fare to the station was 1d.

79. They were single deck, box-like vehicles popularly known as 'Bathing Machines' or 'Pill Boxes'. The driver, who collected the fares, sat on the off-side. The Tramways Company reduced the fare to the station to 1d., in advance of, and to the annoyance of, the Omnibus Company who had advertised that they were to be the pioneers of 1d. fares in Cambridge.

80. On the same routes as those served by the Omnibus Company.

81. In 1899 the British Electric Traction Company bought shares in the Tramways Company with a view to electrifying and extending the tramway system. Cambridge Town Council also showed interest in the scheme but difficulties led to its abandonment. In 1904 the Cambridge Electric Tramways Syndicate decided to buy the Traction Company's tram shares and to negotiate with the Tramways Company for the electrification of the tramway system.

82. Now Darwin College.

83. 21 April 1905.

84. John Berry Walford, proprietor of a small engineering firm and motor works in Egham, Surrey, had previously operated an omnibus service between Egham and Staines. In 1907 he bought the old Cambridge Motor Omnibus Company, then in liquidation, but at first the Corporation would only allow him to operate between the station and St. Andrew's Street with single-deck vehicles. In 1908 double-deck omnibuses, provided there was no over-hang, were allowed in the town centre and additional services were commenced in Huntingdon Road and Mill Road. The Ortona Company was joined, in 1913, by the British Automobile Traction Company Ltd. In 1930 the company became part of the Eastern Counties Omnibus Company which operates in Cambridge today.

85. They were advertised in the sale catalogue as being, 'readily adapted as Sea Side Bungalows, Summer Houses, House Boat Bodies, or for similar purposes'. The tram depot, now a furniture store and shortly to be demolished, was taken over by Mr. J.V. Pryor as a fish store.

INDEX

Adams, William, ix, 3, 11, 44-6, 87, 128
Adams, Mrs., 54, 82, 86-7, 94
Aikin, Miss, 4-5, 16, 17, 35, 44, 57
Aldis, W. S., Senior Wrangler, 154, 155
Alexandra Street, xi, xiv, 137, 143, 179, 182, 207
Allen, J. B., schoolmaster, 162, 163
Amateur Musical Society, 110
amateur theatricals, 126, 175
Anti-Mendicity Society, 182
anti-smoking lecture, 70
apprentices, 1-6, 8-9, 16-17
archery ground, 21

baking powder case, 190
Balfour, J. S., Tramways Company Chairman, 197, 198, 199, 204, 205, 206, 207
balloon, 31, 42, 150, 151
Ballot Act, 146, 152
balls, 31, 152
Bank, Cambridge Savings, 177
Bank Holiday Act, 123
Barnwell, xii, xiv, 27, 183, 186, 192
Barnwell Mission Hall, 193
Barrett
    Agnes, x, 20, 43-4, 53, 56, 60, 61, 77
    Fred, 61, 98, 99, 136
    Harriet, 61, 77, 136
    John, x, 20, 43, 60, 61
    Robert, x, 127
Basham, W. I., woollen draper, 53, 54, 141, 189
bat and trap, 21, 135
Bateson, Dr. W. H., Master of St. John's College, 162-3
Battell, E., tailor, 15, 17
bazaar, 64-5, 109-10
Blumson, Mr., shop assistant, 3, 6, 8, 9, 12, 13, 22, 23, 27, 29
Board of Health, 40
boat race, 129-30

Bond, William, grocer, 72, 73, 124, 137, 177
Bonnett, John, woollen draper, 82-3
Book Club, 127-8
bribery, 67-9
bridge, proposed, 157-8
Bridge Street, 62, 81, 83, 84, 158, 195
British Association, 38-9
Browning, Oscar, author and historian, 186
Bubier, Rev. G. B., 10, 71-2, 153
Building Society, Cambridge, xi, 131
Butler, Dr. H. M., 76, 145
Butler, Mrs. Josephine, 144, 145

Carter, Dr., 117, 172, 173
Castle Hill, 63
Cavendish College, xiii, 181
Cavendish Park, xiii
cemetery
    Histon Road, 87, 128
    Mill Road, 96
charades, 20, 125-6
charities, 133-4, 176
Chartist movement, 28-9
Chater
    Agnes (see also Barrett), 66, 67, 69, 104, 114, 115, 116, 117-8, 125, 126, 130, 136, 150, 171-3, 174, 175, 193, 198, 204
    Alfred, x, 59, 62, 81, 82-4, 98, 99, 104, 136, 140, 146, 171, 172, 173, 174
    Arthur, 119, 187
    Augustine (Gussy), xiii, xv, 171, 172, 173, 183, 203, 209
    Bertram, xv, 206, 209
    Eliza, 58, 59, 61, 67, 78
    Elizabeth (Lizzy), 114, 125, 143, 150, 181
    Ernest, 114, 116, 150, 162, 171, 172, 173, 175, 176, 194, 203
    Ethel, 62, 114, 116, 125, 136, 142, 142, 155, 171, 174, 175